THE **GHANA** COOKBOOK

THE **GHANA** COOKBOOK

FRAN OSSEO-ASARE & **BARBARA BAËTA**
with photos by Fran Osseo-Asare

HIPPOCRENE BOOKS, INC.
New York

Copyright © 2015 Fran Osseo-Asare and Barbara Baëta
Sixth printing, 2022

Photographs by Fran Osseo-Asare

For information, address:
HIPPOCRENE BOOKS, INC.
171 Madison Ave.
New York, NY 10016
www.hippocrenebooks.com

Cataloging-in-Publication Data available from the Library of Congress.

ISBN-13: 978-0-7818-1343-3
ISBN-10: 0-7818-1343-3

Printed in the United States of America.

CONTENTS

Part II: Recipes

ACKNOWLEDGMENTS

It is impossible to adequately acknowledge and thank everyone who has seriously contributed during this cookbook's decades-long gestation and delivery without adding another hundred pages.

Barbara and I are deeply indebted to our publisher, Hippocrene Books, and Priti Gress in particular, for sharing our vision.

We are also grateful to those in Ghana who graciously taught me (Fran) in their kitchens, markets, homes, and offices. Several of you are mentioned by name in the book. I am especially grateful to my late sister-in-law Afua Eunice Osseo-Asare; the staff and students at Flair Catering (particularly those who taught me most directly: Grace Mantey [now Grace Freeman], Favour Anyomi [now Favour Osei-Mensah], Victoria Odoi, and Esther Sowah); as well as Barbara's indispensable office secretary Rosaline Lamptey; and my guide and driver throughout northern Ghana, Abudulai Abubakari. We are also grateful to Comfort Awu Akor in Tamale and the staff at the Tamale Institute of Cross Cultural Studies; Dorcas Nimbo in Bawku; the late Nana Oyeeman Wereko Ampem II for permission to take photographs at the Akuapem Amanokrom Odwira and officials at the Ewe Hogbetsotso (Festival of Exodus) in the Volta Region as well; artist Katie Torda for the use of props from her gallery for several food photographs; other friends and colleagues in Ghana and the U.S. too numerous to list; my virtual supporters, especially fellow African food bloggers, via Betumiblog (you know who you are); the International Association of Culinary Professionals (IACP) for its foresight and pre-contract travel grant; members of the Nittany Valley Writers Network; the TED Fellows community; and family and friends who cheered me on when the going got long and lonely. Again, you know who you are, but especially family members Kwadwo, DK, Masi, Abena, Samuel, Sylvia, Linda, and Patricia. New Leaf Initiative in State College and my creative colleagues provided the perfect place to nurture this work.

I appreciate the enthusiastic support from interns, most notably in managing and helping with the massive recipe testing tasks. From Penn State: Katie Cochran, Morgan Cooper, and Danielle Dombeck, and from Georgia, culinary student Meisha D. Johnson. I also owe my faithful crew of recipe testers a debt of gratitude, and as promised, I name you here: Katherine Ampomah, Kelsey Cantor, Jenny Dang, Joe Fennewald, Janet Ferguson, Morgan Friedrich, Collette Heinze (and helpers), Kelly Lakin, Amy Lorek, Lazarus Lynch, Paulette McLane, Brandi Simpson Miller, Cordialis Msora-Kasago, Megan Orr, Karina Rook, Bethany Spicher-Schonberg, Adam Virzi, and especially the All-Star Team of Janelle Anhwere, Hanna Boakye-Yiadom, Henrieta Esi, Cleopatra Jones, Teki Martei, Angela Rogers, Ozoz Sokoh, and Mary Spak. Sincere apologies if I have missed anyone.

Barbara and I are grateful to photographer Eric Don-Arthur for his lovely portrait of us on Flair's rooftop dining area.

Finally, I thank God for the grace and strength to see this task through. *Gye nyame* ("except for God").

PREFACE
by Fran Osseo-Asare

The Akan people of West Africa recognize what great cooks everywhere know: the secret to good cooking lies in the quality of the ingredients. As they understand in Ghana: "the good soup comes from the good earth" (Twi: "*nkwan bɛyɛ dɛ a, efi fam*").

Let me begin by acknowledging that this book bends several cardinal cookbook rules: some recipes include unfamiliar or exotic ingredients (but with substitutions given where possible), and though many of the recipes are quick and easy, some are not. This book is an unrepentant celebration of West African Ghana's vibrant cuisine and culture. While the book serves as a basic cooking course guiding anyone who wishes to delve more deeply into Ghana's (or West Africa's) culinary cultures, it is also a handy step-by-step cookbook for those with a more casual interest.

Ghana's exuberant cooking is attractive on many levels: the food is fresh, delicious, healthy, economical, user-friendly, varied, efficient, and flexible. Over the years, my appreciation and enthusiasm for it have only deepened.

I agree with the South African food writer Laurens van der Post who wrote in the 1970s that the cuisine of the rising middle classes in West Africa exhibits "… a kind of morning freshness, their taste is exhilarating and exploratory and their inventiveness lively. And their meals stimulate not only the palate but the mind as well; some of the best conversations I have ever had have taken place over food eaten with West African friends." [1]

North Americans continue to explore and embrace new foods, especially ethnic cuisines. The emphases on lighter cooking with more vegetables and complex carbohydrates and less meat, on timesaving meal preparation (while simultaneously rethinking the need for speed via the "slow foods" movement), and on interesting new combinations of foods and seasonings continue to embolden us to broaden our culinary horizons, and to scrutinize some of our prior stereotypes. We have shown ourselves quite open to borrowing and adapting foods from a variety of cultures.

---

[1] van der Post, Laurens, and editors of Time-Life Books. *African Cooking*. New York: Time-Life Books, 1970, p. 62

1

Many books have been written on Caribbean, Cajun, Brazilian, and African-American cooking, all referring vaguely to "African influences." There is also a crop of encyclopedic African or African Diaspora cookbooks, which while fascinating and needed, can overwhelm someone new to the subject. Finally, the flood of international cookbooks, or specialty cookbooks, such as those on hot and spicy foods, offer African recipes with great unevenness in authenticity. Too often books treat the continent and islands of Africa, numbering well over fifty countries, as a single entity, when even within one country like Ghana there are ten regions with cuisines reflecting distinctive geographies, ingredients, cultures, and histories. While most people recognize such variation in other parts of the world, they tend to overlook it in Africa.

This cookbook is for adventurous but inexperienced cooks who are interested in trying new cuisines; for those who like to cook but are pressed for time or might be on a tight budget; for people who have enjoyed some West African food and want to try their hand at cooking it. And what about folks on gluten-free or sugar-free or dairy-free diets? Or those who follow the slow-foods movement? This cookbook is for them as well.

The Ghana Cookbook is designed as an introductory, but comprehensive, cooking course that builds on basic flavors, textures, and cooking principles, and seasons them with stories, photography, and cultural explanations. This project is the culmination of over four decades of learning on my part, including more than ten years of collaboration with my distinguished partner Barbara Baëta. Though I do the writing and speak in my own voice, Barbara's profound influence and experience are evident throughout the book.

Now, we warmly welcome you to our kitchen. As we say in Ghana, "*Akwaaba!*" ("Welcome!")

INTRODUCTIONS

FROM BRISBANE (CA) TO ACCRA — FRAN'S STORY

This cookbook is the one I always wanted to buy and could never find. It is the one I wanted for myself first, and later for my mom, sisters, children, friends, and colleagues—at home, school, work, in my community, and beyond. It is the distillation of decades of living with a foot in two worlds—the United States, where I was born and grew up, and Ghana, my husband's homeland, and now my adopted country, too.

Let me back up.

In 1957, when I was eight years old and living in California, Great Britain's West African colony the Gold Coast became Ghana, the first black African country to achieve its independence from a colonial power. At that time, my family was a typical American family blended from immigrants, with a Norwegian grandfather on one side and Appalachian mountain folk on the other. My parents had met in Virginia where my Montana-born dad was stationed in the navy and Appalachian mom was working as a waitress. They moved west to live in Oregon for a few years and then moved south to the San Francisco Bay area in California when I was two. By 1957 I was growing up oblivious to distant Africa. The big news in Brisbane, California, was that Johnny Cash came to sing at the local barbecue restaurant.

Fast forward ten years. The youngest of three daughters, I left home on a scholarship to attend the University of California at Berkeley in 1967. Over the next four years I fell in love with a brilliant fellow student from the new Ghana, Kwadwo (k-w-AH-j-oh) Osseo-Asare. He was orphaned, the eldest of four siblings. By my graduation we were discussing marriage. I knew I needed to travel alone to Ghana to find out what I would be getting myself into if we married, and also to reassure my parents (and by that time, step-parents as well) that we could successfully navigate a cross-cultural, cross-racial marriage. That difficult experience is chronicled in my first book, *A New Land to Live In* (InterVarsity Press, 1977).

After graduation in August 1971, I traveled alone to Ghana to spend a year getting acquainted with his country while he continued on to gradu-ate school in Berkeley. I had only traveled on an airplane once before and was shy and uncertain of my reception. His "aunt" and what seemed like hundreds of relatives met me at the airport in Accra, the capital city. They threw their arms around me, exuberantly calling out "*Akwaaba!*" (ah-KWAH-ah-bah) which means "welcome" in the Akan language, and captures the essence of Ghana's famed hospitality. In the same way, the delicious one-pots, soups, and stews I enjoyed in the homes of my new family and friends nurtured and welcomed me in a deeply soothing way. When the time came for me to re-create the meals I was learning to love, and that my husband-to-be had been raised on, my sisters-in-law-to-be and friends were willing to help me—and I was eager to learn.

Ghana and its food captivated me. At the end of my year there Kwadwo and I married in Ghana before returning to the U.S., where I entered a gradu-ate program in the School of Social Welfare at the University of California at Berkeley. Eventually we moved to Colorado, then on to Pennsylvania, and had two daughters and a son. I also spent the past four decades traveling back and forth between Ghana and the U.S., deepening my love affair with my husband's homeland and its cuisine. Our children, too, have had the chance to live both in the United States and in Ghana. Along the way, I also returned to graduate school, this time to a doctoral program in rural sociol-ogy at Pennsylvania State University. I wanted to understand how Ghana, blessed with wonderful resources and a decent educational system, as well as creative and hardworking people, could be sliding into social, political, and economic decline.

When they were growing up and learning to cook, I could find no African cookbooks to help me teach my children, so I wrote my own, *A Good Soup Attracts Chairs* (Pelican Publishing Company, 1993). That cookbook also came in handy when we adopted two nephews from Ghana and brought them to live with us in the U.S. after their mother, my husband's sister (and one of my earliest teachers), died.

I always longed for a definitive guide to cooking Ghanaian food, but felt unequal to the daunting task of authoring such a cookbook alone. One of the first African cookbooks I discovered was the African volume of the 1970 Time-Life series on Foods of the World (*African Cooking*), authored by Lau-rens van der Post. It included a full-page color photo of a young Barbara Baëta catering a buffet luncheon in Accra. She was described as "one of Ghana's leading culinary experts," who opened her catering service in 1968. According to the photo caption, "an invitation to one of her dinners is highly prized." I then noticed the name Barbara Baëta reappearing in acknowledgments in books by other authors. I learned of Barbara's famous company in Accra, Flair Catering Services, and discovered that she had authored some influential recipe cards in the 1970s. One day in the early 2000s, while lamenting to my husband that Barbara Baëta would be the ideal person to work with, he mentioned that he had gone to high school in Ghana (Achimota) with her brother Basil, a physician in Canada. How did I not know that?

We promptly made a trip to see him, and left a copy of my Ghanaian primer *A Good Soup Attracts Chairs* to give to his sister when she next visited. A year later Barbara and I arranged to meet face-to-face. We were instantly at ease with one another. She shared that she had tried several of the recipes in my book and they were very good. She also mentioned that people were always asking her to write a cookbook, but she was too busy and not really one to sit down and write. She invited me to spend time at her school and catering company to explore collaboration. I spent several weeks at Flair in 2002 and received a grant from the International Association of Culinary Professionals in 2004 to visit again, as well as to travel throughout the regions of Ghana gathering information for our book. I have made innumerable additional visits to Ghana and Flair since then.

A surprise along my journey was the meshing of my personal and professional interests. The more deeply I researched sub-Saharan African cuisines in general (and Ghana's in particular) the more I became aware of a need for more information about sub-Saharan African cuisine and gastronomy. Despite the welcome explosion of writing and blogging and "YouTubing" about African cuisines, it is sometimes accompanied by naiveté and an uncritical embrace of ingredients and techniques, as well as a lack of information to help translate the cooking from a local, indigenous context to an international one.

Thus the nature of this book has broadened to include not just anecdotes about personal experiences, but information and photos to help place the recipes in context and give detailed instructions to "fill in the blanks."

However, before diving into recipes, let me introduce Barbara.

FROM GHANA WITH LOVE—
BARBARA'S STORY

Barbara Baëta, also known as Amesika Barbara Rose Baëta and fondly called "Auntie Sika" by family and friends, is a beloved national treasure of Ghana.

One of the country's first internationally and formally trained hospitality industry professionals, Barbara has cooked for every head of state of Ghana since it became the first black African country to receive independence in 1957 (Kwame Nkrumah through current President John Mahama, whose wife, incidentally, is a graduate of Flair Catering Services). The list of dignitaries she has served reads like a global who's who; Flair prepared the one state meal served to President Barack Obama and his family during their July 2009 trip to Ghana. She remembers fondly preparing other state meals for well-known figures such as Jimmy Carter, Queen Elizabeth II, U Thant, the Prince of Wales, Emperor Haile Selassie, President Thabo Mbeki, and the Sultan of Brunei.

Barbara comes from a distinguished family. A member of the Ewe ethnic group, she is descended from royalty. Her paternal great-great-great grandfather sailed from Portugal to West Africa to buy rubber and gold, married a Ghanaian king's daughter from Keta, and stayed. For her years of support to her community of Anloga in the Keta District of the Volta region, Barbara was made an honorary "Queen Mother" with the royal name of "Mama Hogbe." Her family represents a global melting pot: a great-great-grandmother was the daughter of a Danish man who came to build the fort along the coast and a local Ghanaian woman. The original Baëta brother who came to Ghana also plied his trade in Brazil. There he and other family members mixed with and acquired Brazilian relatives.

Outstanding men and strong, pioneering, independent women characterize Barbara's family. Her grandmother braved the scorn of the local mission middle school headmaster to become the first girl admitted to the Keta middle school. (He disdainfully asked: "What do you want here . . . All the learning you will ever need is to be able to do sums about chickens [*koko-kunta*, i.e., chicken arithmetic], and that you can do already."[2]) This same grandmother became a teacher and at age eighteen founded the YWCA in Keta in the then Gold Coast. An aunt, Annie Baëta Jiagge, became Ghana's second woman lawyer and first female Appeal Court judge. Barbara's father, Rev. Prof. Emeritus Christian Baëta, was a world-renowned theologian who taught at the Department of Religion at the University of Ghana, Legon.

The eldest of five children, including a sister and three brothers, Barbara herself has always accepted responsibility for looking after and nurturing them and others. She continues to do so, seamlessly combining her personal and professional lives.

At around age four or five, Barbara Baëta began spending holidays at her grandmother's farm at Aflao, near the Ghana-Togo border. She helped cook, learned to make bread, and learned to sew. She looked forward to the visits and they instilled in her a lifelong love of cooking and a fascination with fashion and design.

As she grew from a five-year-old playing under the coconut trees, she pursued her interest in food and the hospitality industry, both academically and practically. After attending the prestigious Achimota Secondary School, she furthered her education in hotel and institutional management at the Huyton College for Girls in Liverpool, England, then at Glasgow and West of Scotland College of Domestic Science, returning to Ghana in January 1960.

She became Director of Food Services and Hostels at the YMCA in Accra. In 1964 while still in her twenties, Barbara was awarded a technical aid 18-month scholarship by the Canadian government to study large-scale food management and interior decoration with top institutions and individuals across Canada. By 1967 Ghana's government appointed her Ghana's official hostess to the 1967 World Expo (the World's Fair held in Montreal that year), and she prepared a Ghanaian banquet for 500 people, renting the equipment and staff she needed, and bringing Ghanaian ingredients with her. She returned to her work at the YMCA, but after a year announced to her parents, "Look, if I can go to Canada and do this kind of function for 500 people by myself, why am I still working for somebody?" Her experience gave Barbara the confidence to establish her own business, borrowing about $200 from Barclays Bank and insisting on doing it by herself.

Before leaving Canada after the Expo, she had dinner with some friends, and announced her aspirations: "I'm going home. I want to start my own

---

[2] Crane, Louise. *Ms. Africa: Profiles of Modern African Women*, Philadelphia: J. B. Lippincott, 1973, p. 16.

business. I want something with F for food, fashion, and flowers. Find me a name." One of her friends thought a while and said "But Barbara, you always do everything with flair anyway." Bingo. "Flair Catering Services" was established in 1968, and has always been distinguished by its sophisticated and quality preparation and presentation of Ghanaian traditional dishes as well as cuisines from other countries. Barbara also established the nonprofit Flair Vocational Training Institute to help equip young people, especially young girls, with marketable skills in the hospitality industry. Over 1,500 young people from throughout Africa have been trained through her institute's efforts.

Barbara exudes Ghana's famed hospitality and generosity. Her disarming smile, humility, and infectious joy and optimism draw even strangers to her and make them feel special and welcome. In 2011 President Mills awarded her one of Ghana's highest medals, the Order of the Volta, for distinguished service to the nation. A deep spirituality and sense of gratitude, coupled with boundless energy, sparkling creativity and belief in the value of hard work make her an inspiration to those around her. I can scarcely remember sitting around her generous dining room table without a host of family and visitors welcomed there.

However, hers is a tough love that has been tested during some dark days in Ghana. She defiantly closed her successful Accra restaurant, The Calabash, after military personnel began "bullying their way through, thinking they could come in and eat free." She escaped by seconds being caught in the crossfire of a 1966 coup when she was the last person to leave the Ghana Broadcasting Company after cleaning up from filming a cooking show. She has weathered food, water, and power shortages, political and economic instability, and social upheaval with persistence and an unshakable confidence in the goodness of God. In short, Barbara epitomizes the "can do" attitude (what I call "*betumi*") now recognized as a key ingredient for successful development anywhere.

Barbara decided early on to keep her company small enough that she could know and supervise her employees personally (several dozen now), and be close to the fifty or so students who attend her catering school each year. This was a conscious decision not to expand into a huge business, but to remain a small efficient one.

Long before "culinary tourism" became an official term, Barbara was regularly traveling to England, France, and North America with her staff and students, exposing them to international standards in the tourism industry while promoting Ghana's cuisine and fashion with her signature "From Ghana with Love" extravaganzas. She could raise many thousands of dollars in a single night while showcasing Ghanaian fashion designers, floral arrangements, and foods. An advocate and role model for women's rights, she has long been an active member of the professional women's group Zonta International.

Now in her seventies, Barbara shows few signs of slowing down. She recently single-handedly began a campaign to upgrade food safety and sanitation skills in Ghana's informal and semi-formal hospitality industry. She has begun by organizing courses that are being expanded to include more sites, and is hopeful that it will soon be possible to establish a nationwide certification program. In characteristic giving fashion she welcomes this opportunity to share her culinary expertise and stories with a larger audience. She has also recently broken ground on a new site and embarked on fulfilling a life-long dream: to expand her current catering school into an African Culinary Institute, capable of educating students to prepare not only Ghana's regional specialties and Asian and Western dishes, but eventually highlighting regional food from across sub-Saharan Africa, from west to east to south.

INTRODUCING GHANA

Ghana is vibrant and intensely alive. Its essence is difficult to capture, for it is a collage of innumerable constantly shifting sights and sounds and smells:

- Fishermen straining and singing in tune with the rhythm of the waves as they stand on the sand along coconut tree-lined coasts and pull in nets
- Wooden pestles rhythmically thumping in wooden mortars, pounding boiled cassava and plantain or African yams into *fufu* while skillful hands turn the dough
- Flutes, drums, keyboards, electric guitars moving bodies and feet and voices in fields, churches, and nightclubs, day and night
- Vendors streaming along streets gracefully balancing heavy loads on their heads or calling out and waving phone cards, plastic bags of plantain chips, peanuts, tiger nuts, whole pineapples, dish towels, sunglasses, dog chains, CDs, chewing gum, green South African apples, chocolate bars, newspapers and magazines, soccer balls . . . a constantly moving roadside market passing by car windows
- Neatly stacked peeled oranges and coconuts ready to quench thirst
- Smiling children eating sweet mangoes with juice dripping down their arms
- Fashionable young women with elaborate hairstyles and in bright, dramatic outfits and high heels smartly moving between offices and shops
- Musical laughter and loud voices everywhere

GHANA

BURKINA FASO

UPPER
WEST

UPPER
EAST •Bolgatanga

BENIN

•Wa

Sisili

Kulpawn

NORTHERN

•Tamale

White Volta

Daka

Oti

TOGO

COTE D'IVOIRE

Black Volta

BRONG AHAFO

Tain

Pru

Afram

Lake
Volta

VOLTA

•Sunyani

ASHANTI

Bia

Tano

•Kumasi

EASTERN

•Koforidua

Ankobra

Ofin

Anum

Bom

Ho

Volta

Todzie

Keta
lagoon

Cape
St Paul

WESTERN

Sekondi-Takoradi

CENTRAL

Cape Coast

Accra

GREATER ACCRA

Accra

GULF OF GUINEA

ATLANTIC OCEAN

LEGEND
● Regional capital
✪ National capital

- Constant construction, with cement and glass skyscrapers and malls and restaurants and overpasses and freeways popping up everywhere (sometimes clogging roads and drains and straining water and electrical systems)
- Gorgeous textiles, classic and new
- A hopeful, youthful energy in the air, fueled by investors, oil, and the "African maker" movement
- New technology everywhere—cars, computers, notebooks, iPads, and ubiquitous cell phones
- The faithful kneeling on prayer mats or chanting
- Opulent gold jewelry and huge, dramatic umbrellas and pomp displayed at durbars with kings and attendants sitting in glory
- In the north, cattle grazing, vegetables and yam slices drying in the sun, skilled leatherwork and woven fabrics, mosques, distinctive round mud-walled architecture, colorful woven Bolga baskets
- Rivers and lakes, tropical rainforest, elephants and crocodiles, red dusty lateritic soil, Guinea fowl along roads and fields, roosters crowing
- A swirling mix of peoples, national and international: Ga, Akan, Dagbani Ewe, Fante, American, Nigerian, Indian, European, Syrian, Chinese . . .

In 1957, at the time of independence, the "Gold Coast" renamed itself after the ancient wealthy West African medieval kingdom of Ghana famous for its gold. The Republic of Ghana is over 92,000 square miles, making it slightly smaller than Oregon, my home state. In the center of West Africa's coast, Ghana's southern coast borders the Gulf of Guinea and the Atlantic Ocean. Its other borders include Côte d'Ivoire (Ivory Coast) on the east, Togo on the west, and Burkina Faso to the north. Coastal Accra is the capital city.

Tropical Ghana lies just a few degrees above the equator, and about 4 percent of the land remains tropical rainforest, about 20 percent is semi-deciduous forest, and there are savannah lands along the coast and in the north, plus transitional zones. The Eastern Region is home to the Akwapim-Togo hills.

Ghana's youthful and rapidly growing population numbers over 26 million people (compared to about 4 million in Oregon). Up to two-thirds of the people are involved in agriculture and animal husbandry in the formal or informal sector. Crops vary with the climate and geography among the ten administrative regions in the country, which are historically loosely affiliated with ethnic groups (i.e., Ewe speakers in the Volta Region, Fante speakers in the Western Region, Twi speakers in the Ashanti Region, etc.).

The land is crisscrossed with rivers, especially dominated by the Volta River (the Black Volta and White Volta and their convergence), its tributaries, and Volta Lake, one of the largest man-made lakes in the world. Fresh and salt-water fish and shellfish from the coast and inland are an important part of the diet, often smoked, salted, and/or dried to preserve them.

Crops include maize (corn), cassava, pepper, plantain, okra, yam, tomato, cocoyam, peanut, leafy vegetables, oil palm, beans and pulses, millet, sorghum, cocoa, rice, banana, papaya, eggplant (garden egg), oranges, pineapple, avocado, mango, sheanut, onion, coconut, cashew, cotton, colanut, sugarcane, lime/lemon, ginger, along with other fruits, vegetables, and staples.

Cattle are raised in the hotter, drier north away from the tsetse flies that transmit animal trypanosomiasis and prevent cattle from thriving elsewhere. Guinea fowl also run wild there. While goat, mutton, pork, and poultry are more prevalent in northern Ghana, in the more central Eastern and Brong Ahafo forested regions cocoa, red palm, and plantain trees thrive, and bush meat like grasscutter (aka, "greater cane rat") has long been a delicacy, along with seasonal mushrooms and giant land snails. Palm trees line coastal areas.

The many languages spoken in Ghana pose a research challenge when writing about foods and ingredients. For example, people may say they use *kakadro* (Twi), *kakatsofa* (Ga), *gometakui* or *nkraosa* (Ewe), or *kakaduro* (Hausa) when referring to "ginger." The spice *Xylopica aethiopica* is known as *hwentia* in Twi, but *etso* in Ewe and *so* in Ga. And sometimes a generic word like *shito* or *mako* may refer to one of any of a variety of peppers, or to a condiment. Okra soup is *nkruma nkwan* in Twi but *enmomi wonu* in Ga, and *fetri detsi* in Ewe. When featuring regional dishes in this book, their local name is sometimes indicated.

Pronunciation Note: In the local names, "ɔ" is pronounced like the "ou" in "ought" and "ε" is pronounced like the "e" in "set."

PART I:
ESSENTIAL FLAVORS
& TECHNIQUES

Just as basic dress patterns are transformed by adjustments in color, texture, and design, so too can West African culinary patterns be creatively altered to provide infinite variety. However, one needs a basic knowledge of West African flavor principles, seasoning techniques, preparation techniques, and soup and stew bases.

The Ghanaian Pantry in North America

To seriously cook Ghanaian food, especially outside of Ghana, requires stocking one's kitchen and pantry with a few special items. While any well-appointed kitchen with stove, oven, microwave, electric blender or food processor, spice grinder, pots and pans, etc. will allow you to cook the recipes in this book the following items are wonderful additions if available:

- An *asanka* (for grinding)
- Wooden masher (*apotoyewa/apotoriwa* or *tapoli*)
- Wooden stirring stick (much sturdier than standard wooden spoons)
- Cheesecloth (for straining to make beverages, puddings, etc.)

For cooking traditional meals, several pantry items may need to be ordered online or obtained at an African or international market (see Resources, page 238). Some of them may also be replaced by more familiar substitutes. Here are the basics I like to keep on hand, listed by priority (see Glossary for detailed descriptions):

- Gari (cassava meal) [*No substitute*]
- Fufu flours (yam, plantain, cocoyam) [*Substitutes: Potato starch and instant mashed potatoes*]
- Palm oil (especially spiced dzomi or zomi) [*No taste substitute; but the color red can be duplicated by adding paprika to vegetable oil*]
- Dried shrimp/crayfish/herrings (includes smoked and dried, ground and whole) [*Substitute: possibly fish sauce*]
- Canned cream of palm fruit [*No substitute*]
- Dried hibiscus flowers (roselle) [*No substitute*]
- Agushi (dried melon seeds) [*Substitute: Hulled pumpkin seeds*]
- Attiéke (cassava couscous) [*Substitute: wheat couscous*]
- Ground red pepper from Ghana (*When "dried ground red pepper" is listed in this cookbook it refers to regular ground red cayenne pepper from the U.S. If substituting Ghanaian ground red pepper, reduce amounts by one-fourth as it is hotter.*)
- Hwentia (*Xylopica aethiopica*) [*Substitute: black peppercorns (Piper guineese)*]

- Ashanti pepper [*Substitute: whole black peppercorns*]
- Stoneground white corn flour
- Toasted corn flour (*ablemamu; see page 29*)
- Fonio, African millet, or African millet flour [*Substitute: any millet or flour*]
- Koko flour
- Bambara beans [*Substitute: garbanzo beans*]
- Hausa koko mix
- Dried white corn [*Substitute: dried hominy*]
- Beef, chicken, shito, and shrimp-flavored Maggi or Royco seasoning cubes. [*Substitute: any seasoning cubes/granules, bouillon cubes, or stock*]. *Note: I prefer not to use seasoning cubes, and substitute stock or seasoned salt and other flavorings, as indicated in many of the recipes.*

Other staples I like to have in my cupboard that are more easily found in the U.S. include:

- Adobo or other seasoned salt
- Canned corned beef (Exeter or other)
- Canned Goya sardines in tomato sauce or oil, or other canned fish
- Canned evaporated milk
- Peanut oil
- Dry-roasted unsalted peanuts
- Natural-style creamy peanut butter or "groundnut paste"
- Hulled sesame seeds
- Dried unsweetened flaked coconut
- Canned coconut milk
- Dried black-eyed peas
- Dried red pepper flakes
- Hot sauce/condiment (shirachi, sambal oelek, shito, etc.)
- Canned tomatoes
- Tomato paste
- Rice (basmati, jasmine, broken, long-grain, medium grain, indigenous red, etc.)
- Curry powder or masala
- Dried herbs such as thyme, basil, aniseed, bay leaves

African markets as well as Latin American and Asian markets in the U.S. are good sources for some fresh produce used in Ghana recipes, such as fresh African yams (especially puna), small green (apim) or large ripe plantains, cassava/manioc, cocoyams/taro, various types of peppers, and garden eggs (a type of eggplant). Other perishable goods I like to keep on hand are:

- Fresh ginger
- Fresh garlic
- Fresh chili peppers such as habanero (Scotch bonnet), cayenne, jalapeno
- Fresh tomatoes

- Onions, shallots
- Tropical fruits as available (papaya, pineapple, oranges, lemons, limes, watermelon, avocado, cantaloupe, etc.)
- Okra
- Spinach or other greens
- Frozen banku dough (*see page 30*)
- Frozen mango and banana chunks
- Smoked fish
- Margarine or butter (*Note: butter is generally not available in Ghana, so people traditionally use margarine; however, butter may be substituted in place of margarine in all recipes.*)

For more detailed information on Ghanaian culinary terms, ingredients, cooking techniques, utensils, dishes, etc., refer to the Glossary on page 231.

Textures, Flavors, & Cooking Methods

Several of the cultural characteristics of Ghanaian cooking listed here are also found in many other parts of Africa as well:

Textures

- There is an emphasis on food texture. Traditionally, food in Ghana is eaten with freshly washed (right) hands. Perhaps because of the intimate, close contact of fingers with food, texture is very important. Generally, pounded food has a very different texture than food that is commercially ground. Some foods are routinely finely ground for many recipes (e.g., sesame seeds, corn, peanuts, onions, wheat flour, cowpeas), while for others a different texture is preferred (e.g., pounding shrimp or tiny dried fish in a wooden mortar or grinding in a ridged clay grinding bowl, tearing rather than liquefying peppers and onions for pepper sauces). At other times, pounding results in a lump-free product, such as when boiled cassava or plantain is pounded to make smooth, elastic *fufu*. Steamed foods are common and have their distinctive firm textures (e.g., *kenkey* or *dokono*, a soured corn and cassava dough steamed in plantain leaves, and *tubaani*, a steamed black-eyed pea pudding similar to Nigerian *moinmoin*). Overall, textures range from creamy to crunchy, from firm or smooth and soft to chewy, or lumpy or crispy outside and creamy inside (as in fried ripe plantain). Similarly, finely ground dried corn or finely grated dried cassava yield different products than coarsely ground or grated. One difficulty in substituting blenders for some recipes that are traditionally pounded in a mortar and pestle is that it significantly alters the texture of the foods.
- A preference for "chewiness" of food is also common, whether that be in meat in a stew or on a stick (*chichinga*), or roasted chicken. My nephews

from Ghana still cannot eat fryer chickens from the U.S. because they feel their soft, mushy meat has neither taste nor substance.

- Eating is a quite sensual experience. There is often a love of viscous textures, such as provided by okra or baobab and some leaves like jute (*ayoyo*). This affinity may be related to the idea that foods are made more palatable by a slippery coating. Oil is especially prized for the way it coats food. Ghana shares this affinity with much of West Africa, and it is indirectly alluded to in Nigerian Chinua Achebe's famous sentence in *Things Fall Apart*, "Proverbs are the palm oil with which words are eaten." In a similar way, *fufu* (a heavy, elastic dumpling) is coated with soup and swallowed without chewing. The peristaltic movement in the throat is similar to that of swallowing an oyster whole. The texture of the *fufu* is also in a sense felt and "tasted" with the fingers before it even enters the mouth.

Flavors

- Flavor principles include an affinity for salt, including smoked and salted fish, for spicy flavors (especially from fresh and dried chili peppers and fresh ginger); for bitter and sour flavors, such as is found in some greens and fermented foods; and for what has come to be known as "umami," found in Ghana's trademark dried ground shrimp/crayfish, as well as other smoked/dried fish.

- One reason for the popularity of Chinese cooking and soy sauce in Ghana may be the similarity in flavor principles, including the use of ginger and chili peppers, the adoption of seasoning cubes (with MSG), and dried/smoked fish. "Rice and stew" is a classic Ghanaian combination, making it easy to adopt much Asian cooking.

- A flavor that is conspicuously absent in Ghanaian main dish cooking is "sweet." While sugar or honey may be added to beverages and breakfast porridges and is found in desserts like fools, puddings, cakes, and frozen treats, it is rarely included in main or side dishes, with the exception perhaps of the sweetness imparted by ripe plantains. Even white sweet potatoes, with their lower sugar content, are preferred over the orange ones popular in the United States. Many Ghanaians coming to the United States for the first time find North American food excessively sweet.

Cooking Methods

- While Ghanaians adore Chinese cooking and stir-fries, a major difference is that many dishes in Ghana are time-consuming to prepare and require long, slow cooking times. Cowpeas, free-range meat, and poultry especially tend to need tenderizing by slow simmering. Including a little smoked fish in a bean stew requires time for the flavors to meld after the beans are cooked. Many Ghanaian recipes are slow-cooker friendly and a good fit with the growing "slow foods" movement. However, a few simple tricks can help to greatly reduce the time spent over the stove.

- Busy Ghanaian housewives have always found ways to speed up cooking time. "*Gari*," a West African convenience food made from fermented, dried, roasted cassava is a regular kitchen staple. A simple "light soup" (*nkrakra* or *nkrankra*) made with fish is also quick to prepare, as are stews made using canned sardines or corned beef.

- In addition to slow simmering on a stove, Ghanaians rely on both shallow-fat and deep-fat frying, generally with a vegetable oil (as in frying ripe plantains for the spicy coated cubes called *kelewele*, or *kose/akara*, black-eyed pea fritters, or yam "chips").

- Steaming, especially in banana or plantain leaves, is popular.

- Grilling, roasting, boiling, and baking all take their place in the repertoire of Ghanaian cooks. Grilling meat, fish, and vegetables in the traditional setting requires a time investment to prepare charcoal or wood fires, but in North America the process of grilling may be greatly simplified.

Seasoning Techniques

Meats, poultry, and fish are generally seasoned before cooking, whether they are to be grilled, baked, or used in soups or stews. The seasoning may be stuffed into slits, rubbed over the item, or the item may be steamed in a little water before continuing on to make a soup or stew or sauce. Steaming is done partly to seal the juices into the meat and flavor it, and partly because meat from free-range cattle and poultry tends to be tough and needs to be cooked for a longer time.

The seasonings most often used in Ghana include salt, garlic, ginger, onion, and chili pepper. More recently seasoning cubes or seasoned salt have displaced some fabulous indigenous spices and traditional seasonings. Grinding on a grinding stone is a common traditional technique for preparing the ginger and garlic, but North Americans can grate the ginger and crush the garlic. Onions are often simply sliced, and seasoning cubes are crushed between the fingers. Seasoning cubes are more common in West Africa than granules, for they are more portable and can be sold individually. Hot dried chili powder is sprinkled over the item being seasoned and/or fresh chili peppers may be simply sliced and sprinkled over it or added whole and removed during cooking once the desired heat is reached. Poultry or fish may be cleansed with lemon or lime juice and a little water before being seasoned. Many, but not all, Ghanaians like spicy foods. It is fine to tone down the heat if a milder experience is preferred.

Basic Seasoning Mixture for meat and poultry

This recipe is a basic seasoning that can be used on almost anything. The amounts of ingredients are flexible and forgiving, and can be adjusted according to your preferences. This preparation works for both stews and soups, depending on the recipe. It makes enough for 2 pounds of meat or poultry.

Ingredients

2 heaping teaspoons crushed garlic

½ to 1 cup chopped onion

1 or 2 small chicken, beef, or shrimp-flavored seasoning cubes, crumbled (optional)

½ teaspoon salt or seasoned salt (or to taste)

½ teaspoon dried ground red pepper (or to taste)

A little fresh red chili pepper (your choice; see heat chart, page 37), sliced (including seeds, unless a less spicy flavor is preferred); or ¼ teaspoon or more dried ground red pepper

Directions

In a bowl, sprinkle all the ingredients over the meat or chicken, and toss well. Put the meat or chicken into a pot with ½ cup of water or stock, cover tightly, and steam on medium heat for 15 minutes.

Variations:

In place of seasoning cubes, increase the salt/seasoned salt and substitute a little dried ground shrimp and spices like thyme or basil or black or white pepper, or use stock in place of the water.

Basic Seasoning Mixture for fish

To make above seasoning mixture for use with grilled fish, grate rather than chop the onion and mix the prepared ingredients together in a bowl with a tablespoon of vegetable oil. Cut slits into the sides of a whole, cleaned fish, and stuff the seasoning into the slits and rub on the outside of the fish. (For example, see the recipe for Grilled Tilapia on page 134.)

Tankora Powder

Tankora powder (aka *yaji* powder; *chichinga* powder) is a West African rub for meats, poultry, etc. that is most famously used for West African kebabs. Like curry powders, it's a blend of several dried, powdered ingredients. There are many versions, but most commonly they contain dried ground red pepper, ginger, some kind of black or white pepper, salt, peanut powder, and various other spices. Some versions call for mace, cloves, Maggi cubes, or garlic, and in Ghana people commonly mix in some toasted corn flour.

I recommend going "all out" and making the rub from scratch. As with a curry powder, freshly made is best. You can mix and match the ingredients you happen to like in the quantities you prefer. I usually make this just before I need it, but it could also be stored in the freezer. In this book Tankora Powder is used in making Ghana-Style Beef/Liver/Chicken Kebabs (pages 74-75).

Ingredients

½ cup peanut flour

¼ cup toasted corn flour (*page 29*)

½ teaspoon dried ground red pepper (or to taste)

1 teaspoon ground dried ginger (or to taste)

½ to 1 teaspoon salt or seasoned salt (or to taste)

Optional: other ingredients as desired, e.g., ½ teaspoon dried powdered green bell pepper; ¼ teaspoon mace or nutmeg; ½ teaspoon ground black, white, or Ashanti pepper; shrimp-flavored or other seasoning cube, crumbled

One of the best kebabs (called *chichinga* or *tsitsinga*) I had in Ghana was made from tender beef (often *chichinga* is made from very tough meats and quite chewy), and the vendor (from the North) told me he made his own *tankora* powder that included: white pepper, dried sweet green pepper powder (the only time I've ever heard of that in *tankora* powder), dried powdered ginger, ground nutmeg, Maggi and Royco shrimp seasoning cubes, salt, peanut powder, and dried red pepper.

Directions

Mix all the ingredients together.

Removing Skins From Black-eyed Peas

Several Ghanaian (and other West African) dishes first require removal of the outer coating (skins) from black-eyed peas. While it is possible to purchase pre-hulled and pre-ground peas in some African stores, I have found such packages unacceptable due to the presence of small stones and grittiness. Also, a food scientist suggests that my displeasure also had to do with the fine size of ground beans making it hard to attain the right fluffiness in the batters. Many others find them helpful, however. If using them, simply soak the dehulled beans and omit the manual, labor-intensive dehulling process described here.

Allow plenty of time for this step. I regularly do it several hours before I actually need to use the dehulled beans, storing them in the refrigerator. Dehulled beans are most commonly used in making *Akara* (Black-eyed Pea Fritters, page 78) and can also be used in preparing *Tubaani* (Black-eyed Pea Steamed Pudding, page 76).

To dehull a cup of dried black-eyed peas:

1. Pick over the black-eyed peas and discard any unacceptable ones, rinse, and soak them in about 3 or 4 cups of water for at least 30 minutes.
2. Fill a large bowl with water and add the beans. Take up a handful of beans and rub them between your palms and/or thumb and fingers to loosen the skins so they pop off. The skins will float to the surface and you can pour them off or add more water to the bowl and have them float out.

Or to save time, especially with large batches use a food processor:

2. Put the beans in a food processor in several batches, along with a very small amount of the water they soaked in, and pulse very briefly, just a few seconds, three or four times. The goal is to loosen the skins, not to grind the beans themselves. Pour the beans out of the food processor and back into a large bowl. Fill it with water and tilt and shake the bowl slightly from side to side. The skins will begin floating to the top and over the edge of the bowl. It is a good idea to have a colander handy in case some of the beans start to also slip out. Supplement the removal by also rubbing the remaining skins between your palms and your thumb and fingertips.

Cracking the Mysteries of the Coconut

Coconuts are widely used in many world cuisines, including African, Brazilian, Asian, and Indian. "Fresh" coconuts in North America mean the brown hairy ones with hard shells sold in the produce section. In Ghana they call those "dried," and when they say "fresh" coconut they mean the literally fresh green ones right off the trees, often sold with the tops whacked off with a machete right in front of you. Those coconuts are soft and gelatinous inside, and you can drink the coconut water right out of them, scooping the meat up with a spoon or a piece of shell.

Opening Coconuts & Extracting Coconut Water

There is more than one way to crack open a hard brown coconut. This is a fun activity to do with children and young adults—just make sure that they stand back when someone is swinging the hammer. If your coconut shows any signs of mold, return it to the store where it was purchased and get a refund. I generally buy two coconuts when I need one, just in case.

Tools
hammer

ice pick or similar sharp implement (I've used screwdrivers, clean
nails, and the meat pick from a nut cracker set)

newspapers

large towel

cup, tall glass, or small pitcher

fine strainer

knife and/or vegetable peeler

Remember that the liquid extracted in Step 3 is NOT coconut "milk" (see page 28). It is coconut water, found both in the brown and the green coconuts. It makes a healthy, refreshing drink and has become somewhat of a fad in grocery stores in North America, where its health benefits are increasingly exalted and it is hailed as a sports drink and anti-aging wonder drink. It is sold canned, but is easy to obtain directly from a coconut.

For those with more patience and less preference for hammering, one can also put a cracked-open coconut on a cookie sheet or baking dish in a medium preheated oven (350 degrees F) for about half an hour or until the meat pulls away from the shell.

Directions

1. I usually crack open coconuts in my garage where I have a cement floor, but it can also be done indoors. Spread a few newspapers under the coconut and turn it up so you see the three "eyes" at one end. Place the ice pick, or whatever you are using, in the center of one of the eyes, and hammer it through the eye to make a hole and then wiggle it around to enlarge the hole and remove it. Repeat the process with the other 2 eyes.

2. Turn the coconut over a glass, cup, or small pitcher (use a tea strainer to keep out bits of shell) and let the coconut water run into it. Always try to buy a "juicy" coconut (shake them in the store before you buy).

3. After removing the liquid from the coconut, move the glass or cup to a safe place, and wrap the coconut with a towel to avoid flying coconut pieces. Put the coconut down on the floor and begin hammering away. Many times there will be a small line around the center of the coconut that has been made to make it easier to crack the coconut open. If there is such a line, aim at it or otherwise at the center (not the ends). When the coconut begins cracking open, keep pounding away until many of the pieces of the white meat have broken off from the shell (they will have a brown coating on one side). The rest can be pried off carefully with a knife. You may have to unwrap it a few times to check, and even leave the towel off near the end.

4. Use a vegetable peeler to remove the brown skin from the coconut, which can be cut or broken into pieces and served that way, or grated or chopped into fruit salads or other recipes.

Making Coconut Milk

Coconut milk is made from the meat of the coconut, either fresh or dried. While canned coconut milk is available and convenient, it is expensive and has emulsifiers/preservatives in it. It is possible to hand-grate fresh coconut meat for this recipe (no need to remove the brown peel after taking off the shell) but I prefer using organic dried grated unsweetened coconut.

Tools and Ingredients
blender

cheesecloth

strainer or colander

large bowl

Scant cup dried unsweetened grated coconut (preferably organic)

1½ cups hot water

Directions
1. Put a scant cup of the dried coconut into a blender container. Pour in 1 cup of the hot water and blend for 2 or 3 minutes.
2. Place the colander or strainer over a large bowl and line it with the cheesecloth. Pour the coconut-water mixture from the blender into the cheesecloth, using a spatula to scrape it all in.
3. Pick up the cheesecloth from the ends and twist to get all the liquid out and into the bowl. Put the coconut in the cheesecloth back into the blender and add another ½ cup of hot water and blend again for 1 or 2 minutes and then repeat the process with the cheesecloth. Discard the coconut dregs or use for added fiber in baking.
4. Pour the coconut milk into a jar and store for up to a few days in the refrigerator.

Make ahead: I always use my coconut milk as soon as I make it, but you can also freeze leftovers in an ice cube tray to use later. After freezing, store the cubes in the freezer in a covered container.

To use: The coconut cream rises to the top and can be used like cream or stirred back into the milk when using.

Toasting and Grinding Corn Flour

Ablemamu

Toasted corn flour is a key ingredient in several Ghanaian classics. While it is easy to buy this corn flour in Ghana, those of us outside Ghana may need to make our own unless we have access to an international or online market where it is sold. One solution is to simply toast cornmeal in a dry frying pan, but I prefer this "make-do" version. This produces a toasted corn that is still not quite as fine as Ghana's, but quite acceptable.

Ingredients
1 cup white popcorn kernels

Directions
1. Preheat a heavy skillet over medium heat. Toast the popcorn on medium heat, shaking it constantly for about 6 minutes, or until just before the kernels pop.
2. Quickly pour the kernels onto a cool plate so that they do not continue to heat and pop.
3. Grind the kernels in a coffee grinder, straining them through a fine tea strainer and regrinding the chaff until getting the amount needed.

To serve: *See recipes on pages 154, 162, and 197.*

Fermented Corn and Cassava Doughs

Fermentation is an important culinary technique in tropical countries such as Ghana, especially of starches such as maize (corn) and cassava (also called yucca or manioc). While it is easy to buy freshly prepared corn dough or cassava dough in Ghana, in North America there are generally three choices: 1) make your own; 2) buy an imported "instant powder" version; 3) buy pre-frozen dough from Ghana. For many years, my only option was to make my own, but today with advances in processing techniques and transportation, I am more likely to buy frozen dough, such as Nina's fermented corn meal (no cassava) or corn and cassava dough. I still find the instant powders do not suit me. Note: While *Banku* in Ghana is made from both corn and cassava dough, in the U.S. I was taught to make it only with corn dough, which was easily available. I follow that custom here.

In case you do not have access to imports, the traditional "Western" way of making your own dough is given here.

I once asked a food scientist in Ghana why the fermented corn dough in Ghana tastes different from the one I make here in the U.S. I already knew that the dry milled corn flour was coarser than the wet milled corn found in Ghana. He explained that it may partially be because they are different varieties of corn and different bacteria, but primarily because the starches change to sugar differently in the unground and ground corns. Finally, while some people express (possibly excessive) concern about possible aflatoxins on corn that has not been properly dried and processed, this is not a problem for commercially available cornmeal in the United States.

Fermented Corn Dough
Banku Dough

When I was first married, I tried valiantly to ferment *masa harina*, only to discover that the lime processing of that flour prohibited fermentation from taking place. Here is one way to make your own dough. Note that it takes several days before the fermented dough is ready to use. While people generally prefer white cornmeal in Ghana, yellow cornmeal may be substituted.

Ingredients
3 cups white Indian Head cornmeal or similar stone ground cornmeal
1 tablespoon cornstarch

Directions
1. Put 3 cups of cornmeal into a nonreactive container, like glass or ceramic. Add 1 tablespoon of cornstarch and mix them together well using a wire whisk.
2. Add 2½ to 3 cups of lukewarm water (add a little more if the dough seems very dry). Mix thoroughly with a whisk, cover lightly with a cloth or paper towel and leave to sit in a warm place (counter, stovetop, or oven) for several days, stirring once a day.
3. The dough should begin to bubble up as it ferments. If any mold forms on top, carefully scrape it off. The longer it ferments, the sourer it will become. I usually give mine about 3 days, depending on how warm the weather is. (Some people suggest adding a little vinegar to get the sour taste, but I do not.)

To serve: See recipes on pages 186 and 187.

Fermented Cassava Dough

The Ewe people number between 3 and 6 million, mostly living in Southeastern Ghana in the Volta Region and also southern parts of neighboring Togo and Benin. While Barbara Baëta can and does prepare dishes from all ten regions in the country (and far beyond), she is an Ewe woman and her heart belongs to places like Keta along the coast. On her own table, she displays a love of dishes featuring the riches of the sea and coast along with dishes including cassava dough, such as *Akple* (page 189), the Ewe version of *Banku*. It is my understanding that the main difference between the two is fermentation and the cassava dough (*Banku* is mostly made from fermented corn dough and some cassava dough in Ghana, though I usually make my *Banku* with just fermented corn dough; *Akple* is made from unfermented corn and cassava dough).

Here is my approach to creating the cassava dough. Finding fresh cassava is the first challenge. It is a root and will likely be called yucca in U.S. markets. It does not keep well and will probably be coated in wax. Ask someone in the produce department to cut a few tubers in half before you buy them to make sure they are not rotten.

Ingredients
1 pound tubers of fresh cassava/yucca

Directions
1. Peel the cassava and drop them in some water. To peel: cut the ends off, cut the cassava root in half at the center, and then use a sharp knife to peel back the dark bark and remove it. If you also cut the pieces horizontally, you will see a stringy piece running down the center of the cassava; pull it out or grate it along with the rest of the cassava.
2. Grate the cassava into a clean bowl. I use the "fine" side of a box grater. You should end up with around 2½ cups of grated cassava.
3. Put the cassava in a nonreactive bowl (glass, plastic, stainless steel) and add ½ cup of water and swish the cassava and water around with your fingers or a spoon.
4. Drain the wet mixture. My strategy is: put the grated cassava into a clean pillowcase and double it over, then place the pillowcase on a latticed patio chair or similar surface outside with a plastic pan under it to catch the starchy water draining out. (Put a paper towel between the chair and pillowcase). Then place a bowl weighted down with rocks on top of it, and leave it outside in warm, dry weather (a garage would be an alternative). Not elegant, but it works.*
5. After 2 or 3 days, you should have a dry, tightly pressed together clump of cassava. Place 1 cup of water (or more, if necessary) and the cassava in a blender, and blend to a smooth dough/paste. This dough may be used immediately or frozen. (See recipe using it: *Akple*, page 189).

* This process is awkward and cumbersome (which is why I don't usually make my own), but the toxins in cassava, and the need to weight it down heavily and allow the liquid to drain out, mean it isn't something I'd do in the kitchen. To avoid the mess, one should just buy frozen cassava dough, if available.

Tomato Tips

Tomatoes in all forms are indispensable in the Ghanaian kitchen. Many of the recipes call for tomatoes, and generally one can use fresh or canned tomatoes interchangeably. In Ghana one usually adds whole fresh tomatoes to the soup broth to soften them while cooking the soup, then they are removed, the skins slipped off, and then ground in an *asanka* or electric blender. Some people prefer to deseed the tomatoes, others do not. When slicing or chopping tomatoes into a stew, often the peelings are left on, but they may be omitted as well.

Certainly, sun-ripened tomatoes fresh off the vine are wonderful, but they are not always available. My second choice would generally be canned plum tomatoes, pureed in a blender. (I like to remove the seeds by straining pureed tomatoes through a strainer, but that is a personal preference.) Tomato sauce can be used in a pinch, but it will add other flavors besides the tomato, and is sometimes sweetened, something Ghanaians would never do. Note that canned already-pureed tomatoes tend to be thicker than when pureeing canned tomatoes oneself. I find them too sweet so prefer to puree them personally.

And finally a word about **tomato paste**—Ghanaians love tomato paste. In 2006 it was reported that Ghana was the world's second largest importer of tomato paste after Germany. Tomato paste finds its way into many soups and sauces and stews. It is easy to buy small tins of it any season of the year, when fresh tomatoes may not be available. Also, it is highly concentrated, and only takes a fraction of the amount of fresh tomatoes. It can flavor and thicken soups and stews without making them watery. In a pinch, tomato paste may be thinned with water to replace fresh or canned tomatoes. In most of the recipes, it is a personal choice which to use.

On a health note, tomato paste is said to be a great source of lycopene, a cancer-fighting antioxidant optimally helpful when eaten during a meal that contains a little fat. According to the Heinz Institute of Nutritional Sciences one serving of raw tomato provides 3.7 mg of lycopene, whereas a serving of tomato paste provides 13.8 mg. Another reason to love it. Oh, and it also adds that umami flavor.

To peel/deseed/puree fresh tomatoes:

To peel: Bring enough water to cover the tomatoes to a boil in a small saucepan. Take it off the heat and put the tomatoes into the hot water and let sit until their skins begin to split, about 2 minutes. Remove them with a slotted spoon and plunge them into cold water to loosen the skins. Peel off the loose skin.

To deseed: Cut the tomatoes into halves or quarters. Place a strainer over a bowl and hold the tomato pieces over the strainer while using your fingers to remove the seeds. The juice will be saved in the bowl.

To puree: After peeling and removing the seeds, puree the tomatoes using an electric blender, and add back in the juices lost in seeding.

APPROXIMATE YIELDS WHEN USING FRESH TOMATOES (not including plum tomatoes, which have more pulp). This is not an exact science and actual amounts may vary:

1 medium tomato (approximately 4 ounces) yields about:
    cored, sliced or chopped: ¾ cup
    blended (with peel and seeds): ⅔ cup
    peeled/seeded/chopped: ½ cup + 2 to 3 teaspoons juice
    peeled/seeded/blended: ⅓ cup
    grated (peel and core discarded): ½ cup

1 large tomato (approximately 7 ounces) yields about:
    cored, sliced or chopped: 1⅓ cups
    blended (with peel and seeds): 1 cup
    peeled/seeded/chopped: ⅔ cup + 2 tablespoons juice
    peeled/seeded/blended: almost ⅔ cup
    grated (peel and core discarded): ¾ cup

Cooking with Peppers

PEPPERCORNS

When reading recipes in Ghanaian or other African cookbooks, never assume that "add pepper" means adding "black pepper" in the Western sense. Ghanaian cooking is noted for its liberal use of a variety of chili peppers in cooking, both fresh and dried. However, long before Portuguese explorers arrived in Ghana in 1471, likely bringing chili peppers with them, Ghanaians were using other types of pepper in their cooking. They still use them today. Those listed below are similar in shape and color to the familiar black peppercorns (*Piper nigrum*) commonly used in Western cooking. However, they all have distinctive flavors and are worth adding to one's repertoire. If unavailable, *Piper nigrum* can generally be used as a substitute.

Grains of Paradise (*Aframomum melegueta*): Called *fom wisa* in Twi, but also known as melegueta pepper, Guinea grains, or Guinea pepper, the name refers to the seeds of an indigenous spice from West Africa related to the cardamom family. (Melegueta pepper should not be confused with the Brazilian malagueta pepper, a *Capsicum frutescens* chili pepper.) In the 1700s, while Ghana was noted for its gold (Gold Coast) and Côte d'Ivoire or Ivory Coast for its ivory, much of present-day Liberia was known as the "Pepper Coast" or "Grain Coast" after this spice. *Fom wisa* seeds were highly sought by medieval spice traders as a substitute for black pepper in the fourteenth and fifteenth centuries. Ghanaians continue to value the seeds as a flavoring for food. *Aframomum melegueta* is used interchangeably with the closely related "alligator pepper," which technically belongs to the family *Aframomum danielli, A. citratum*, or *A. exscapum*.

Ashanti pepper (*Piper guineense*): Another peppercorn from West Africa, it is known as *masoro* in Hausa, or *soro wisa* in Twi. Other names are West African pepper, Benin pepper, false cubeb, Guinea cubeb, or uziza pepper.

Hwentia (*Xylopia aethiopica*): *Hwentia* is the Twi name for the seeds and seedpod of an African tree/shrub. *Hwentia* is also known as Grains of Selim, kimba pepper, African pepper, Moor pepper, Negro pepper, *Kani* pepper, *Kili* pepper, Sénégal pepper, or Ethiopian pepper. When cooking with *hwentia* (see the recipe for *Kelewele*, page 52), both the seeds and the seedpod are crushed.

CHILI PEPPERS

Chilies vary in size, shape, length, aroma, and color, but it is primarily the variation in their heat from capsaicin oil that distinguishes them. They range in color from red and green to yellow and orange, and are used both fresh and dried. Though originally from the Americas, they have spread throughout the world.

There are five basic species of Capsicum peppers, though hundreds of varieties: *C. annuum, C. baccautum, C. Chinense, C. frutescens, C. pubescens.* The most common chili peppers in Ghana come from the C. Chinense family. Ghanaians (especially outside of Ghana) love Scotch bonnet or habanero peppers. My personal favorite from Ghana is the green *kpakpo shito* with its distinctive fruity aroma. I cherish the hope that this pepper will one day find its way across the ocean.

Handling chili peppers:

A habanero or Scotch bonnet pepper can be from 40 to 140 times hotter than a jalapeno. That explains why cooks are advised to wear rubber gloves and use extreme caution when working with chili peppers, especially the hotter varieties. Some people advocate using goggles to protect the eyes. Neither gloves nor goggles are used in Ghana, except perhaps in professional kitchens. When using fresh peppers such as habanero, never touch a pepper directly. I hold the washed pepper with a fork and use a sharp knife to deseed it or remove membranes. Incidentally, capsaicin oil is not water soluble, which is why drinking a lot of water or rinsing a hand with water will not help ease the burn. It is fat soluble, so drinking milk or rubbing oil or even milk on a hand will help alleviate the heat.

Using chili peppers in my recipes:

It is a challenge to indicate exactly how much chili pepper to use in the recipes in this book. It depends on the type of pepper and personal preference. Often I add a slice or two of a chili pepper to a stew or soup and taste the stew as it cooks, removing the slice if the stew seems to be getting too hot. Sometimes I simply slice off the end and cook the pepper whole in a soup. Once cooked, the pepper can be gently squeezed with a spoon (in the soup to avoid squirting one's eyes) and the heat can be gradually released into the soup; or it can be sliced and served alongside the soup or stew, allowing diners who wish more heat to help themselves. I often combine both fresh and dried chili peppers. Sometimes part of a chili pepper can be blended with tomatoes or other spices like garlic or ginger before adding to the soup or stew. Much of the heat in the chili peppers is contained in the seeds and inner membranes, so one way to reduce the heat is to deseed and cut out the membranes.

When using chilies, it is best to be cautious and conservative. For those new to chili peppers, it is wise to begin with dried ground red pepper, gradually increasing the amount until the desired spiciness is obtained—remember, more can be added but the reverse is not true. Be aware that dried hot ground red pepper directly imported from Ghana is hotter than that commonly sold in North American grocery stores.

CHILI PEPPER HEAT

The heat in capsicums is commonly rated using the SHU (Scoville Heat Units). While helpful, its accuracy is limited, as the same variety of pepper can have widely varied intensity or pungency, depending on soil, climate, or even location on the same bush. Below are listed some common SHU of peppers and sauces, in ascending order of heat:

Habanero (*C. chinense Jacquin*)	100,000 to 350,000 SHU
Scotch bonnet (*C. chinense*)	100,000 to 325,000 SHU
Kpakpo shito (*C. chinense*)	70,000 to 100,000 SHU
Cayenne (*C. annuum*)	30,000 to 50,000 SHU
Jalapeno (*C. annuum*)	2,500 to 5,000 SHU
Tabasco Original Pepper Sauce	2,500 to 5,000 SHU
Paprika (*C. annuum*)	0 to 300 SHU
Bell peppers (*C. annuum*)	0

Ghanaian Basic Tomato Gravy

Just as Brazilian cooking often begins with preparation of a base called a *refogado*, or Spanish Caribbean cooking uses a *sofrito*, in Ghana many stews begin with a simple "gravy," made from oil, sliced or chopped onions, sliced or chopped fresh tomatoes (or canned tomatoes or tomato paste), likely chili peppers (fresh or dried and ground), and sometimes fresh garlic and/or ginger. The oil may be canola, soy, peanut, corn, palm, coconut, or other vegetable oil, each with a distinctive flavor. In contemporary middle-class Ghanaian homes, expensive imported olive oil is more often finding its way into recipes for stews and sauces. This popularity is based on the perception that olive oil is healthier than traditional oils. It does, however, impart a "non-Ghanaian" flavor to the food.

From this combination, other vegetables and/or protein sources can be added. This list includes an endless variety of greens, eggplant, pumpkin, cowpeas, eggs, fresh and/or smoked/dried fish and shrimp, seeds, and nuts. The gravy is also a base for one-pots where rice or *gari* (cassava meal) are added to make Ghanaian classics reminiscent of fried rice, Spanish rice, or paella (see *Gari Foto* and *Jollof Rice* recipes, pages 152 and 156). This basic sauce can also stand on its own merits and be served with many of the recipes in this book, from Rice and Beans (*Waakye*) to *Jollof* or Coconut Rice, *Banku*, *Ampesi* (Boiled Starchy Vegetables), or Fried Ripe Plantains, etc. Also, it is easy to add things to it, from fresh or dried or smoked fish and seafood, poultry, snails, mutton, pork, beef, or goat to vegetables or ground seeds or nuts, singly and in combination.

But classically, tomato gravy only requires oil, onion, tomato, chili pepper, and salt. For health reasons, I have halved the amount of oil used in Ghana.

North American vs. Ghanaian: Ghanaian gravy is not your typical American gravy. After I married and invited my brother-in-law Kwaku and his family to my home in Pennsylvania to experience a typical "American Thanksgiving," Kwaku kept looking past that brown stuff at the table for the familiar red sauce that would make his bland mashed potatoes and roast turkey edible. Several times he asked "But where's the *gravy?*" before I realized what was happening.

Makes about 2 cups

Version 1: Everyday Tomato Gravy

Ingredients

2 to 4 tablespoons vegetable oil (palm, peanut, canola, etc.)

1 large onion or several scallions, peeled and sliced or chopped (1 cup)

1 heaping teaspoon crushed or minced garlic (optional)

1 heaping teaspoon grated or minced fresh ginger (optional)

2 cups sliced or diced tomatoes

Chili pepper, to taste (use as much of a seeded and chopped habanero or Scotch bonnet [hot] or jalapeno [mild] as desired—for beginners, a thin slice will do); or ⅛ teaspoon dried ground red pepper to begin with and adjust to taste (more can be added, but the reverse is not true)

½ teaspoon salt or seasoned salt (or to taste)

1 heaping teaspoon canned tomato paste

½ cup water or stock

Directions

1. Heat the oil in a skillet on medium heat for 2 minutes. Add the onions to the hot oil and sauté for 2 minutes. Stir in the garlic and ginger, if using, and sauté 2 or 3 minutes more.
2. Stir in the tomatoes, chili pepper, and salt. Stir in tomato paste and water or stock.
3. Simmer about 15 minutes on medium-low heat, or until the gravy has thickened to the desired consistency, stirring occasionally. Adjust the seasonings.

Version 2: A Smoother Tomato Gravy

Ingredients
1 large onion, peeled and coarsely chopped

2 cloves garlic, peeled

1-inch piece fresh ginger, peeled and coarsely chopped (optional)

3 or 4 medium tomatoes or 1 (14.5 ounce) can diced tomatoes

¼ cup oil

⅛ to ¼ teaspoon dried ground red pepper (or more to taste)

1½ teaspoons canned tomato paste

½ teaspoon salt or seasoned salt (or to taste)

½ cup water or stock

Directions
1. Put the onion, garlic, and ginger into a blender or food processor. Add 2 table-spoons of water. Blend until smooth, pausing and using a spatula to push mixture down if necessary. Pour the mixture into a bowl and set aside while preparing the tomatoes.
2. Peel (and deseed, if desired) the tomatoes. Put them in the (unwashed) blender or food processor and puree.
3. Heat oil in a large frying pan on medium heat for 2 minutes. Add pureed onion mixture and sauté for 5 minutes on medium-low heat.
4. Stir in the pureed tomatoes, ground red pepper, tomato paste, salt, and ½ cup water or stock (use the water to rinse out the blender container before adding it to the pan, if desired).
5. Simmer about 15 minutes on medium-low heat, stirring occasionally, until the gravy has thickened to the desired consistency. Adjust seasonings. This "gravy" should be a thick sauce, too thick to pour.

Variations: Cooks often add their favorite seasonings to the gravy, such as a little ground nutmeg, white pepper, curry powder, or a crumbled seasoning cube.

Basic Stocks and Soups

Most soups in Ghana start with a basic stock. There are three main foundations for Ghanaian soups and some stews. The cornerstone of them all is a simple broth or stock that is the basis of what are called "light soups." It contains no added fats, and is a broth made from poultry, meat and/or fish, onion, tomato, chili pepper, salt, probably garlic and ginger, and sometimes other seasonings. (Timesaver hint: In most cases, a commercially produced meat, poultry, fish, or vegetable stock can be substituted.)

The second stock is for "groundnut soups," or what might be better called "peanut soups" in the U.S. (Peanuts, legumes that grow in the ground, are called "groundnuts" in England and Ghana was once a British colony.) In Ghana, where fresh milk and cream are not readily available, the basic soup stock is often thickened with creamy roasted and pounded peanuts.

The third basic soup category is those with a palm butter base, made from the pulp of the red palm fruit, known as "palmnut soups."

After mastering a basic "light soup," one can confidently proceed to make any of the soups in this book. *Lovely Light Soup with Goat* is the first soup I learned to make in Ghana, when I was in my early 20s, so I have presented it here for you to try. It is still hard to beat. It is a basic stock made from vegetables and goat meat. Other broths may be made substituting poultry, beef, or fish, including bones, singly or in combination, and the seasonings may vary depending on personal preference.

Lovely Light Soup with Goat
Apɔnkye Nkrakra

Makes 6 to 8 servings

This recipe is adapted from a version served at Flair. This simple version is hard to beat. No added fats, either, it is the original "lite" soup. I enjoy it best with some *Fufu* (Ghana-Style Dumplings, page 190). Ahhhhhh! It should be called "Goat Light Soup for the Soul."

Ingredients

1 pound goat meat with bones, cut into chunks

1 large or 2 or 3 medium whole tomatoes

1 onion, peeled and quartered

Fresh whole red chili pepper to taste (your choice, see chart page 37; try using just a slice of a Scotch bonnet or 1 whole jalapeno if not used to cooking with chili peppers), trimmed and seeds removed if desired; or ⅛ teaspoon or more dried ground red pepper

1 tablespoon tomato paste

Meat Seasoning

1 heaping teaspoon grated fresh ginger

2 or 3 cloves garlic, peeled and crushed

½ teaspoon ground aniseed (*sekoni*) or other seasoning of your choice

1 to 2 teaspoons salt or seasoning of your choice (many Ghanaians would likely use Adobo or other seasoned salt and Maggi or Royco seasoning cubes)

½ to 1 teaspoon dried ground red pepper (or to taste)

2 small bay leaves, left whole

Directions

1. Put the goat meat in a large soup pot and add all of the meat seasoning ingredients and ½ cup water. Stir well. Cover, bring to a boil, lower the heat and let the meat simmer while preparing the broth.

2. Bring 4 cups of water to a boil in another large pot. Slice the top off the chili pepper. Add the whole tomatoes, quartered onion, and chili pepper, and simmer 10 minutes or just until the vegetables are soft. Remove the vegetables with a slotted spoon and grind in a blender or *asanka*. If desired, discard the chili pepper or deseed it and slice and grind with the other vegetables, gradually adding the slices little by little till you have the desired heat. Return the ground vegetables to the water in the pot and add 4 more cups of water. Stir in the tomato paste. Pour the broth mixture into the pot with the seasoned meat.

3. Let the soup simmer until the goat meat is tender (this may take several hours as goat meat tends to be tougher than beef).

4. Optional Step: To make a clearer soup, once the goat meat is tender, remove the goat meat with a slotted spoon and strain the broth through a sieve into a large pot or bowl, using a spoon if necessary to help force some of the ground vegetables through the sieve (scrape the underside of the strainer with a spoon also), then return the meat and broth to the pot and adjust the seasonings (salt, onion, tomato, dried red pepper, etc.) to taste. Add a little more water if necessary.

½ cup chopped onion

1 small jalapeno pepper (mild); or 1 small cayenne pepper (medium); or 1 habanero (hot); or 3 kpakpo shito peppers (hot); or ¼ to ½ teaspoon dried red pepper to begin (or to taste), optional

Variations:

Cook some eggplant or zucchini in a saucepan, then blend and add near the end for a thicker soup.

Add other vegetables like okra or mushrooms; and/or add other herbs or seasonings depending on what you have on hand.

PART II: RECIPES

SNACKS, STREET FOODS & APPETIZERS

PLANTAINS

Plantains, those large, starchy relatives of the bananas we eat in North America, must be cooked before eating. This book contains recipes for them at all stages: green and hard, yellow and soft, and black and yellow and almost "reddish" when "over-ripe." Ghana is reportedly the largest producer of plantains in West Africa—only Uganda and Rwanda are said to produce more on the continent. In Rwanda, plantains, sometimes called "cooking bananas," are an important dietary staple and have been called "potatoes of the air." Perhaps this is because, like potatoes, they are a major starch eaten with meals and they grow on trees rather than in the ground. Major growing areas in Ghana are the Eastern, Ashanti, and Brong-Ahafo regions.

COCOYAMS (TARO)

A variety of the tropical plant taro (*Colocasia esculenta*) is called "*cocoyam*" or "*mankani*" in West Africa. Both its leaves and the root (called a corm) are edible. Cocoyams can be peeled and thinly sliced and fried following the same procedure as for Green Plantain Chips (opposite page). They are slightly harder to slice because they are more slippery when peeling and slicing, but worth the effort. Use one small cocoyam per person. I usually buy cocoyams at an Asian market. They should be fresh, firm, hard, and hairy, with rings around the corm and no sprouts. Cocoyam chips have a different flavor and texture than potato chips, though they are also mild. As with plantains, the thinner the chips are cut, the crispier they are. I make mine paper thin, using a Y vegetable peeler.

When my husband and I were (literally) poor graduate students and married in Ghana in 1972, we cooked and served these at our wedding reception. They were inexpensive but elegant.

Green Plantain Chips

Makes 5 servings (6 strips each)

This is a popular snack food throughout western Africa. Inexpensive and easy to make, these are a sure way to impress your friends in the U.S. Freshly made plantain chips beat the store-bought ones any day. They are not sweet, quite unlike dried dessert banana chips.

Ingredients

2 large green plantains (each plantain makes 12 to 18 strips, depending on size)

Several cups of vegetable oil (like canola) for deep frying

Salt to taste

Troubleshooting: If a strip of plantain dropped into the oil sits on the bottom, the oil is too cold. If as soon as it is dropped in it comes to the top and almost immediately begins to brown, the oil is too hot.

Thinly sliced and fried plantain chips or strips are readily available in Ghana both salted and spiced. Other "chips" are increasingly being sold commercially in Ghana made from root vegetables such as sweet potatoes (*atomo*), cassava (*duade*), or cocoyams.

Directions

1. Rinse the plantains and peel by slicing off the end tips and making a slit lengthwise through the peel without cutting into the plantain itself. Use the tip of a knife to pry the peel loose to get started, then remove the peel by hand. Scrape off any fibrous strings on the plantain.
2. There are different ways to slice the plantain (see variations). I prefer making long very thin slices using a y-shaped vegetable peeler or a standard peeler. Lay them out flat on a large tray or baking sheet without touching one another as they are cut.
3. Fill a heavy pan or deep fryer no more than halfway with oil and heat the oil to 365 degrees F. (On my stovetop, the medium-high setting gives approximately the correct temperature, but it must be monitored and turned up and down to keep it there.)
4. Get about 18 slices ready and add to the preheated oil a few at a time. Do not add them all at once or they will clump. Nudge them as they are added to prevent them from sticking to each other. Stir with a long-handled spoon to ensure even cooking. Remove the chips with a slotted spoon in a few minutes when they are golden and crisp and drain them on a paper towel-lined colander or platter. (If the chips bend they are not fully cooked: they should be crispy, like potato chips.)
5. Salt to taste while they are still warm. After cooling, store in an airtight container.

Variations:

Sprinkle the chips with salt mixed with dried ground red pepper to taste.

Instead of strips, cut the plantain into thin rounds or ovals.

Savory Plantain Pancakes
Tatale

Makes 10 to 12 (using ½ cup batter)
or 15 to 18 (using ⅓ cup batter)

I grew to love plantains in Ghana, and am especially partial to them when they are ripe (yellow) or over-ripe (black and yellow and squishy). One of my favorite ways to prepare them is as a simple savory pancake (no syrup, please). It is customarily eaten with boiled *bambara* ground-nuts, which also grow in the northern regions of Ghana.

The first challenge is to procure ripe-to-overripe plantains. In some parts of North America one must buy green (unripe) plantains and let them ripen at home. As a rule, buy twice as many plantains as required, two or three weeks before they are needed.

Ingredients

3 or 4 large over-ripe plantains (about 1½ pounds after peeling; about 3 cups when sliced)

½ cup finely grated onion or shallots

3 teaspoons grated or ground fresh ginger

1 to 2 teaspoons dried ground red pepper (more or less to taste)

Scant ⅛ teaspoon calabash nutmeg or regular nutmeg (optional)

¼ to ½ teaspoon salt (or to taste; optional)

⅓ to ½ cup (2 ounces) rice flour or cornmeal

⅓ to ½ cup (2 ounces) all-purpose flour

About 1 cup palm oil for pan frying

Directions

Make batter:

1. Cut the ends off the plantains and slit horizontally along one side, then peel and slice them. Put the plantain slices into a large mixing bowl and mash them. Traditionally these would then be pounded in a mortar with a wooden pestle, but if you must use a blender or food processor, keep some of the mashed plantain out and add after blending the rest so there are still some pieces remaining.

2. Stir in the onions or shallots, ginger, dried ground red pepper, nutmeg, if using, and salt.

3. Add the rice flour (or cornmeal if you prefer) and all-purpose flour and stir. Add 1 cup of water and stir again. Let the mixture sit for 20 to 30 minutes before cooking the pancakes.

Cook pancakes:

4. Heat a heavy skillet or griddle as for regular pancakes (medium-high heat). Use a pastry brush to brush palm oil generously on the pan, then drop the batter onto the griddle using ⅓ to ½ cup batter for each pancake. Use a spoon to spread the batter into a circle shape.

5. When the pancake is firm enough to turn without breaking, turn it over with a pancake turner, pressing the turner down firmly on the pancake to flatten it. Continue doing this every few minutes while the pancakes cook. Barbara and I like our *tatale* quite brown and

In Ghana, *tatale* with *aboboe* makes a wonderful, elegantly simple party snack, especially pleasant when washed down with cold glasses of beer. It is hearty enough for non-vegetarians to adore. Interestingly, *tatale* with *aboboe* is the only Ghanaian dish I know of, apart from porridge, where sugar is served on the side and may be added to the beans to taste. Still, some purists insist that even that is a foreign intrusion.

"crusty", but they may be fried to suit individual preference.

6. Set the pancakes on paper towels to drain off excess oil. Avoid stacking them as you cook—spread them out to drain. Continue cooking pancakes until all batter is used, brushing fresh palm oil on the pan for each batch.

Make ahead: The cooked *tatale* can be kept warm in a low oven, but will become tough if heated too long. A better alternative is to heat them a few seconds in the microwave before serving them.

The batter may be made up to a day ahead and refrigerated, covered, until cooking time.

To serve: *Tatale* is classically eaten with Stewed Bambara Beans (*Aboboe*, page 142) or Bean Stew (*Red-Red,* page 124). When *bambara* beans/groundnuts are unavailable, an acceptable substitute is garbanzo beans (chickpeas). Peanuts have supplanted *bambara* beans/groundnuts in much of West Africa. Fresh boiled peanuts could also be used as could roasted unsalted peanuts.

Spicy Fried Plantain Cubes

Kelewele

Makes 4 to 6 servings

Kelewele is one of my all-time favorite snack foods from Ghana. It is generally described as something like "spicy fried plantain cubes," but that description is like calling a sunset "beautiful." Western cookbook versions I've seen are anemic versions of the best *kelewele* as prepared in Ghana, where it is often served accompanied by dry roasted unsalted peanuts. The sweet, spicy, and chewy plantain is a perfect counter to the mild crunchy/creamy flavor and texture of the peanuts. Years ago my husband and I used to go for walks in the evenings in Ghana to the roadside vendors whose lamps and candles flickered in the night and where the women neatly wrapped our hot, freshly cooked kelewele in clean newspaper.

Kelewele and peanuts go well with ice-cold beer or a drink like Ginger Beer (page 203) or Hibiscus Iced Tea (*Bissap*, page 205). The following recipe is a U.S. adaptation of Flair's version.

Ingredients

2 tablespoons coarsely chopped yellow or red onion

2 to 4 ounces fresh ginger, peeled and coarsely chopped

1 slice or more fresh red habanero or Scotch bonnet or other red chili pepper, seeds removed for milder flavor; or dried red pepper flakes or dried ground red pepper to taste (if you are new to chili peppers, begin with a small amount, such as 1 slice or ¼ to ½ teaspoon dried ground red pepper and add more gradually until the desired heat is achieved)

1 teaspoon whole cloves

1 teaspoon anise seeds

⅛ teaspoon finely grated calabash nutmeg or regular nutmeg (optional)

3 or 4 sticks hwentia (optional)

¼ teaspoon salt (or to taste)

4 large slightly over-ripe plantains (somewhat black and soft, but not completely), peeled

Vegetable oil for deep-frying

Directions

Prepare seasoning mixture:

1. Place the onion, ginger, chili pepper, cloves, anise seeds, nutmeg (if using), and 2 or 3 tablespoons of water in a mini food blender or processor along with 3 or 4 broken inch-long pieces of *hwentia* (*hwentia* adds a nice spicy, peppery, but not hot, flavor). Coarsely blend (it should not be completely blended and still have small pieces of cloves, aniseed, and hwentia).

Note: Sometimes you can use a small standard canning jar on a regular-size blender if you don't have a mini blender. It may be necessary to remove the jar and shake it a few times to blend the seasonings. If you use a regular-sized blender container, it may require stopping several times to use a rubber spatula to push the mixture down as it is blended. Alternatively, one can crush and mix all the ingredients by hand in batches in a small marble mortar with a pestle.

2. Pour the seasoning mixture into a small bowl, stir in the salt, and let it sit while preparing the plantains. (If desired, squeeze out the fibrous strings and use mostly the seasoned liquid left behind in the blender, discarding the large coarse fibers and broken spices.)

Prepare plantains:

3. Cut each plantain in half lengthwise, then cut each half in half lengthwise again, and slice each quarter on a diagonal into diamonds, or at 90 degree angles into small cubes. The size of each piece may be quite small (such as ½ inch or a little larger, depending on your preference.)
4. Sprinkle a few tablespoons of the seasoning mixture over the cut plantains and stir well to coat. Taste the mixture and adjust seasonings as necessary. Let the coated plantains sit for several minutes while preparing oil.

Fry plantains:

5. Heat oil in a deep fryer or heavy-bottomed pan to about 350 degrees F. Make sure the oil is shallow enough that it will not bubble over when adding the plantains.
6. Using a long-handled slotted spoon, put some of the seasoned plantain pieces into the hot oil, stirring to make sure they do not stick together. When they are nicely browned on all sides, remove and drain them on paper towels. Continue cooking the remaining plantains in small batches.

To serve: These are best eaten immediately or soon after cooking, preferably with dry roasted unsalted peanuts.

Spicy Plantain Balls
Kaklo / Kakro

Makes 12 to 24 balls

Never throw out squishy, moldy black plantains. They are perfect for many things, such as this recipe, reminiscent of both Savory Plantain Pancakes (*Tatale*, page 50) and Ghana-Style Donuts (*Bofrot/Togbei*, pages 84-86). Many Ghanaians choose these balls as a favorite snack or side dish, especially when served with a Fresh Pepper Sauce (page 168) or *Shito* (page 170). They also pair well with Bean Stew (*Red-Red*, page 124). While the seasoning ingredients are similar to those for *tatale*, the texture is quite different. This recipe is from Flair.

Ingredients
3 over-ripe plantains, or enough to yield at least 2 cups mashed

3 tablespoons finely grated onion

½ teaspoon dried ground red pepper

1 rounded teaspoon grated or finely minced fresh hot chili pepper, variety of your choice, such as jalapeno (mild) or cayenne (medium) or substitute additional dried ground red pepper (optional)

1 teaspoon salt

Scant ½ cup unfermented corn dough (page 189); or 1 cup toasted corn flour (page 29) mixed with ⅓ cup water

2 tablespoons all-purpose flour

1 heaping teaspoon baking powder

Vegetable oil for frying

Directions
Prepare the plantain balls:
1. Peel and mash the plantains to get a good 2 cups (a Ghanaian wooden mashing tool called an *apɔtɔyewa* or *apotoriwa* is perfect for this but you can used whatever tool you have in your kitchen).
2. Sprinkle the grated onion, dried ground red pepper, fresh chili pepper, and salt over the plantains, along with 2 or 3 tablespoons of water.
3. Add just enough water, a tablespoon at a time, to the corn dough to make it smooth, and add to the bowl with the plantains. Add the flour and baking powder, and stir well. If the dough seems very soft, add a little more flour; if it seems too dry, add a little more water.

Fry the plantain balls:
4. Heat oil in a heavy pan or deep fryer not more than half-filled to 360 degrees F. Do a temperature test: when the oil is hot enough, a small amount of dough dropped into the oil will quickly rise to the surface.
5. When the oil is hot, slip a long-handled spoon into the oil to coat it, then scoop up a spoonful of batter (balls should be about 2-inches in diameter). Using another spoon (also coated with oil) quickly slide dough into the oil. Cook the *kaklo* in batches until they are quite browned on all sides. They will likely turn over as they cook, but use a long-handled slotted spoon to stir and turn them if needed.

6. Use the slotted spoon to lift them out into a paper towel-lined colander to absorb the extra oil and cool.

To serve: *Kaklo* can be eaten warm or at room temperature.

Variations:

Some earlier recipes omit the flour and baking powder. If choosing to do this, decrease the amount of water, or omit it altogether.

Some recipes include fresh ginger and some include a little sugar as an optional addition.

Some historic Ghana cookbooks (e.g., Alice Dede's *Ghanaian Favorite Dishes*, 1969; and *Ghana Recipe Book*, 1970) show how creative Ghanaian cooks have never limited themselves to making these fried balls with plantains. There are recipes using cassava instead of the plantains and serving them with coconut. Other recipes use mashed sweet potatoes in place of the plantains, eggs, butter or fat, water or milk, and coat the balls with breadcrumbs. They are then fried to be served with meat or fish stew.

Grilled Ripe Plantain Slices with Peanuts

Kofi Brokeman

Since living in Ghana I have become addicted to ripe plantains cooked in many different ways. They make a healthful (cooked) snack naturally low in sodium, but high in potassium, vitamins B6, C, and fiber, and are heartier than bananas. When ripe plantains are plentiful in Ghana, roadside vendors sell grilled slices along with small wrapped packages of shelled roasted peanuts with their skins still on. The combination provides a complete inexpensive but satisfying meal that goes by the popular nickname "*Kofi Brokeman*" (in other words, *Kofi* is "broke"—has no money).

Ingredients

1 ripe plantain per person

Roasted peanuts (*opposite page*)

In Ghana, if someone is eating *Kofi Brokeman* on a bus or in a public place near you, they will likely gesture politely to you and say "You are invited" (i.e., you are invited to join me), an ingrained hospitality gesture of Ghanaians.

Directions

1. Build a fire in a charcoal grill or fire up a gas grill. Brush oil on the grill rack to keep the plantain from sticking. (Alternatively, use "no stick" aluminum foil and put the peeled and sliced plantain directly on that.)
2. Cut the ends off the plantain, make a shallow cut just through the peel from end to end on one side, peel it and remove any stringy fibers. Cut the plantain on the diagonal into a few slices.
3. Spread out the coals, and place the rack a few inches above the charcoal. Grill the plantain pieces until they are brown and cooked on each side (about 5 to10 minutes per side). Be careful the slices do not burn. If they darken too quickly, raise the rack or move slices to the outside of the grill away from the direct heat.

To serve: These are best eaten warm off the grill with a few handfuls of dry roasted unsalted peanuts.

Roasted Peanuts

Makes 8 (¼ cup) servings

Market women in Ghana roast shelled peanuts with skins on in large pans filled with sand so the nuts heat and cook evenly. In the 1970s, they were served unsalted and tended to be small Spanish-type peanuts. Nowadays larger Virginia peanuts are common as well.

Raw shelled (or unshelled) peanuts may be found in international (especially Asian) markets or health food stores in the U.S. Whether serving peanuts as a snack or using them in cooking, roasting raw peanuts is not complicated.

Ingredients

2 cups raw peanuts, shelled, with or without skins

Salt (optional)

Directions

1. Preheat oven to about 325 degrees F.
2. Line a cookie sheet (or similar pan) with foil (optional), and spread 2 cups of peanuts in a single layer. Place the pan in the preheated oven and roast the peanuts for 3 to 5 minutes. Remove and shake the pan gently and return it to the oven to roast for another 3 to 5 minutes. Remove again and allow the peanuts to cool until you can taste them. (The skins will have turned dark and they will continue to cook after removing them, so make sure they are not overly brown.) Taste and if more cooking time is needed, shake the pan again and roast for a few more minutes.
3. After they are cooked and cooled, remove the skins by rubbing the peanuts between your palms. (I take my pan outside and fan it so the skins blow away.) Salt, if desired, while still warm. Cool and store in a covered container.

To serve: These are often served in Ghana along with Grilled Ripe Plantains (opposite page) to make *Kofi Brokeman*.

Boiled Peanuts

Makes 6 to 8 servings

In Ghana, as in many parts of the Southern U.S. and Asia, raw peanuts are enjoyed as a snack when boiled. Raw peanuts are called "green" when they are freshly dug up and contain moisture. In Ghana, people buy large quantities of the raw, dried peanuts still in their shells. The dried peanuts are soaked in water overnight, then boiled covered in salted water for several hours until the peanuts are soft. This is a great snack for eating outdoors. In the U.S., raw peanuts are commonly sold already shelled, and are available at health food stores or Asian markets.

Ingredients
2 cups shelled raw peanuts

1 teaspoon salt

Directions
1. Rinse the peanuts and soak in a bowl of water overnight.
2. Bring about 6 cups of water to a boil in a large saucepan. Drain the peanuts and add to the boiling water. Add 1 teaspoon of salt (or more).
3. Lower the heat to medium and cook the peanuts in the salted water until they are soft like beans. This may take anywhere from 1 hour to 4 hours depending on how fresh the peanuts are. Add more water as they cook, if needed. Drain the water off, and serve.

To serve: These may be eaten alone, but in Ghana boiled peanuts/groundnuts are sometimes served with boiled corn or cassava.

Peanut Balls
Kuli-Kuli

Makes 16 small balls

Ingredients

¾ cup peanut flour

8 tablespoons hot water

Salt to taste (optional)

Peanut oil for frying

Directions

1. Gradually add the hot water to the peanut flour to achieve the correct consistency for forming the dough into balls, adding more water or flour as needed. Mold the dough into small balls. (It helps to lightly flour one's hands with a little peanut flour before shaping the dough.)
2. Deep-fry the balls in hot peanut oil for a few minutes until they are crisp and brown on the outside. Drain in a colander or on paper towels.

Note: Do not try to use already prepared peanut butter to make these—the balls will simply disintegrate when you try to deep-fry them.

I observed some amazingly strong, skilled women in Bawku in Northern Ghana make *kuli-kuli*. After roasting, removing the skins, and grinding a metal drum full of peanuts, they removed the excess peanut oil by kneading the paste. They made this look easy, but it requires tremendous hand strength. After squeezing the mixture tightly into balls, they deep-fried them to remove more oil. Finally, they pounded the balls with a pestle in a wooden mortar to make another paste that was seasoned with salt and rolled into ropes thinner than pencils that were then joined together to form irregular circles, and deep-fried again. These final shapes are called *"kuli-kuli,"* though there are other versions, such as balls, with the same name. After years of laboriously duplicating the process (I actually put the ground peanuts between two cutting boards on the floor and stomped on them to extract the extra oil), a hugely labor-saving product has entered the U.S. market: "peanut flour" (e.g., Protein Plus).

Spicy Coated Peanuts

Makes 8 to 10 servings

Coating ingredients with a batter before deep-frying them is a common cooking technique in Ghana. In the U.S. we are most likely to coat peanuts with something sweet (as in the recipe for Peanut Toffee, page 212), but this savory snack/appetizer recipe is guaranteed to wake up those party peanuts! To locate raw unsalted peanuts with their skins on try an Asian market or health food store.

These are a perfect snack to eat while sipping ice-cold Star or Club beers, fruit juices, *bissap* (aka *sobolo*), ginger beer, or iced tea. In winter in North America they also go well with a hot drink like mulled wine, spiced cider, coffee, or tea. The hot oil somehow steams the peanuts so they're still chewy, but the crispy, spicy coating gives them a kick. Eat them soon after making them.

Ingredients

4 cups canola or other vegetable oil for deep-frying

1½ cups shelled raw unsalted peanuts with skins on

Batter

Heaping ¾ cup (4 ounces) unsifted all-purpose flour

¾ to 1½ teaspoons dried ground red pepper (or to taste)

¾ teaspoon salt (or to taste)

⅛ teaspoon (a pinch) white pepper

½ teaspoon baking powder

1 egg

1 can evaporated milk

Directions

1. Pour vegetable oil into a deep fryer or a deep heavy saucepan. Do not fill over half full. Heat the oil to about 360 degrees F while making the batter.

Prepare batter:

2. Sift together the five dry ingredients into a medium bowl.
3. In a separate bowl, beat the egg with a fork or wire whisk. Shake the can of evaporated milk then open it and add ⅓ cup to the egg along with ¼ cup water and beat to combine. Stir the wet ingredients into the dry ingredients.

Note: The first tricky part in this recipe is determining if the batter is the correct consistency: neither too thick so that the peanuts clump together, nor so watery the batter slips off the peanuts. If the batter seems too thick, add a tablespoon of water; if it seems too thin, add another tablespoon of flour.

Fry peanuts:

4. Put a spoonful of batter into a small bowl, and mix in an equal amount of peanuts. Add the peanuts to the hot oil.

Note: Here is the second tricky part—the goal is to get the peanuts to cook individually. I scoop a spoonful of coated peanuts onto a long-handled spoon over the fryer, then use the tip of a long-handled knife to carefully tap each peanut into the oil without splattering.

5. When the nuts are in the oil, stir frequently with a long-handled metal or wooden spoon to ensure they brown evenly. It will take about 5 to 6 minutes for them to cook.
6. As soon as they turn quite brown (the browner they are, the crispier they will be, but be careful they do not cross the line to burned), remove with a slotted spoon and drain them on paper towels or paper. Continue until all the peanuts are cooked. Serve hot or warm.

Troubleshooting:

If small drops of batter separate from the peanuts into the oil, the batter is too thin.

If long tails string out from the peanuts as they drop from the spoon, or the skin of the peanut is showing, likely the batter is too thick.

If the coated peanuts sink to the bottom of the pan and stay there, the oil is not hot enough.

If the peanuts are soggy, the oil is also not hot enough.

If the peanuts barely hit the oil before they start to brown, the oil is too hot.

Toasted Corn

Makes 6 to 8 servings

In Ghana, people frequently snack on seeds and nuts like tiger nuts, groundnuts/peanuts, and cashews, often combined with something else, such as fresh coconut or corn. While corn is boiled (and eaten alone or with fresh coconut) or popped, it is also toasted. African toasted corn requires the right type of dried corn—hominy, white Indian, or even yellow field corn. Popcorn kernels or dried sweet corn will not work. I have the best luck purchasing the corn in African specialty grocery stores.

The corn can be prepared several different ways: deep-frying, toasting in a pan on a stove top, or oven roasting. My husband claims this snack is a great stress reliever, especially when eaten with dry roasted unsalted peanuts. Note that this is not a snack for children, nor for anyone with weak teeth. Also, it is best eaten shortly after it has been cooked and cooled as it becomes harder as time passes.

Ingredients
2 cups dried corn

Vegetable oil (not olive oil)

Salt

Directions
Prepare corn:
1. Soak the corn in water for at least 3 days in the refrigerator but make sure it does not begin to sprout.
2. Rinse and drain the corn in a colander, and after allowing the water to drip off, blot the corn dry with paper towels or a clean cloth.

Deep-frying Method *(Note: This method is not for young people or anyone with little confidence or experience with deep-frying.)*

3. Fill a heavy frying pan with a cover no more than half-full with vegetable oil and heat on a stovetop on medium-high for 5 to 10 minutes. To test the temperature: Carefully, using a long-handled slotted spoon, lower a kernel of corn into the hot oil. If it sinks to the bottom and stays there, the oil is not hot enough; if it bounces up to the top immediately, the oil is too hot; if the oil bubbles and the corn gracefully floats up, it is perfect.
4. When the oil is ready, using a slotted spoon with a long handle, carefully pour the corn into the hot oil, give it a quick stir, and cover it immediately (I use a clear glass lid). It will begin to splatter as soon as the corn hits the oil (the reason for blotting the water off the drained corn). Depending on your stove, you may wish to turn the heat down to medium at this point.
5. After 5 minutes, with the edge of the lid away from you, using a potholder, carefully lift the lid halfway up (the edge of the lid in front facing down and the edge of the lid in back almost facing straight up). Quickly and carefully peek at the corn (around the lid) to see if it has turned golden or slightly brown. If not, continue cooking and check again in 2 minutes. You can also remove a kernel, let it cool, and taste to see if it is crunchy. If so, remove the pot from heat and use a slotted spoon to quickly remove the corn and drain it on paper towels. Add salt to taste while the corn is still warm.

Stove-top Method

3. After draining the corn and blotting it dry, pour it into a bowl and add 1 to 2 teaspoons of oil and a little salt. Stir well.

4. Heat a frying pan on medium heat for 5 to 10 minutes. Coat the bottom of the pan lightly with a little oil (I use a pastry brush). Add the corn and cook until it is lightly browned (about 15 to 20 minutes), shaking the pan (or stirring) several times to ensure it cooks evenly. If the corn seems to be browning too quickly, lower the heat. Watch carefully because the corn can quickly burn. Keep a lid handy just in case the corn begins to "jump."

5. Line a colander or pan with paper towels or simply put paper towels on a counter, and place the toasted corn on it to cool. Add salt to taste while the corn is still warm.

Oven-Roasting Method

3. Put the rack in the middle of the oven and turn on the oven to preheat to 400 degrees F. Line a cookie sheet with foil and lightly brush vegetable oil on the foil.

4. Pour the corn into a bowl and add 2 tablespoons of vegetable oil and some salt and stir well (more salt can be added later). Spread the corn evenly in a single layer on the cookie sheet.

5. Cook in the oven until lightly golden brown, about 15 to 20 minutes, shaking the pan every 5 or 7 minutes to make sure the corn cooks evenly. Add additional salt to taste while the corn is still warm.

Crab or Lobster Ramekins
Akontoshie

Makes 4 or 5 servings

Barbara Baëta has adjusted the traditional recipe for *Akontoshie* to create a chic but easy first course dish for a luncheon or dinner party that can be made from crab or lobster meat. Irish baking dish seashells lend a nice presentation and ambiance to the dish. It can also be served in a crab shell, a ramekin, or other small ovenproof cup.

Ingredients

1 slice bread (enough to make ½ cup breadcrumbs)

6 ounces fresh or canned crabmeat or lobster meat, drained and flaked with a fork or your fingers

Ghanaian Tomato Gravy

2 tablespoons vegetable oil

½ cup minced or grated onion

1 heaping teaspoon pressed or crushed fresh garlic

1 teaspoon grated fresh ginger

1 to 2 tablespoons minced, grated, or ground sweet bell pepper; or 1 minced chili pepper of choice (e.g., seeded jalapeno for mild, cayenne for medium, habanero for very hot); and/or ½ teaspoon or more dried ground red pepper

1 tomato, seeded and grated or blended (½ cup with juice)

1 heaping teaspoon tomato paste

1 teaspoon additional seasoning of choice (e.g., dried ground shrimp, ground white pepper, no-salt seasoning)

Salt to taste (begin with ¼ teaspoon)

Special equipment

4 or 5 ovenproof shell-shaped dishes, ramekins, or crab shells (about 6 ounces each)

Directions

Prepare breadcrumbs:

1. Put a slice of bread into a blender and pulse the blender to make crumbs. (If the bread is too fresh and soft, let it sit out for a while to dry, or pop it into a toaster for a minute before blending.) It should make about ½ cup of crumbs. Put a clean, heavy pan on the stove and toast the breadcrumbs over medium heat until they are browned and crisp, stirring or shaking the pan frequently. Remove the pan from heat and pour the crumbs into a bowl to prevent further cooking. Set aside.

Make gravy:

2. Put a frying pan on the stove to heat on medium heat, then add the oil and minced or grated onion. Sauté for a few minutes, then add the garlic, ginger, and fresh bell or chili pepper. Stir well and cook for another minute or two. Add the tomato, tomato paste, and seasonings. Cook for a few minutes until well blended.

3. Add the flaked crabmeat or lobster meat to the gravy and stir well. Let it cook for several minutes for the flavors to blend and thicken as some of the liquid cooks out. (If using fresh crabmeat, make sure it is cooked through.) Taste and adjust seasonings and add salt to taste.

Fill the shells or ramekins:

4. Fill the ramekins/shells with the stew—you should have a little over a cup of stew, enough for 4 filled with ⅓ cup of stew each, or 5 filled with ¼ cup each.

5. Sprinkle a couple of teaspoons of toasted breadcrumbs over the stew in each ramekin/shell (or increase the amount up to 2 tablespoons for a crunchier topping).
6. Place the filled ramekins/shells on a baking sheet in a moderate oven (350 degrees F) and bake for 15 to 20 minutes, or just until heated through, making sure the crumbs do not burn. Voila! A delicious, impressive first course to a meal.

Make ahead: Even better, the stew and breadcrumbs may be prepared ahead of time. Just fill the ramekins or shells and refrigerate. Then sprinkle on the breadcrumbs and heat them at the last minute (allow a little more time to heat). These should be served warm.

Variations:
Ghanaians would likely use more oil in the gravy than suggested. Sometimes butter replaces the oil. Sometimes cheese is added.

Tuna Fish Ramekins
Akontoshie is best made with fresh or canned crabmeat or lobster meat but you can substitute a 6-ounce can of chunk tuna (preferably in water).

Squid or Octopus Appetizers

Octopus and squid are both known as *bosra* among the Ewe people. While this recipe was not part of the traditional diet, Barbara has adopted classic seasoning and deep-frying techniques to produce what has proven to be one of Flair's most popular appetizers. This recipe calls for octopus or squid, or a combination, but other firm fish or shrimp could be substituted. There are two ways to prepare this dish: with a batter and without.

When preparing it where I live in North America, only cleaned and prepped baby squid is available. I do not buy the tentacles, just the tubular part of the body. Also, I buy baby octopus which is softer than the octopus in Ghana. Thus, this recipe recommends a pound of the baby squid (but over a pound of the octopus, unless intending to also cook the tentacles). This recipe is the one that convinced my cautious teenage nephew Sam to try (and like) squid and octopus. They complement beer, red or white wine, soda, or juices as an appetizer, or are a savory snack with tea or coffee.

Ingredients

1 pound squid (or substitute a little over 1 pound octopus, or a combination of each)

1 fresh lemon

4 cups vegetable oil like canola for deep-frying

Batter (optional)

1½ cups all-purpose flour plus a little extra to dust the squid/octopus before coating

1 teaspoon baking powder

Heaping ½ teaspoon salt or seasoned salt (or to taste)

½ teaspoon ground dried red pepper (or to taste)

1 small shrimp-flavored seasoning cube, crushed; or 1 teaspoon fish masala or ground dried shrimp (optional)

2 medium or 1½ large eggs

¼ cup evaporated milk

Directions

Prepare the squid/octopus:

1. Cut squid into small strips the long way, about ½ inch wide, and cut the strips in half or thirds. With large octopus, cut them into strips about 1½ inches by 1¼ inches. With baby octopus, simply cut them into small pieces. Add 2 cups of water to a small bowl, and squeeze the lemon juice into the water. Wash the squid/octopus pieces in the liquid, swishing them around well, then shake the excess water off, and place them in a colander lined with paper towels to drain.

Prepare the batter (optional):

2. Sift the flour into a large bowl. Add the baking powder, salt, ground dried red pepper, and crushed seasoning cube or other seasoning option.
3. Break eggs into a small bowl, and stir with a fork or wire whisk. Add the evaporated milk along with 1 cup of water. Stir, then add to the dry ingredients.
4. Mix together with a wire whisk, adding more water a tablespoon at a time if necessary to get a thick batter that will stick to the squid/octopus. If the batter becomes too thin, add more flour a tablespoon at a time.

Seasoning Paste

1 heaping teaspoon ground or grated fresh ginger

1 heaping teaspoon ground or grated onion or shallot

2 cloves garlic

1 heaping teaspoon dried ground red pepper (or to taste)

1 to 2 teaspoons salt or seasoned salt (or to taste)

1 small shrimp-flavored seasoning cube, crushed (or substitute 1 teaspoon seasoned salt, fish masala, or ground dried shrimp powder)

Equipment

A deep-fryer or heavy pan with a lid

Prepare the seasoning paste:

5. Place the ginger, shallot/onion, and 2 cloves of garlic into a small blender and adding a teaspoon of wter at a time grind thoroughly. (If a mini-blender is not available, crush, grate, or grind all the ingredients and mix them together manually.)

6. After blending the ingredients, remove any extra water by straining the paste over a bowl and pressing to remove the liquid (save the liquid to use to flavor a gravy for stew). Mix the blended solid ingredients with the dried ground red pepper, salt, and fish seasoning.

Fry the squid:

7. Heat the vegetable oil in a deep fryer or deep heavy pan to about 360 degrees F (never fill the pot more than halfway, but make sure there is enough oil to cover the squid/octopus).

8. Dry the squid/octopus pieces well with paper towels and lightly dust them with flour. Coat them with the seasoning paste.

9. The seasoned squid pieces can be deep-fried as they are or dipped in the batter and coated before frying. Place them carefully in the hot oil in batches, using a long-handled spoon or tongs and watching out for splatters. As soon as the first batch is in, cover the pot or fryer for a couple of minutes, then remove the lid and stir the pieces to make sure they brown on both sides. When they are nice and crispy, in just a few minutes, remove to a paper-lined colander or tray to drain. Repeat until all are cooked.

To serve: At Flair they often dip the cooked pieces in a Ghanaian tomato gravy (see page 38) and serve them on a skewer like a kebab, alternating the fried octopus with fried squid, sweet bell pepper, tomato, and/or onion slices. They also serve them with little steamed cassava "pancakes" called *yakayake*. Sometimes, they sprinkle the fried squid or octopus over a large cooked fish as a garnish. In the U.S., I serve the squid and octopus with a hot sauce and a horseradish cocktail sauce. They also go well with *Shito* (page 170), or any hot sauce like sriracha or sambal oelek, or even ketchup.

Tuna Fish Turnovers
Ekan Kotoku

Makes 2 dozen turnovers

"Meat pies" commonly refers to turnovers filled with a meat, fish, or other filling and are popular appetizers/snacks/street foods in Ghana and other parts of West Africa. The filling may include items ranging from canned corned beef to leftover fish to cooked meat or ground beef or even vegetables.

Here is a family-favorite (and easy) version. It is lighter than those often served in Ghana. Double this recipe to make party snacks or to take to community or school functions. Our family eats the turnovers as a light supper or a portable make-ahead picnic lunch, accompanied by a salad or side vegetable and fruit. Fish turnovers are mildly reminiscent of Indian or East African *samosas* or *sambusas*, which are deep-fried rather than baked.

Ingredients

Filling

2 tablespoons margarine or butter

1 tablespoon minced onion

1½ teaspoons tomato paste

1 tablespoon all-purpose flour

½ teaspoon salt (or to taste)

1 to 2 dashes dried ground red pepper (just a little—these are generally not spicy)

½ cup canned tuna fish in water, drained (or flaked leftover cooked tuna fish)

1 hardboiled egg, peeled and mashed with fork

Pastry

2 cups all-purpose flour, plus extra for rolling out pastry

1 teaspoon salt

⅔ cup shortening

6 to 7 tablespoons cold water

Directions

Prepare filling:

1. Melt the margarine or butter in a skillet over medium-low heat. Add the onion and cook for a few minutes. Then turn the heat to low and stir in 2 tablespoons water, the tomato paste, flour, salt, and ground red pepper. Flake the tuna fish and stir into the sauce along with the mashed egg. Cook for 2 minutes then set the pan aside to prepare the pastry.

Prepare pastry:

2. Sift the flour and salt into a large mixing bowl. Using a pastry blender, two knives, or your hands, cut the shortening into the flour until it is in pieces the size of small peas.

3. Sprinkle 2 tablespoons of cold water over part of the flour mixture, then gently mix it and push it to the side with a fork. Continue to add the cold water in the same manner until all the pastry is moistened. Dust your hands with flour and form the dough into two balls.

4. Dust a work surface and rolling pin with flour then roll out one of the balls (cover the other ball and/or put it in the refrigerator while working), moving from the center to the edges until it is between ⅛ inch and ¼ inch thick. If the dough is too crumbly, add a little more water and if it is too sticky, add a little more flour. (I prefer dough rolled out closer to ⅛ inch—it is lighter and will also make more turnovers.)

5. Using a biscuit cutter or glass (or even a knife), cut the dough into circles about 3 inches in diameter and place them on a cookie sheet. Reserve the scraps of dough. Repeat with remaining dough ball.
6. Collect the reserved scraps of dough from the first and second balls together and form into another ball, and roll it out and cut out more circles. (Only use the scraps once, if you do this a third time your dough will become tough.)

Prepare turnovers:
7. Preheat the oven to 400 degrees F.
8. Fill a small glass or bowl with water. Put a heaping teaspoon of the filling in the center of a circle. Dip your finger into the water and moisten the edges, then fold the pastry over to form a half circle. Dip a fork in flour, then crimp around the edges of the turnover to seal it well. Prick the top several times with the fork so steam can escape. Place on a large baking sheet. Repeat until all the dough and filling is used.
9. Bake turnovers for about 20 minutes (check after 15 minutes) or until they are crisp and golden. Cool on a wire rack. Store refrigerated in an airtight container. They also freeze well.

Variation:
The turnovers can be made in other shapes and sizes by cutting larger or smaller circles or squares to form the turnovers into triangles. Smaller circles make nice appetizers.

Fish Cakes

Makes about 12 fish cakes / 4 servings

Ghana-style fish cakes (and Fish Balls, page 72) make a delicious snack and a great party appetizer. They can also be served as a unique breakfast or brunch item.

Ingredients

1½ pounds fresh fish or leftover cooked fish (such as red snapper, grouper, halibut), flaked (about 2 cups)

½ teaspoon dried ground red pepper (or to taste)

½ teaspoon salt (or to taste)

1 teaspoon fish spice (such as Indian fish masala or curry powder)

¼ cup finely grated or minced onion (optional)

1 egg (optional)

¼ cup well-packed breadcrumbs (preferably made from white slightly stale bread), or cooked and mashed African yam

Oil for frying (not red palm oil)

Directions

Cook fish (if not using leftover):

1. Preheat oven to 350º F. Place a piece of aluminum foil on the bottom of a baking pan and grease the foil lightly. Wash the fish and season with salt and black or red pepper, and place the fish in the baking pan and roast until barely cooked, about 20 minutes, or until it flakes easily. Remove from the oven and allow the fish to cool enough to handle . Remove the skin and all the bones and discard; flake the fish.

Assemble fish cakes:

2. Put 2 cups of flaked fish in a bowl and mash it with a fork or your fingers or a wire whisk until it looks like breadcrumbs. Add the ground red pepper, salt, fish spice, onion (if using), and egg (if using) and mix thoroughly. Add the breadcrumbs or mashed yam and mix again. Add just enough water to allow the patties to hold together (about ⅛ to ¼ cup).

3. Put a piece of waxed paper onto the work surface, and put about 2 tablespoons of the fish mixture on it. Using the blade of a table knife, flatten it into a patty about ½ inch thick and 2 inches square. These patties are quite delicate, but should hold together. Continue forming patties with the rest of the mixture.

Cook fish patties:

4. Put ¼ to ½ inch of oil in a large heavy frying pan and heat it for about 5 minutes to a medium-high temperature of about 375 degrees F. Carefully lift a fish patty using a pancake turner or spatula and slide it into the oil using a spoon or knife or another spatula. Repeat until the pan is filled with as many

patties as will fit in without crowding. It will only take a couple of minutes for them to brown on one side. Gently turn the patties over with a slotted spatula. When browned on both sides, put them on paper towels to cool and soak up any excess oil.

To serve:
Serve with hot pepper sauce, *Shito* (page 170), or ketchup.

Make larger patties and serve as a main dish with sautéed onion rings, yams or rice, and Ghanaian Basic Tomato Gravy (page 38).

Serve as a first course with cucumber, tomato, onion, and lettuce salad with a vinaigrette dressing.

Make ahead: These fish cakes can be made ahead and reheated before serving.

Troubleshooting:
If the patties do not stick together, try adjusting the fish mixture by either blotting off some of the moisture with paper towels, adding more breadcrumbs or yam, or adding an additional egg. Also try pressing more firmly together.

If the patties brown too quickly, the oil is too hot.

If they disintegrate in the oil, check the temperature of the oil and raise the heat or adjust the binding. (Even in pieces, use them as a delicious salad topping or garnish.)

Fish Balls

This recipe is similar to that for Fish Cakes (page 70) but replaces the breadcrumb or yam binder with a cream sauce. The fish mixture is shaped into balls, coated in egg and breadcrumbs, and then fried.

Ingredients

1½ pounds fresh fish or leftover cooked fish (such as red snapper, grouper, halibut, or any fleshy fish), flaked (about 2 cups)

½ teaspoon dried ground red pepper (or to taste)

½ teaspoon salt (or to taste)

1 teaspoon fish spice (such as Indian fish masala or curry powder)

¼ cup finely grated or minced onion (optional)

1 egg

½ cup well-packed breadcrumbs (preferably made from white slightly stale bread for a lighter color)

Oil for frying (not red palm oil)

Cream Sauce

1 cup milk

1 tablespoon cornstarch

2 tablespoons margarine or butter

¼ teaspoon salt

⅛ teaspoon dried ground red, white, or black pepper

Directions

Cook fish (if not using leftover):

1. Preheat the oven to 350 degrees F. Place a piece of aluminum foil on the bottom of a baking pan and grease the foil lightly. Wash the fish and season with salt and black or red pepper, and place in the baking pan. Roast until barely cooked, about 20 minutes, or until it flakes easily. Remove from the oven and allow the fish to cool enough to handle. Remove the skin and all the bones and discard them. Put the fish into a bowl and flake.

Prepare cream sauce:

2. Put the milk and cornstarch in a small pan and stir until smooth. Add the butter or margarine, salt, and pepper. Heat on the stovetop over medium heat, stirring constantly until it comes to a simmer. Let simmer for 1 minute or until thickened, then remove from the heat.

Assemble fish balls:

3. Place 2 cups of flaked fish in a bowl and mash it with a fork or your fingers or a wire whisk until it looks like breadcrumbs. Add the ground red pepper, salt, fish spice, onion (if using), and mix thoroughly. Add ¾ cup of white sauce. (Note: begin with ¾ cup of white sauce and then add the rest if it will not make the balls too soft to hold their shape.)

4. Break egg into a small bowl and mix with a fork. Put breadcrumbs on a plate. If desired, place a sheet of waxed paper on the work surface.

5. Shape about 2 tablespoons of the fish mixture into a ball in your hands, then dip it into the beaten egg, and roll it in the breadcrumbs. Continue until all of the fish mixture is used.

Fry the fish balls:

6. Heat several cups of oil in a deep fryer or deep pan on the stove to about 375 degrees F. Make sure never to fill the oil over half full since it could bubble over when adding the fish. Add the fish balls a few at a time to the hot oil and fry until golden. Remove with a slotted spoon drain them on paper towels.

Make ahead: The fried fish balls can be kept warm in an oven, or reheated quickly in a microwave or oven just before serving.

To serve:

Milder flavored and moister than the fish cakes, these fish balls make delicious appetizers served with hot pepper sauce, *Shito* (page 170), or ketchup.

At Flair catering, these are sometimes served in a Ghana-style tomato gravy (page 38), with or without curry powder: gently set the fish balls into the pot with the gravy just before serving and shake to coat them.

Ghana-style Beef Kebabs
Chichinga

To pronounce *Chichinga*, the first "i" is pronounced like the "i" in "it," and the second one like a long "ee", with the emphasis on the second syllable [chiCHEENga]. It's also spelled "*kyinkyinga*," in which case the first "n" is silent. In Nigeria it is called *tsire suya* (*sooya*), often shortened to simply *suya*.

This popular street food, appetizer, and party snack is common throughout West Africa. *Chichinga* is usually made from a variety of protein sources, such as liver or beef (more traditional), chicken (more contemporary), lamb, or goat. It should be possible to adapt it to vegetarian choices like mushrooms or tofu as well. The distinctive taste comes from the rub, the *tankora/yaji/chichinga* powder, which includes roasted cornmeal, pulverized, fried, and then re-ground peanuts, dried ground ginger and red pepper, and salt, as well as other spices. Ghana meats are often tough and *chichinga* sometimes taste overcooked to Western sensibilities.

Ingredients

12 ounces tender boneless beef, such as top sirloin

1 cup Tankora Powder (page 24)

2 tablespoons peanut oil

6 to 8 (8-inch long) bamboo skewers, soaked for an hour before using

Marinade

1 to 2 teaspoons tomato paste

⅓ to ½ teaspoon dried ground red pepper (or to taste)

½ teaspoon grated fresh ginger

1 or 2 cloves garlic, ground, grated, or crushed

2 tablespoons grated onion

1 teaspoon salt or seasoned salt (e.g., spicy Adobo)

½ teaspoon ground white or black pepper (or to taste)

2 teaspoons peanut or other vegetable oil

Directions

Marinate meat:

1. Mix all the ingredients for the marinade together in a medium mixing bowl, stirring well.
2. Trim all the fat from the beef and cut into thin strips roughly ¼ inch thick (you should have about 18 to 21 pieces).
3. Coat the meat evenly with the marinade and refrigerate, covered, for at least 30 minutes.

Prepare kebabs:

4. When ready to grill the *chichinga*, preheat a broiler or prepare the grill. If broiling the kebabs, line a broiler pan or baking sheet with foil to ease the cleanup.
5. Place a half cup of the tankora powder in a plastic or paper bag. Add 6 pieces of the marinated meat at a time and shake them well to coat. Repeat until all meat is coated.
6. Thread 3 pieces of meat onto each skewer. Do not push the pieces tightly together. Using a pastry brush, lightly brush the kebabs with a little peanut oil.

Grill or broil kebabs:

7. Place the kebabs about 5 inches from the heat source (under broiler or on the grill). Turn after about 5 minutes and cook for another 5 minutes, or until they are cooked through.

To serve: *Chichinga* goes very well with a lager beer (like Club or Star in Ghana), Ginger Beer (page 203), ginger ale, or Hibiscus Iced Tea (*Bissap*, page 205).

Variations:

Ghana-style Liver Kebabs

Beef or chicken liver can be prepared the same way, making sure the liver is completely cooked. The USDA advises an internal heat of 160 degrees F.

Ghana-style Chicken Kebabs

Chicken can be cooked using the identical process as above. Since North American chickens tend to be soft, it may be more flavorful to use a roasting or free-range chicken. You will need 12 ounces boneless chicken breast and/or thigh meat, cut into roughly 18 to 21 thin strips.

Black-eyed Pea Steamed Pudding
Tubaani / Tubani

Makes 6 to 8 servings

Ghana has a simple steamed black-eyed pea paste pudding called *tubaani/tubani*. I learned to make it in Tamale in Northern Ghana. *Tubaani* provides a healthy, hearty vegetarian snack or meal accompaniment.

We made our *tubaani* using flour from black-eyed peas, and that is the recipe included here. However, one could substitute the same basic paste obtained after soaking and dehulling dried black-eyed peas as on page 25. Or substitute Nigerian *moin-moin* flour available in African markets.

Ingredients
2 cups ground dried black-eyed peas or black-eyed pea flour

3 cups warm water

About 8 plantain (banana) leaves for wrapping, or aluminum foil (nonstick is nice), or parchment paper

1 tablespoon baking powder or 1 teaspoon baking soda

Special Equipment
Deep pot with insert for steaming and tight-fitting lid

> A related dish in Nigeria called *"moinmoin"* includes additions to the (dehulled) black-eyed pea mixture, such as pieces of hard-boiled egg, meat, seafood, or vegetables, along with additional seasonings and a little palm oil. You can also vary the size of the packets.

Directions
Prepare pudding paste:
1. Sift 2 cups of black-eyed pea flour into a bowl. (If grinding your own dried black-eyed peas, pick through, and rinse, if necessary, before grinding them a cup at a time in an electric blender, straining the flour several times and regrinding the larger pieces. Discard any pieces that cannot be ground fine.)
2. Add 3 cups of warm water to the flour while stirring with a fork. Allow the mixture to sit for 1 hour.

Prepare the leaves/foil/parchment:
3. If using frozen plantain leaves, defrost them. The leaves impart a delicate flavor to the *tubaani*, but if they are not available, foil or parchment are the easiest substitutes. If using foil/parchment, tear off about 18 inches, lay it on the table so the shiny or nonstick side is up, and fold in half horizontally (so the shiny or nonstick side is on the inside of the packet). This makes a long rectangle about 18 inches by 6 inches. Cut the foil/parchment into thirds to get 3 packets about 6 inches long. Fold the two cut ends of each packet over about ¼ inch and repeat folds once or twice more until you have little packages with one end open. (The folds are important so that the pudding does not seep out the sides while it is steaming.) Use your hand to open the packet slightly to make room to add the dough. Repeat the entire process as necessary until you have enough

packets to contain all the pudding paste—2 cups of flour will make about 8 balls using the size of foil described. Remember to have the packets ready before you beat the pudding paste with the mixer.

Prepare packets and steam pudding:
4. Put several cups of water into a pot with a steamer insert (or improvise one using a metal colander or similar item).
5. After the pudding paste has sat for an hour, beat the mixture with an electric or rotary beater on medium-high for about 5 minutes to beat air into it and make it a bit fluffy, kind of like whipped heavy cream. Near the end of the 5 minutes add the baking powder or soda and mix it in thoroughly.
6. When the pudding paste is ready, bring the water in the steamer to a boil while filling the packets. Using a spoon, fill each foil/parchment packet about two-thirds full with the batter. Do not fill them more than about two-thirds full, to allow room for expansion as they steam. If using the leaves, make a slight "cup" in your palm and holding a leaf with the underside up, spoon a spoonful of the pudding paste into it, then fold one side over, then the other, then the two ends, one at a time. Repeat with the remaining leaves.
7. Place the packets on the steaming tray and put into the pot and steam them for about 45 minutes. They should be firm but not hard. Remove one from the steamer after half an hour and check for doneness.

To serve: Serve warm or at room temperature in any of the following ways:

Open the packets, cut the pudding into pieces on the diagonal, then sprinkle with a mixture of coarsely pounded salt and pounded dry red pepper. (This is how it was served in Tamale.)

Slice half a large onion and fry it in several tablespoons of oil (such as sheanut or peanut oil), and serve over or alongside the *tubaani*.

Slice the *tubaani* and sprinkle with salt, dried red pepper, and sliced onion.

Serve the *tubaani* with a simple gravy or stew.

Black-eyed Pea Fritters
Akara

Makes 24 small or 8 to 10 large fritters

Akara (also called *accara, akla, kose, koose, kosai*) is a hugely popular West African pea/bean fritter. This dish has many variations. Ghanaians treasure it and it is also popular in Nigeria. A version that traveled to Brazil is known as *acarajé*. In Ghana, *akara* is commonly made from black-eyed peas. The initial step is to remove the skins from the black-eyed peas and grind them. A second option is to use finely ground black-eyed pea powder. While this may be convenient, for the best *akara*, I prefer soaking and dehulling dried black-eyed peas and grinding them myself. (It is also possible, though less common, to make the *akara* without first removing the skins.)

Ingredients

1 cup dried black-eyed peas

½ cup minced or grated onion

3 to 4 teaspoons grated fresh ginger

½ teaspoon salt (or to taste)

½ teaspoon dried ground red pepper (or to taste)

Vegetable oil for deep-frying

Directions

Prepare the fritters:

1. Remove the skins of the black-eyed peas as described on page 25. While soaking the peas, prepare the other ingredients, and put the oil into a deep fryer or a large heavy pot. Never fill the fryer or pot more than half full.

2. After removing the skins of the black-eyed peas, grind half of them thoroughly in a blender, using up to ¼ cup water and pushing down the sides with a spatula several times if necessary. This will take several minutes. Alternatively, grind them in a food processor. Avoid using any more water than necessary.

3. Empty the first batch into a bowl and repeat the process with the second half of the beans. When they are fairly well ground, add the onion, ginger, salt, and ground red pepper, and continue mixing until the paste is well blended.

4. Empty the bean paste in the blender into the bowl with the first batch, and whip using a mixer, whisk, or spoon for about 2 minutes or until air is incorporated into the batter to make it light (mixture should be a little thicker than egg whites or whipped cream).

Fry the fritters:

4. Preheat the oil. If using a deep fryer, set the temperature to 350 to 360 degrees F. When using a heavy pot on my electric stove, I need to alternate between a medium-high and high heat as the batter is added and removed.

Troubleshooting:
If the fritters sink to the bottom of the pan, the oil is not hot enough; if they brown immediately without having time to cook through to the center, the oil is too hot.

6. Depending on the size of *akara* desired, choose a long-handled spoon for putting the batter in the oil: a teaspoon size for tiny fritters, a tablespoon or serving spoon size for larger fritters. Dip the spoon into the oil to coat it, then dip it into the paste and scoop out some batter. Quickly use another spoon to carefully slip the batter off into the oil. Repeat until the fryer or pot is filled but not crowded.
7. If the fritters do not turn over by themselves, turn them over halfway through cooking time. Cooking time depends on the size of the fritters, but it will take several minutes until they are nicely browned.
8. Remove fritters with a slotted spoon as they brown and drain them on paper towels to cool and absorb extra oil. After cooling the first batch, break open a fritter to confirm that it is fully cooked, and adjust the temperature of the oil if necessary for cooking the remaining dough.

To serve: The fritters can be eaten warm or at room temperature, alone or with a dip. Bite-size fritters may be served with toothpicks and a hot sauce and/or version of a peanut sauce as a party appetizer. In Ghana, larger fritters are classically served with porridge for breakfast, or eaten as a snack.

African Yam Balls
Yele Kakro

Makes about 2 dozen balls

Like many flexible Ghanaian/West African recipes, there is plenty of room for improvisation in making yam balls, especially with seasonings. Fresh puna yams from Ghana are especially nice (do not use the yams or sweet potatoes commonly found in U.S. markets).

Ingredients

4 cups peeled and chopped African yams (about 2 pounds)

3 medium tomatoes

¼ cup vegetable oil plus enough for deep-frying

1 large or 2 small onions, minced

½ teaspoon dried thyme or a similar herb

½ teaspoon salt (or to taste)

½ teaspoon dried ground red pepper (or to taste)

2 eggs, beaten

A few tablespoons flour

Directions

Prepare vegetables:

1. Put the yam cubes into a large pot and cover with water (and add a little salt, if desired). Bring to a boil, lower the heat, and cook until soft, about 20 minutes, depending on the size of the cubes.
2. While the yams cook, scald the tomatoes in boiling water and then plunge them into cold water and remove their skins. Core, and seed, if desired, then chop finely. Set aside.
3. When the yam cubes are tender, drain off the water and mash while still warm, using a potato masher, the wooden mashing tool called *apɔtoyewa* or *apotoriwa* in Ghana, or a rotary or electric mixer, making sure they are thoroughly mashed and not lumpy.

Make batter:

4. Heat ¼ cup vegetable oil in a skillet on medium heat. Add half of the minced onion and cook for a couple of minutes, then add half of the chopped tomatoes. Cook for a few more minutes, just until the onion is soft but not browned, stirring occasionally. Stir in the thyme, salt, and ground red pepper.
5. Put the mashed yams or potatoes in a bowl. Stir in the cooked onion-tomato mixture and the uncooked tomato and onion. Add the beaten eggs and mix everything well.

Fry the yam balls:

6. In a deep heavy saucepan or an electric deep fryer put enough oil to fill the pan halfway and heat the oil to 375 degrees F.

7. Sprinkle a little flour on a flat work surface (a pastry mat or wax paper will reduce cleanup time), put a little oil or flour on your hands and shape spoonfuls of the mashed yam mixture into balls a little smaller than a golf ball.
8. When the oil is hot (sprinkle a drop of water in and see how it sizzles to judge if it is hot enough) put several balls in and cook them a few minutes until they are golden brown on all sides. Remove with a slotted spoon and drain the excess oil off on paper towels. Repeat until all yam balls are cooked.

To serve: Eat as a snack or serve as a side dish with a meal while they are still warm, possibly accompanied by some Fresh Pepper Sauce (page 168) or *Shito* (page 170).

Variations:

Add a little leftover cooked meat or fish, or two or three minced garlic cloves to the mixture before forming the balls.

If African yams are not available you can substitute 5 cups peeled and chopped russet potatoes and 2 heaping tablespoons flour.

African Yam Cakes

Follow the directions for yam balls, but omit the tomatoes, and reduce the egg to one. When the yam mixture is ready, dust your hands with flour and roll the yam mixture out into a cylinder. Using a sharp, moistened knife, cut the cylinder into thick slices (or you can simply form patties by hand). Brush the slices with some egg white, dust them with flour, and fry each side for several minutes on a greased griddle or pan, turning carefully. These may be kept warm in the oven or reheated in a microwave.

Savory Pastry Chips
Chin Chin

Makes 6 to 8 servings

This is a popular party snack in Ghana. Flair Catering uses a pasta machine, but they can be easily made without one.

Ingredients

2⅔ cups all-purpose flour, plus extra for rolling dough

2 tablespoons margarine or butter or butter-flavored shortening

1 teaspoon salt

¼ teaspoon dried ground red pepper

¼ teaspoon ground white pepper

1 teaspoon crushed or ground garlic cloves

¼ cup ground or finely grated onion

½ teaspoon baking powder

Vegetable oil for deep frying

1 or 2 bay leaves to season the oil (or a few slices of onion)

Special equipment

Pasta machine or rolling pin

Directions

Make dough:

1. Sift flour into a large bowl, then rub or cut the margarine or butter into it, using your hands, a pastry cutter, or two table knives, until it looks like cornmeal.

2. Add the salt and peppers and mix all together. Add the garlic and onion, mixing some more. Add the baking powder and continue mixing.

3. Measure out ½ cup of water. Sprinkle a few tablespoons over part of the dough in the bowl and mix it in with a fork. Push the moistened flour to the side and add a little more water (a couple of tablespoons), mix and push to the side of the bowl. Continue adding the water until the dough is just wet enough to hold together.

4. Knead the dough lightly in the bowl for half a minute. Divide the dough into 2 pieces.

Form pastries:

5. To make cleanup easier, dampen a work surface with a little water and put waxed paper on it, then sprinkle the waxed paper with a little flour. Otherwise, simply sprinkle some flour directly on the work surface.

6. Roll one piece of dough out to about ⅛ inch thick. (If using a pasta machine, cut the dough into sizes that will fit into it.)

7. Gently fold the dough on top of itself several times, then cut it into strips about ⅛-inch to ¼-inch wide (the thinner, the crisper). Unfold the dough, and cut the strips into pieces about 1¾ inches long. Or cut them into many tiny squares if preferred. Repeat with remaining piece of dough.

Fry the pastries:

8. Heat about 5 cups of oil to 350 to 375 degrees F in a deep fryer or heavy pot on the stove, never filling over half full. Season the hot oil by adding a bay leaf or a couple of slices of onion briefly and removing them before they burn.

9. Put the strips (or squares) of dough carefully into the pot a couple dozen at a time using a long-handled slotted spoon and stirring the oil occasionally while they cook. Within a few minutes, when they are a light golden color, remove with slotted spoon and drain on paper towels. Cook smaller squares separately from the strips. They will cook in just a minute or two and should be nice and crunchy when cool.

Make ahead: These chips can be frozen, or stored tightly covered in an airtight container for up to a week.

To serve: At Flair they often serve these chips with plain peanuts or Spicy Coated Peanuts (page 60) in small cocktail baskets set around the room. After making this once, you can decide how you prefer to adjust the seasonings.

Ghana Wine-Raised Doughnuts
Togbei / Bofrot

Makes 12 to 18 doughnuts

When I lived in Nungua along Ghana's coast in the 1970s I became attached to a chewy dough-nut that the Ga people call *Togbei*, which delightfully enough means "goat's balls." The Akan people call it *Bofrot* (roughly pronounced "boff-row"). They are a popular street food. I remem-ber buying them by the roadside in Nungua, freshly made and wrapped in newspaper. They make a nice snack with tea.

The doughnuts are made from a raised wheat dough that traditionally uses palm wine in place of yeast. The palm wine gives them a distinctive taste, but as palm wine is not available outside Ghana, yeast and/or dry white wine may substitute. Some people claim unpasteurized beer or lemon juice in evaporated milk can also replace the palm wine.

In contemporary Ghana, people also make a version of *Bofrot* that is a larger cousin to North America's cake "donut holes," substituting baking powder for the yeast/palm wine (see page 86). Try that recipe if you are pressed for time. This recipe for the traditional chewy type can be doubled, tripled, quadrupled, etc. to make large batches.

Ingredients

⅓ cup warm water

3 tablespoons dry white wine or water, warmed

3 tablespoons plus 1 teaspoon sugar

1 teaspoon yeast (rapid rise or regular)

1 egg

½ cup plus ⅓ cup unsifted bread flour

¼ teaspoon ground nutmeg

⅛ teaspoon baking powder

Pinch of salt

Vegetable oil for deep frying

Directions

Make the dough:

1. Pour warm water and wine, if using, into a large bowl, and stir in the sugar to dissolve. Sprinkle in the yeast and let it sit for a few minutes to allow the mixture to begin to bubble.
2. Beat the egg, put it in a measuring cup and measure out one-third of it (this recipe uses awkward measurements, but they work). Once the yeast begins to foam, add the one-third of the egg and mix.
3. Gradually pour the flour through a strainer into the liquid, mixing well. Stir in the nutmeg, baking powder, and salt. Mix all together well, cover the bowl with a cloth and allow it to sit in a warm place for at least 2 hours. The dough should at least double in size, so make sure your bowl is large enough to accommodate.

Fry the doughnuts:

4. When ready to fry the *bofrot*, heat oil to 375 degrees F in a deep fryer or large heavy pot (only fill pot half full). Line a colander with paper towels.
5. In Ghana, experienced chefs efficiently and quickly scoop up the batter in the hollow of

their right hand and drop it into the oil in a perfect ball. For the rest of us, dip a long-handled soup spoon in the oil to coat, then scoop up a spoonful of the dough and slide it off the spoon into the oil with another spoon (also dipped in oil first). You can fry a few doughnuts at a time but be sure not to over-crowd the pot. Ensure the doughnuts cook evenly on all sides, turning them over as necessary. When they are dark (a bit darker than you would probably think they need to be) remove them to drain the excess oil in the paper-towel-lined colander.

To serve: These are delicious at breakfast or as a snack with tea or coffee: chewy and less sweet than most American doughnuts.

Troubleshooting:
If the balls of dough flatten out, there is likely too much liquid in the batter—try adding a little more flour.

If they sink to the bottom, the oil is not hot enough.

If they brown on the outside but do not cook on the inside, the oil is too hot.

Ghana Cake Doughnuts
Togbei / Bofrot

Makes 12 to 18 doughnuts

This recipe is adapted from one used by Barbara at Flair. These are faster to make, with a different texture from the wine-raised version (page 84)—more coarse and crisp, just as a muffin differs from a regular slice of bread. Either way is tasty.

Ingredients

1 cup unsifted bread flour

Rounded ¼ teaspoon salt

3 tablespoons margarine or butter

3 tablespoons sugar

½ teaspoon ground nutmeg

Rounded ½ teaspoon baking powder

1 egg

¼ cup evaporated milk plus ½ cup water, or ¾ cup regular milk

½ teaspoon vanilla extract

Vegetable oil for deep-frying

Troubleshooting:

The dough should be shaped like a ball. If it flattens out there is likely too much liquid in the batter—try adding a little flour to the dough.

Directions

Make the batter:

1. Sift the flour and salt into a bowl, and cut in the margarine or butter (use your hands or 2 table knives) until the mixture resembles cornmeal. Stir in the sugar, nutmeg, and baking powder.
2. In a separate bowl, beat the egg, then add the milk (and water, if using), and vanilla extract and mix well. Make a hole in the center of the flour mixture and add the liquids all at once, blending with just a few swift strokes to keep the batter from becoming tough. Let the batter sit for 30 minutes.

Fry the doughnuts:

3. Line a colander with paper towels to drain the *bofrot* after cooking them.
4. About 10 minutes before the 30 minutes are over, heat vegetable oil in a deep fryer or deep, heavy pan to 360 to 375 degrees F. (Do not fill the pan with oil more than half full.) Do a temperature test: when the oil is hot enough, a small amount of dough dropped into the oil will quickly rise to the surface.
5. The doughnuts are usually prepared larger than a golf ball but a little smaller than a tennis ball. When the oil is hot, slip a long-handled spoon into the oil to coat it, then scoop up a spoonful of batter. Using another spoon (also coated with oil) quickly slide dough into the oil. Cook the doughnuts in batches until they are quite browned on all sides. They will likely turn over as they cook, but use a long-handled slotted spoon to stir and turn them as necessary.
6. Use the slotted spoon to lift them out into the paper towel-lined colander to absorb the extra oil and cool. They can be eaten warm or at room temperature.

Fresh Corn and Coconut Snack

Snacks in Ghana are known as "small chop." A simple popular snack is roasted corn and fresh crunchy coconut pieces. This is a great snack on a hot summer afternoon or evening, especially when accompanied by an ice-cold beverage of your choice, like Ginger Beer (page 203), Hibiscus Iced Tea (*Bissap*, page 205), Tamarind Drink (*Puha*, page 208), or beer.

Ingredients

1 coconut

1 or 2 ears of fresh corn per person

This recipe assumes you are using sweet corn. If you were using corn grown in Ghana, the cobs would have to be cooked much longer. The first time my sister-in-law cooked corn in the U.S., she boiled it for hours, to everyone's dismay.

Directions

1. Crack open and prepare the fresh coconut as described on page 26. Cut or break the coconut meat into bite-size strips or chunks.
2. Shuck the corn and bring a pot of salted water to a boil. Add the corn cobs and cook them just until tender, 5 to 10 minutes. Alternatively, you can grill the corn over an open fire, or cook them in a microwave oven (about 6 minutes for 1 ear on high heat, turning once).
3. Serve pieces of corn on the cob and coconut together.

FRESH FRUIT SNACKS

One of the most popular (and healthiest) snack foods in Ghana is simply seasonal fresh tropical fruit. Fruit is also one of the most common desserts. Three typical examples are fresh mangos, fresh oranges, and avocados (called "avocado pears" in Ghana).

Mangoes

In Ghana, the local variety of mangoes are generally very sweet, smaller, and much more fibrous than the larger ones. When these are in season and ripe, they fall from trees in abundance, and there is no experience quite like the joy of eating fresh juicy sweet mango. The larger mangoes are often sliced lengthwise just above and below the large seed in the center (think "filleting" the mango) to get two large halves. Here is one common way of cutting and serving them:

Slice the mango lengthwise and split in half. Turn the halves with the flesh side up, and use a knife to score the flesh lengthwise about half an inch apart down to but not through the peel. Then, score them at a 90-degree angle to make small square cubes. Holding the two ends, a slight push on the skin in the center turns the cut mango out, and the half is placed on an individual serving plate, peel side down. Or, the cubes can be sliced off and the skin removed.

Oranges

Similarly oranges (often with green skin in Ghana, with many seeds and thick fibrous membranes) are enjoyed multiple ways. They are served as a kind of juice snack needing no cup: vendors along the roadside or at bus stops neatly strip off the top skin of the orange, exposing the pale thick membrane under it, then they slice off the very tip. Purchasers squeeze the orange as they suck out the thirst-quenching sweet juice from the opening at the top.

Oranges are also served as halved slices or as wedges. They make a surprisingly simple, neat, and classy snack or dessert served on a tray garnished with fresh mint leaves.

Avocados

Avocados are versatile in Ghana. They may be served sliced alongside other food, in place of butter on bread, mashed into a kind of Ghanaian guacamole, or stuffed with a seafood salad.

MAIN DISH SOUPS

Meals are not commonly served as separate courses in Ghana, and a soup (or stew) is usually served as a main dish, accompanied by a filling starch. See pages 41-43 for an overview of basic stocks used as a base in Ghanaian soups. Also included there is a recipe for a foundational "light soup" using goat. Light soups can be made with basically any clear stock, whether vegetarian, poultry, meat, or fish-based. Some "light" soups have added greens or fresh or dried vegetables such as eggplant (or garden eggs in Ghana), okra, tomatoes, and/or mushrooms. Another category of soups includes those thickened with ground seeds (like *agushi*, a kind of melon seed, or sesame seeds) or ground "nuts" (such as peanuts/ground-nuts, beans, and palmnut fruit, the pulp or "creams" of the red oil palm).

Plain Light Soup
Nkrakra

Makes 4 to 6 servings

This is a basic recipe for a clear broth based on water (or stock), tomatoes, chili pepper, onion, and salt, enhanced as desired by spices (garlic, ginger, herbs, etc.) as well as vegetables, bones, or a little meat, chicken, or fish. It is a soothing recipe and considered a good soup for those who are ill or weak. Much more recently, it is seen as an appropriate soup for a first course.

Ingredients

3 medium tomatoes

1 medium onion or a few shallots, coarsely chopped

½ to 1 teaspoon dried ground red pepper (or to taste), or chopped fresh chili pepper equivalent in heat

6 cups water or stock

1 teaspoon salt or seasoned salt (or to taste)

Optional seasonings to taste

2 cloves garlic

1-inch piece fresh ginger, coarsely chopped

Chopped herbs like thyme, basil, *akoko besa*, etc.

Optional ingredients

1 small eggplant or 3 garden eggs, peeled and cut in large chunks

½ pound meat of choice or chicken cut into chunks; or fresh fish, skin and bones removed;   and/or soup bones (up to 1 pound)

2 tablespoons tomato paste

Directions

1. Grind the tomatoes, onion or shallots, dried or fresh chili pepper, and other optional seasonings with 1 cup of water in an electric blender about 45 to 60 seconds.
2. Pour in a soup pot with 5 cups of water or stock, and salt to taste and bring to a boil, then lower heat to simmer. If using soup bones, add them to the pot at this point along with eggplant and any meat or poultry, if using. Stir in tomato paste, if desired.
3. Simmer mixture until meat and poultry are tender. (If using eggplant, remove it when soft; remove the skins and puree in a blender; return to the soup pot when the meat or poultry is almost tender.)
4. If using fish, break it into pieces and add to the soup about 15 minutes before serving the soup. Remove any bones before serving.

To serve: May be served alone or with any preferred starch.

Variations:

Thicken the soup by cooking a starch, like peeled yam or plantain or potato, and adding some of the liquid in which the starch was cooked to the soup (or cook the slices right in the soup).

A little freshly pounded *fufu* (not the powder version) is also sometimes added.

Add additional meat, chicken, or fish.

Include smoked fish or ground shrimps as an additional seasoning.

For a vegetarian alternative: use vegetable stock and add other soft, mild vegetables such as mushrooms or summer squash.

Chicken Light Soup with Carrots and Zucchini

Makes 4 servings

This is a quick and simple version of a light soup that has a delicate sweetness from pureed carrots. It is slightly thickened by using zucchini squash.

Ingredients

12 to 16 ounces boneless skinless chicken

4 cups chicken stock

1 or 2 large carrots, peeled

1 whole onion, peeled

1 medium zucchini squash

2 large tomatoes (peeled and deseeded first, if desired)

1 inch fresh ginger, peeled and coarsely chopped

¼ teaspoon dried ground red pepper (or more to taste)

½ teaspoon dried thyme or other herb (or to taste; optional)

Directions

1. Cut chicken into desired serving sizes and put into a pot with the stock, whole carrot(s), onion, and zucchini. Bring to a boil, reduce heat, and simmer for about 10 minutes or until the carrot, onion, and zucchini are softened.
2. Remove the carrot, onion, and zucchini and put in an electric blender, along with the tomatoes, ginger, and 1 cup of broth from the pot. Puree and then return to the soup pot.
3. Add the thyme, if using, and allow the soup to simmer for another 15 minutes while the flavors blend. Taste for seasoning.

To serve: Serve this soup with Ghana-Style Dumplings (*Fufu*, page 190) or other starch of your choice.

Variation: Substitute tomato sauce for the fresh tomatoes.

Light Soup with Lamb, Eggplant, Mushrooms, and Zucchini

Makes 4 to 6 servings

Here is a healthy, simple, and delicious soup. As explained earlier, "light soup" is the English name in Ghana for a light stock-based soup so-named long before the West started talking about "light" foods. There are an infinite variety of light soups, easily adjusted according to what is on hand, but including onion, a little chili pepper, and probably tomato. When preparing this soup In Ghana one would probably substitute garden eggs for the eggplant, and use *kpakpo shito* peppers.

Ingredients

Meat seasoning:

1 tablespoon grated fresh ginger

2 cloves garlic, crushed

2 tablespoons chopped or minced onion

Light sprinkling dried ground red pepper

Light sprinkling salt or seasoned salt

Soup:

1¾ pounds lamb round shoulder chops, fat trimmed and cut into chunks

1 cup tomato sauce

1 cup chopped onion

1 whole small Japanese eggplant, or ⅓ to ½ larger regular eggplant, peeled and cut into quarters

1 medium zucchini, cut in half

1 small jalapeno or other chili pepper (or use ground dried red pepper to taste, if desired, beginning with ⅛ teaspoon)

1½ teaspoons salt or seasoned salt (or to taste)

1 tablespoon tomato paste (optional)

Directions

Season the meat:

1. Put the lamb and any bones in a soup pot with 1 cup of water. Sprinkle all the seasoning ingredients over the meat. Cover the pot tightly, bring to a boil, then lower the heat and let it simmer while assembling the other ingredients, about 10 to 15 minutes.

Prepare soup:

2. Add the tomato sauce, onion, eggplant, zucchini, and chili pepper to the pot with the meat, along with 5 cups of water. (If you like things spicy, use the whole chili pepper; if not, cut it in half and remove the seeds and membranes first.) Add the salt and any additional seasoning of choice, stir well, bring it back to a boil, then let it simmer, covered, until the vegetables soften, about 10 to 15 minutes.

3. Use a slotted spoon to remove the eggplant, zucchini, chili pepper, and some of the chopped onion floating in the soup and put into a blender or food processor. It may be necessary to add a little broth from the pot, or do this in 2 batches. Blend the vegetables until smooth and return to the soup. Rinse the blender container with some of the broth or a little water and pour into the soup.

6 ounces fresh mushrooms (any type), washed and cut in half or quartered (depending on their size)

Additional seasonings of choice:

2 teaspoons grated fresh ginger

Additional chopped onion

2 cloves garlic, minced or crushed

Sprinkling of dried ground red pepper

½ teaspoon dried thyme (or to taste)

4. Continue to simmer the soup until the meat is tender, about 30 minutes, depending on the toughness of the meat. When the meat is nearly tender, add the mushroom slices. For a stronger tomato flavor, add the tomato paste. Stir, cover, and allow the flavors to blend for another 10 to 15 minutes. Before serving, adjust the seasonings to taste, and skim any fat that may have risen to the surface.

To serve: This soup goes well with Ghana-Style Dumplings (*Fufu*, page 190), Rice Balls (*Omo Tuo*, page 179), or thick slices of bread.

Variations:

Adjust or omit the eggplant, zucchini, etc. to suit your tastes.

Cube the vegetables instead of pureeing them.

The recipe makes a fairly thick soup; add additional water or some stock for a thinner soup.

Ghanaian women overseas tend to be innovative cooks. It was a Ghanaian neighbor who first shared with me her discovery that pureed zucchini makes a nice complement to (or substitute for) Ghana's "garden eggs" in light soup. Similarly, my friend and colleague in Canada shared her discovery that pureed carrots are a fabulous addition to chicken light soup, and my sister-in-law blended red bell peppers to get the color she wanted in her soups.

Dried Okra Soup

Makes 4 to 6 servings

In Northern Ghana, many meats, fish, fruits, vegetables, and starches are dried as a means of preserving them. Okra (commonly referred to as *okro* in Ghana), for example, is dried and powdered and added to soups, as are baobab leaves or locust beans (*dawadawa*). This is an easy soup that could also be prepared in a crockpot. Dried ground okra is often available in West African food markets or you can follow the instructions here to make it yourself.

Ingredients

1 pound boneless or 2 pounds bone-in meat (beef, goat, lamb), cut into cubes (or may be shredded if boneless)

¼ to ⅓ cup powdered dried okra

1 large onion, chopped

3 medium tomatoes, peeled, chopped or pureed

1 teaspoon salt or seasoned salt

Optional Seasonings

2 cloves, crushed

1 teaspoon minced or crushed fresh garlic

1 heaping teaspoon grated fresh ginger

¼ teaspoon or more dried ground red pepper or flakes

Directions

1. Place the meat and all other ingredients in a soup pot along with 5 cups of water.
2. Bring to a boil, cover, and simmer until the meat is soft, about 60 to 90 minutes.

To serve: Serve with starch of your choice, e.g., Ghana-Style Dumplings (*Fufu*, page 190), or Rice Balls (*Omo Tuo,* page 179).

Variations: Use other types of meat, and/or add powdered dried shrimp or smoked fish.

DRYING OKRA

Okra can be dried quickly in a microwave or slowly in a low oven. In Ghana, it is usually sundried. Microwaved dehydrated okra preserves more of the ascorbic acid and bright color of fresh okra.

Yield: 5 or 6 good-sized fresh okra (5 to 6 ounces) yield about 3 tablespoons of dried okra powder

Microwave Method (2450 MHz)**:**
Use only firm, fresh, green okra. Wash the okra, cut off the tips, and slice into rounds about ¼ inch thick. Spread them out evenly on a microwave safe plate and cook on high for 5 minutes. After 5 minutes, loosen the okra from the plate with a spatula or your fingers. If the plate in the microwave does not rotate automatically, turn the plate. Microwave on high another minute at a time, for up to 5 more minutes being careful not to burn the okra. If it still bends when pressed, continue microwaving it on a lower heat (level 3 on my microwave) for 1 minute at a time until it is fully dried but not browned. At this point it may be ground in a dry blender, crushed between your fingers, or powdered in a mortar and pestle. Store any extra in the freezer.

Oven Method:
Rinse and dry whole okra and place them on racks on a baking sheet in a very low oven (130 degrees F). Let them slow roast overnight or for about 12 hours, depending on the size of the okra.

Ewe-style Light Okra Soup with Chicken

Fetri Detsi

Makes 4 to 5 servings

Okra, aka "Lady Fingers," that Cinderella of vegetables, is indigenous to West Africa. Among the Ewe people of the Volta Region, there is a short fat type known as *Anlo fetri* after the region where it originated. (The Ewe word for okra is *fetri*, and the word for soup or stew is *detsi*.) This version is one we prepared at Flair Catering. Though it is somewhat time-consuming to prepare the okra this way for this soup, the result rewards your efforts. It is a delicious way to try okra if you never have before.

Ingredients

Chicken
1 chicken cut into 8 to 12 pieces, including the giblets (heart and gizzard) and neck, but not the liver (or buy already cut-up chicken pieces)

1 lemon for cleansing the chicken

2 teaspoons grated fresh ginger

1 teaspoon minced or ground fresh garlic (or to taste)

1 to 2 teaspoons seasoned salt or no-salt seasoning mixture (or to taste)

A pinch dried ground red pepper

¼ cup sliced onion

A little fresh coarsely sliced chili pepper (*kpakpo shito* if available, or your choice; see page 37)

Okra
8 ounces fresh okra

½ cup coarsely chopped onion

Soup
¼ cup vegetable oil (e.g., peanut, safflower, canola; not palm)

1½ teaspoons tomato paste (optional)

Directions

Prepare chicken:
1. After cutting the chicken, remove extra fat. Put the chicken pieces in a bowl and add half a cup of water and toss to wet. Cut the lemon in half and rub one half over the chicken pieces to cleanse and season them; then empty the bowl and repeat with the other half of the lemon. Rinse the chicken in 2 cups of water.
2. Put the chicken in a soup pot with the ginger, garlic, salt/seasoning, and a little ground red pepper. Mix it well to coat the chicken (easiest to do this with your hands), then add ¼ cup sliced onion, the fresh chili pepper, and about ¼ cup water.
3. Turn on the heat to high, bring mixture to a boil, immediately lower the heat, cover the pot, and allow the chicken to steam for 10 minutes. Remove from the heat, and let the chicken cool while you prepare the other soup ingredients.

Note: Traditionally this is the point at which the chicken would then be fried, but along with Barbara, I omit that step.

Prepare okra:
4. This is the fun part. Wash the okra, then cut off the tip of the top and tail of each. Cut through almost all the way to the end and then make another cut so the okra is cut into 4 pieces that are still held together at one end. Remove the seeds—this takes a bit of effort and the tip of a knife (or fingernails). (Barbara removes the seeds "to keep it tidy" but says that in poorer families they would not remove the seeds.)

"Ewe" is not prounounced in 1 syllable like the English word for a female sheep, but with two syllables: "Eh-vey" or "Eh-way"

1 tablespoon ground dried shrimp/ crayfish

1 to 2 teaspoons chicken seasoning (e.g., salt, no-salt seasoning of choice—in Ghana they would likely use a large chicken-flavored seasoning cube)

1 heaping teaspoon grated fresh ginger

1 teaspoon dried ground red pepper (or to taste)

5. Now you will need a good-sized cutting board and a sharp knife. Stack several of the seeded okra together and slice through them. Continue until all the okra is chopped. Gather the chopped okra together on the board and sprinkle the onion on top and mix it in. Fill a cup with water. Pour a couple of tablespoons of water onto the okra-onion mixture and mince them together, then continue mixing and mincing and adding a little more water every couple of minutes. (It will probably take about ¾ cup of water all together.) The okra mixture will thicken and foam and bind itself together to become a mucilaginous dough. Use a knife and a large spoon to lift the mass into a bowl.

Prepare soup:

6. When the okra is ready, heat 2 tablespoons of oil in another soup pot. Add the tomato paste and ½ cup of water to the pot and stir.

7. Remove the chicken from the pot it was steamed in onto a platter. Then strain the liquid into the pot with the tomato paste mixture and discard solids. Add the ground dried shrimp/ crayfish, another teaspoon (or 2) of salt, the chicken seasoning, and 2 cups of water. Bring to a boil, then lower the heat to simmer.

8. Remove and discard the skin and any extra fat from the chicken, and then add the chicken to the broth mixture along with the ginger and dried ground red pepper.

9. Add 1 cup of water to the okra "dough" in two batches, mixing rapidly with a spoon (or your hand) to break it up. Mix the okra into the soup and let the soup simmer for 5 to 10 minutes. Adjust seasonings to taste.

Troubleshooting:

If the chicken is very fatty it may be desirable to skim some of the oil off the top of the soup at the end, or omit the 2 tablespoons of oil.

Add a little more water if the soup seems too thick.

To serve: This soup goes well with *Banku* (page 186) or the similar Ewe *Akple* (page 189).

Okra Soup with Gboma Leaves and Crab
Fetri Ma

Makes 4 to 6 servings

Gboma leaves have a beloved somewhat bitter taste. This soup is an example of an Ewe dish flavored with them. If gboma leaves are not available, substitute spinach or another dark green leaf. The added oil adds to the soup's "heaviness." Ewes tend to use a lot of ginger, garlic, dried shrimp, and smoked fish. They often feel food is too bland without them. This recipe supports that claim.

Ingredients

Meat
1 pound beef (with bone in), cut into chunks (about 20 pieces)

1 teaspoon ground or grated fresh ginger

½ teaspoon ground or grated fresh garlic

1 beef or shrimp seasoning cube (or seasoned salt)

1 cup sliced shallots

8 *kpakpo shito* peppers, sliced; or fresh chili pepper of choice in desired amount (see chart page 37; optional)

1 teaspoon dried ground red pepper

Soup
4 (4-ounce) fresh soft-shelled crabs, or large crabs, or king crab legs

8 ounces smoked dried fish (about 3 to 4 ounces with skin and bones removed)

2 tablespoons pounded dried shrimp

1 beef or shrimp seasoning cube or some seasoned salt (optional)

1 small piece saltpeter (potassium nitrate) to help thicken the soup (optional; *some claim health concerns in using this*)

Directions

Prepare beef:
1. Rinse the beef in a little water and drain. Put the meat in a pan and season with the ginger, garlic, seasoning cube (or seasoned salt), shallots, chili peppers, and dried ground red pepper. Stir well, add ¼ cup water, and put on the stove on medium heat, covered.
2. Simmer, reducing the heat if necessary to keep the water from evaporating (and adding more water as necessary), until meat is tender. The length of time depends on the toughness of the meat. Check it after 20 to 30 minutes.

Prepare crab and fish:
3. If using soft-shelled crabs, cut off the sharp ends of the legs and clean out underneath the mouth.
4. Break off the heads of the fish, if desired (Ghanaians would likely leave them on). Remove skin and bones from the fish.

Prepare soup:
5. Once the meat is tender, add 3 cups of water to the meat in the pot and bring it to a boil. Add the dried shrimp and half of a beef or shrimp-flavored seasoning cube (or ½ teaspoon seasoned salt), if using.
6. Add the crab and smoked fish. (If using the saltpeter, add a small piece "to draw out the stickiness of the okra.") Cover the soup and let it simmer for about 5 or 6 minutes.

GBOMA

There is an indigenous African eggplant known commonly in Ghana as *"gboma."* Its scientific name is *Solanum dasyphyllum*, though the French also call it *aubergine africaine*, the Portuguese *berinjela africana*, and Swahili names include *ngogwe*, *nyanya*, and *nyany chungu*. The plant prefers humid coastal areas and is found throughout the African continent and parts of the diaspora (notably Surinam and the Caribbean). Though the fruit of this plant is eaten, its (usually young) leaves are an important vegetable enjoyed in soups and stews.

8 ounces fetri okra or any okra (fresh if possible), thinly sliced

1 cup good-quality palm oil, preferably *zomi*

1 cup firmly packed gboma leaves or spinach or green leaves of choice, washed

A few sliced seeded chili peppers: jalapenos (mild), or green cayenne peppers (hot), or 1 to 2 habanero peppers (very hot), or 16 *kpakpo shito* peppers, crushed slightly (*for those unused to spiciness, use any peppers sparingly*)

¼ cup sliced onion

7. Place the okra on top of the other ingredients. Shake or stir the palm oil to mix it and add to the soup. Stir in the gboma or spinach leaves. Add the fresh chili peppers and sliced onion.
8. Simmer for several minutes to allow the flavors to blend.

To Serve: Serve this soup with starch of your choice. It is also good reheated the next day.

Variations:
Reduce the amount of palm oil.
Increase the onion and/or water.
Substitute smaked goat with skin on for the beef.

Green Abunabuna Soup with Snails

Ntohuro Nkwan / Kontomire Nkwan

Makes 5 to 6 servings

My husband, an Akwapim from the Eastern Region, loves this Akan soup that is notable for its green color. Unlike him, I am not fond of snails, but it can also be made with smoked game and fish (see Variations). Ghanaians' beloved fermented fish (*momoni*) or *kobi* (salted tilapia) give this soup a distinctive flavor that is generally unavailable to those of us outside Ghana, though adding a little salted cod and/or a dash of Thai fish sauce approximates it. Akans commonly include the spice known locally as "*prɛkɛse*" but Akwapims do not.

Here we give you an adapted recipe for Western kitchens. (I am grateful to Emelia Kwapong, owner and director of Tasty Treats at the Nogouchi Canteen at the University of Ghana; Legon, my husband's favorite place for abunabuna soup when he's in Accra, and especially Georgina Twum, the assistant director, for walking me through the process, increasing my understanding, and answering my questions.)

Ingredients

5 to 12 snails (*depending on whether each person wants 1 or 2 snails*)

1 pound cocoyam/taro/kontomire leaves or other greens (e.g., collard greens, mustard greens, spinach), or frozen spinach

8 ounces dried smoked fish of choice (such as mackerel, whitefish, or whiting)

Chili peppers, to taste (in Ghana, they would likely use about 5 small green *kpakpo shito* peppers; you could substitute 1 small seeded jalapeno [mild], or 1 small green or red seeded cayenne [hot], or 1 green seeded habanero [hot], or 2 red seeded habanero or Scotch bonnets [very very hot], or ½ teaspoon [mild] or ¾ teaspoon [medium] ground dried red pepper)

Directions

Prepare snails:

1. Scald the snails in boiling water to kill them. Wash the snails with water and remove from shells with a fork. Wash again with water and a little lemon or lime juice. Put a little cornmeal on your fingers to remove the sliminess. Take scissors or a knife and remove the heads. Rinse snails again to remove any sand.

2. After cleaning the snails, simmer in a small saucepan with water about 5 minutes (do not overcook). Remove from the pan.

Prepare other ingredients:

3. Wash the greens, removing any tough stems, and cook whole for just 2 or 3 minutes in a little water on the stovetop or covered in the microwave. (The bright green is characteristic of the soup so do not overcook.) Set aside. (Alternatively, defrost a package of frozen whole leaf spinach or other green. No need to cook it).

4. Wash and debone the dried fish and remove the skin. Break into pieces if desired, and set aside.

1 square inch salted cod and/or a dash of Thai fish sauce (optional)

1 large or 2 medium onions, chopped

2 medium red or green tomatoes

1 teaspoon ground fresh ginger (optional)

Several fresh mushrooms of your choice (e.g., about 6 cremini), rinsed, wiped dry, the tip of the stem removed, halved or sliced if desired (optional)

1 teaspoon powdered herrings if available (or to taste), or substitute seasoned salt

Salt to taste (*do not add until the end as smoked/salted ingredients will add saltiness*)

5. Remove the stem ends of the fresh chili peppers; if desired also remove the seeds and membranes for a less spicy soup; slice.

6. Soak the salted cod, if using, in boiling-hot water for a few minutes to reduce saltiness. Drain.

Prepare soup:

7. Put 6 cups of water into a soup pot and add the cooked snails, prepared chili peppers, chopped onion, and whole tomatoes. Bring to a boil and lower the heat and simmer until the tomatoes and peppers are softened, about 5 to 10 minutes.

8. Add the salted cod, ginger, and mushrooms, if using, and continue to simmer. Taste the soup as it cooks and remove the pepper slices when the soup is spicy enough for you and discard them.

9. As soon as the tomatoes are softened, remove them with a slotted spoon. If preferred, remove the tomato skins. Blend them together in a blender with the lightly cooked greens. Return the ground ingredients to the pot.

10. Add the prepared smoked fish and powdered herring or seasoned salt, and another cup of water, if desired, and simmer. After the flavors have blended add salt to taste.

To serve: This soup is traditionally served with Ghana-style Dumplings (*Fufu*, page 190), but also goes nicely with rice or mashed yam.

Variations:

Like many Ghanaian dishes, this recipe is highly flexible. While some people prefer fresh red tomatoes, others like green tomatoes.

Many recipes include variations, such as adding a little groundnut paste (peanut butter), ground beans, or crabs, or omitting the mushrooms.

Substitute 2 pounds (bone-in) or 1 pound (boneless) smoked turkey or game for the snails, cut as desired. Add with the smoked fish.

Substitute dried smoked snails for the fresh ones.

Spinach and Mushroom Soup with Smoked Turkey
Baa Wonu

Makes 6 servings

This soup traditionally uses young cocoyam (*kontomire*) leaves, but spinach makes an acceptable alternative. Smoked turkey substitutes for traditional smoked game. However, in parts of the United States, smoked turkey is difficult to locate except around the Thanksgiving to New Year holidays, which might make this a good holiday meal choice.

Ingredients

2 pounds smoked turkey with bones (or 1 pound boneless)

3 tomatoes

4 scallions

8 ounces fresh young spinach leaves

8 ounces mushrooms, sliced

Salt or seasoned salt to taste

½ teaspoon dried ground red pepper or to taste; or *for the adventurous*, add 1 fresh seeded jalapeno (mild), or 1 sliced seeded cayenne pepper (hotter), or 1 or 2 whole unseeded habaneros with the tops sliced off (hottest)

Directions

1. Remove the skin from the smoked turkey, if desired. Cut the smoked turkey into pieces, and put in a pot, along with 8 cups of water. (If using turkey legs or wings, leave uncut and remove from the soup later to cut.)
2. Wash and trim the ends of the tomatoes, scallions, and spinach and puree them in a blender and add to the pot.
3. Add the sliced mushrooms and salt (remembering that the smoked turkey also has salt). Add a pinch of dried ground red pepper (more can be added later) or the chili pepper, if using.
4. Simmer for 20 to 30 minutes for the flavors to blend. Taste soup while it is cooking and remove the chili pepper(s) when the desired spiciness is obtained. Adjust seasonings, and add another cup water, if desired. Remove bones before serving.

To serve: This goes especially well with Ghana-style Dumplings (*Fufu*, page 190).

Variations:
Use any smoked meat (e.g., ham or ham hocks, game) in place of the turkey, adjusting cooking time as necessary.

Add a little tomato paste, shallots or onions, etc. in addition to, or in place of, the tomatoes and scallions.

Chop the scallions and spinach rather than pureeing them.

Melon Seed Soup
Agushi Nkwan

Makes 4 servings

Ghanaians frequently use ground seeds and nuts to thicken soups. This recipe uses a kind of melon seed that gives it a mild nutty flavor. If *agushi* seeds are not available, use pumpkin seeds. This soup is reminiscent of peanut/groundnut soup, and a good substitute for anyone with peanut allergies.

Ingredients

8 ounces boneless or 1 pound bone-in meat (goat, oxtail, lamb, beef, etc.), fat trimmed and cut into 12 pieces

1 large onion or 3 shallots, finely chopped

Salt or seasoned salt to taste

1 or 2 garlic cloves, crushed or minced (optional)

1 teaspoon grated fresh ginger (optional)

¼ to ½ teaspoon dried ground red pepper (or to taste) or a small amount of fresh chili pepper—for habanero, this would likely be a thin slice (see heat chart, page 37)

6 ounces smoked fish (not smoked and salted herrings)

2 large tomatoes, peeled and chopped

1 cup agushi or pumpkin seeds

To serve: This soup is classically served Ghana-style Dumplings (*Fufu*, page 190). An alternative would be Rice Balls (*Omo Tuo*, page 179).

Directions

Season meat:

1. Put the meat into a soup pot with 1 cup of water. Add half the chopped onion/shallots, ¼ teaspoon salt, the garlic, ginger, and ground red pepper or chili pepper.
2. Stir, cover, and simmer on low heat until the meat is almost tender, about 30 minutes, depending on the cut of meat. Add a little more water while the meat simmers if necessary.

Make soup:

3. While the meat cooks, remove any bones and skin from the fish and break the fish into pieces. Set aside.
4. When the meat is almost tender, add another 5 cups of water and bring to a boil, then lower the heat to simmer.
5. Grind the tomatoes and remaining chopped onion/shallots in a blender and add to the soup pot. (NOTE: Traditionally, people would throw the whole tomato into the hot soup and let it soften for a few minutes, then remove and slip off the tomato skin before the tomato is pureed. Omit or include this step as desired.)
6. Grind the agushi or pumpkin seeds in a blender, using a little of the water from the soup pot to make a paste. Add 1 more cup of the soup broth to the blender and puree to make a smooth paste. Stir the paste into the soup.
7. Add the smoked fish. Allow the soup to simmer for 20 to 30 minutes or until the flavors blend and the meat is soft.
8. Taste and adjust seasonings, if necessary, and cook a few more minutes.

Chicken Peanut Soup
Nkate Nkwan

This is a famous West African soup. Centuries ago, peanuts were introduced into West Africa from South America via the Portuguese and supplanted the native *bambara* groundnuts. At the same time, in much of Ghana, the prevalence of the tsetse fly made cattle-rearing impossible, which led to a diet without milk and dairy products. Thus, to make rich, creamy soups or stews, thickeners like ground legumes, nuts or seeds, pureed vegetables or okra, or palm butter were used. Ground peanuts were a wonderful addition.

A delicious introduction to West African cooking, this soup is very accessible to the North American palate. Commonly made from a basic chicken stock, it is wonderfully flexible: one can use more or less peanut butter, or add a variety of vegetables from eggplant to mushrooms. Also, the recipe is easily adapted to a vegetarian version. Besides the peanut butter, however, the tomatoes, chili peppers, and onions are necessary ingredients. They are a holy trinity in much of Ghana's cooking.

Ingredients

3 to 4 pounds bone-in chicken parts, skin and fat removed

2 cups chopped onion

2 or 3 garlic cloves, minced, pressed, or ground

1 heaping teaspoon grated fresh ginger

1½ teaspoons salt (or to taste)

Dried ground red pepper to taste (at least ¼ teaspoon), or fresh hot chili pepper of choice (see page 37)

1 8-ounce can tomato sauce

1 to 2 tablespoons tomato paste

½ to 1 cup creamy natural-style peanut butter (no sugar added)

About 8 fresh okra or 5 ounces frozen okra, tails removed, left whole or chopped

Directions

1. Put chicken pieces into a heavy pot with ½ cup of water. Add 1 cup of the chopped onion, the garlic, ginger, salt, and ground red pepper. Cover and steam the chicken over medium-low heat for about 10 minutes, making sure the water does not cook away.

2. Stir in the tomato sauce and paste, the remaining 1 cup of chopped onion, and 5 more cups of water. Bring the soup to a boil and then reduce the heat to simmer.

3. Ladle about 2 cups of the soup broth into a medium saucepan, and mix in the peanut butter. Heat the mixture on medium heat, stirring constantly, until the oil separates and rises to the surface. This may take 15 to 20 minutes. Be sure to stir the mixture constantly or it will scorch. Add a little more soup broth as necessary. (NOTE: One can simply stir the peanut butter/broth mixture directly into the soup, but I was taught to cook it separately. It somehow flavors the peanut sauce more, like browning would.)

4. When the oil has begun to separate out, ladle some more of the soup broth into the peanut sauce, stir it, and carefully stir the mixture into the soup.

5. After a few minutes, add the okra. Allow the soup to simmer for about 20 to 30 more minutes, until the flavors blend and the chicken is cooked. Add more water for a thinner soup. Check the seasonings and adjust salt, red pepper, etc., to taste.
6. Before serving, skim off any oil that rises to the surface. If the soup is not going to be eaten immediately, remove the chicken pieces to prevent them from overcooking, and return them to the soup just in time to heat them through.

To serve: Use cooked okra or fresh chopped scallions as a garnish and instead of bread or rolls, serve the soup with mini-rice balls. Serve dried ground red pepper or red pepper flakes on the side so that people can add more spiciness if desired. *Nkate Nkwan* is traditionally served with Ghana-style Dumplings (*Fufu*, page 190), boiled African yam, or Rice Balls (*Omo Tuo*, see page 179). Boiled potatoes or thick slices of whole-grain bread are easy Western accompaniments.

Variations:
When serving this to large numbers of people, the cooked chicken may be deboned and cubed and then added back into the soup.

There are several short-cut options, especially if this soup is served as a first course/starter: use prepared chicken broth in place of the water and add all the other ingredients but omit the chicken pieces; and/or add the peanut butter after mixing it with the hot broth without simmering the mixture first.

Cook and serve the okra separately so that people can decide whether or not they wish to add it.

For a change of pace, make the soup using turkey pieces in place of the chicken.

Instead of the tomato sauce, substitute 1½ cups ground, seeded, fresh or canned tomatoes (do not use canned tomato puree, however).

For a smoother soup, remove the chicken and strain the broth before preparing and adding the peanut butter mixture, or puree the second cup of onion.

Chicken Peanut Stew
To make this a stew, simply add less water (about 3 to 4 cups). The stew can be served over rice like a curry, with small bowls of condiments (see recipe for Vegetarian Peanut Stew on page 126 for a list of suggestions).

Vegetarian Peanut Soup

Makes 4 to 6 servings

This excellent creamy soup uses up to eight kinds of vegetables along with protein-packed peanut butter and eggs to make a hearty soup that pairs wonderfully with Ghana-style Dumplings (*Fufu)*, Rice Balls (*Omo Tuo*), or for a Western touch, crusty French bread.

Ingredients

3 cups peeled and cubed eggplant

1 large onion, finely chopped

4 to 6 cups vegetable stock; or water flavored with seasoning cubes

2 cloves garlic, minced (optional)

2 teaspoons grated fresh ginger (optional)

¼ teaspoon dried ground red pepper, or some chopped fresh chili pepper of choice (see page 37)

1 to 2 cups canned or fresh tomatoes, pureed (do not use canned puree)

1½ teaspoons salt (or to taste)

1 cup creamy natural-style peanut butter (no sugar added)

8 ounces mushrooms, cut in half or thick slices

8 fresh okra or ½ 10-ounce package frozen okra, ends trimmed, whole or sliced

2 medium zucchini or yellow squash, cut into cubes (optional)

4 to 6 hardboiled eggs, peeled

Directions

1. Put the eggplant in a saucepan, add 3 cups of water and bring to a boil. Lower the heat to simmer and cook until soft, about 10 minutes. Use a slotted spoon to remove the eggplant. Save the water. Set both aside.

2. Put the onion into a large soup pot with 4 cups of vegetable stock. Add the garlic, ginger, and chili pepper, if using.

3. Puree all or part of the eggplant using a blender or food processor (add some of the water in which it was cooked if desired) and add all the eggplant to the soup pot.

4. Add 1 cup of the pureed tomatoes and the salt and allow the soup to simmer while preparing the peanut butter.

5. Remove 2 cups of broth from the soup and mix it in a saucepan with the peanut butter to make a smooth paste. Cook the paste over a medium heat, stirring constantly with a long-handled spoon, being careful to avoid both scorching the peanut butter (lower the heat if necessary) and being splattered. After about 15 to 20 minutes, the oil will begin to separate from the paste. At that point add another cup of soup broth to the saucepan, mix well, and slowly stir the mixture from the saucepan into the soup pot.

6. Add the mushrooms, okra, and squash to the soup. For a thinner soup, add additional stock or water. Cover the soup and allow it to simmer about 20 minutes or until the vegetables are cooked. Adjust the seasonings to taste. Add the whole hardboiled eggs a few minutes before serving.

To serve: Serve as directed for Chicken Peanut Soup, page 105.

Palm Nut Soup
Abε Nkwan

Makes 10 to 12 servings

Palm nut soup is a much beloved dish. When my adopted nephew from Ghana celebrated his 23rd birthday, I asked this Americanized young Ghanaian what he wanted for his special dinner (Mexican, Italian, Asian, Indian, Ghanaian, "American," etc.). Two years in a row he answered: "palm nut soup and cocoyam (taro) *fufu*." It took some time to scout around and come up with the necessary ingredients, however, the end result (and his hearty enjoyment) made everything worthwhile.

Palm Nut Soup is also a family favorite at our house for ringing in the New Year. Here I give you a special rich birthday or holiday version. It is loaded with seafood, meat, and vegetables, and adapted to our local environment. This includes a number of "extras," but can be simplified to make an "everyday" version, mixing and matching ingredients of your choice.

For this particular soup, apart from fresh palm nuts there is no substitute for the canned cream of palm fruit. If none is available from a nearby West African or international market, there are sources available online.

Ingredients
1 to 2 pounds meat (beef, lamb, goat, or a combination)

1 to 2 pounds soup bones (optional)

2 cups chopped onion

3 or 4 cloves garlic, crushed or chopped

4 teaspoons grated fresh ginger

¼ to ½ teaspoon dried ground red pepper (*for the adventurous:* instead add 1 fresh seeded jalapeno [mild], or 1 sliced seeded cayenne pepper [hotter], or 1 or 2 whole unseeded habaneros with the tops sliced off [hottest])

2 teaspoons salt or seasoned salt

3 cups peeled and cubed eggplant

1 (28-ounce) can plum tomatoes, pureed in a blender (seeds strained out and removed, if desired)

1 (29-ounce/800-gram) can cream of palm fruit

Directions
Season meat:
1. Remove and discard fat and gristle on the meat, then cut it into chunks and put in a soup pot, along with the soup bones, if using, and ½ cup water.
2. Add the onion, garlic, ginger, chili pepper, and salt. Stir meat and seasonings with a wooden spoon and place the pot over a medium heat to steam, covered, for about 15 minutes, checking to make sure water hasn't evaporated.

Prepare eggplant:
3. While the meat is steaming, put the eggplant in a saucepan with a few cups of water. Cover the pan and bring to a boil over high heat, then simmer for about 10 minutes. When the eggplant is soft, remove the pan from the heat and use a slotted spoon to transfer the eggplant to a blender or food processor in two batches. Add a little of the water used to cook the eggplant to the blender and puree. (If desired, but being careful not to make the soup too spicy, transfer a piece of fresh chili pepper you cooked in the soup broth to the blender and blend with some of the eggplant.)

(ingredients & directions continued on page 109)

PALM NUTS / FRUIT

Palm nuts are used throughout Western and Central Africa to make a variety of soups and stews or sauces. Ghana's palm nut soup is often called by its Akan name: "*abɛ*" (pronounced ah-BEH) for the palm nuts, and "*nkwan*" (soup). Cameroon has its *mbanga* soup, and in Nigeria, a version is *banga* soup.

I once enthused "it is as hard to capture the essence of the palm fruit as it is to describe the hues of sunset to a blind person. The fruit has a color like paprika or glowing coals, with the softness of red velvet, the silkiness of a fine sari, and the richness of fresh cream."

The African oil palm, *Elaeis guineensis*, is indigenous to the tropical forests of Western Africa, and has been called "the most useful tree in West Africa." Its fruit, date-like clusters of bright orange-red palm nuts, is in some ways the "olive" of West Africa. While the fruit is not eaten the same way olives are, there are a variety of types, and the oil and processing methods produce differences in taste and quality. The carotene-rich pericarp or pulp of the palm nut produces a thick, rich, creamy "palm butter," or "cream of palm fruit" (called *sauce graine* or *noix de palme* in French-speaking West African countries) that has no equivalent. (Unfortunately, many people confuse the pericarp/pulp with the highly saturated palm kernel oil of the hard inner seed, which is often used in soaps and personal care products.)

While some countries in western and central Africa make their soups with the orange-red palm oil, in Ghana palm nut soup is prepared with the creamy pulp of the palm nut, while the oil is generally reserved for frying and making stews.

Palm Nut Soup (continued)
Abε Nkwan

> As the soup simmers in step 5, you can use a spoon to skim off any red palm oil that rises to the surface but traditionally in Ghana a thick layer of palm oil on top of the soup is a sign of respect and honor, of generosity, nurturing, and wealth.

8 ounces fresh mushrooms of choice, cleaned and left whole or sliced in half

6 ounces smoked fish (e.g., smoked mackerel, white fish, whiting or salmon; avoid smoked herring with its pungent flavor), skin and bones removed

20 to 25 fresh okra, trimmed and sliced or whole, or 1 (10-ounce) package frozen okra, whole or sliced

1 to 2 tablespoons powdered dried shrimp or prawns (optional)

1 pound fresh shrimp with shells, deveined

3 crabs or king crab legs, cleaned and rinsed (optional)

Assemble soup:

4. After the meat has steamed for 15 minutes, add the pureed eggplant, pureed tomatoes, cream of palm fruit (use a swish of water to get all of it out of can), and 4 to 6 cups of water (depending on desired thickness of soup). Stir well and allow the soup to simmer for about 30 minutes. Taste soup as it begins to cook and remove the chili peppers, if used, when the desired spiciness is obtained.
5. Add the mushrooms, smoked fish, okra, and powdered dried shrimp, if using, and stir. Cover the soup pot and allow to simmer on low for about 20 more minutes, until the vegetables and meat are soft and flavors have blended together.
6. About 10 minutes before the soup is done, add the shrimp and crab, if using, and continue to simmer until they are cooked and flavors have blended.
7. Taste for salt and ground red pepper and add more as needed.

To serve: Serve this lovely, filling soup with Ghana-style Dumplings (*Fufu*, page 190), or Rice Balls (*Omo Tuo*, page 179), or thick slices of sourdough or any hearty bread.

Make ahead: This soup tastes even better reheated the second day, but before reheating remove the shellfish to prevent overcooking them and add them back when the soup is almost ready to serve.

(continued on next page)

Palm Nut Soup (continued)
Abε Nkwan

Variations:

Include a pound of a firm white fish, like cod in addition to or in place of part of the meat. Add near the end of the cooking time with the shrimp and crab.

For a velvety soup, strain the soup after it has simmered for 30 minutes, before adding the mushrooms, okra, etc. (save the "dregs" to use another day in a sauce, or puree them in a blender and return to the soup).

This makes a large pot of soup. More recently, smaller 400 gram cans of palm fruit are becoming available. For a less rich version, one could use the smaller can in the recipe. Alternatively, the recipe could be cut in half.

Peanut Palm Nut Soup
Nkatsebenkwan

Before adding the mushrooms, okra, etc., to the pot for Palm Nut Soup, in a separate bowl mix 1 cup of natural-style peanut butter with some of the soup broth to form a smooth paste, then stir it into the soup. Let boil for a few minutes before continuing with recipe. This version of the soup also goes well with *Banku* (page 186), *Ga-style Kenkey* (page 187), or hearty slices of bread.

Sesame Soup with Poultry

Makes 4 to 5 servings

Sesame soup is popular in Northern Ghana. While in Tamale shadowing Mrs. Comfort Awu Akor, we went to the local outdoor market for ingredients to make ours, including guinea fowl and sesame seeds. Comfort wanted two specific types of seeds, but we had to settle for what was available. Preparations were quite labor intensive. Our Muslim driver Abdul did the honors of slaughtering the guinea fowl—cutting its head off after saying a prayer. We boiled water to clean the fowl and remove its feathers, and cut it into serving pieces. To prepare the sesame paste we rinsed the seeds, dried and toasted them, and pounded them into a smooth paste in a mortar. I have been unsuccessful in duplicating that process using either a coffee grinder or blender, even with the addition of sesame oil. Therefore, this recipe substitutes tahini.

Ingredients

4 pounds guinea fowl, Cornish game hens, chicken, or pheasant

1 cup coarsely chopped onion (red if available)

2-inch piece fresh ginger, coarsely chopped

3 or 4 cloves garlic

1 to 3 chili peppers, or to taste (jalapeno for milder, cayenne for hotter, and habanero for very hot), seeded and stems and membranes removed to decrease heat, if desired

1½ teaspoons salt or seasoned salt (or to taste)

6 small-to-medium peeled tomatoes or half a 28-ounce can tomatoes

1 cup tahini

Directions

Prepare the poultry:

1. Rinse the poultry (if desired, cut off the end of the tails and the tips of the wings) and remove any extra fat and loose skin. Keep the neck but discard the liver. Cut each fowl into serving pieces: for a guinea fowl or chicken, 8 to 10 pieces; for the game hens, quarter each (or cut into more pieces if serving to a crowd, in which case, be fearless and whack away at the bones with a heavy butcher knife).

2. Put the onion, ginger, garlic, and chili peppers in a blender. Add just enough water (a tablespoon or two) to grind them into a paste.

3. Put the poultry pieces into a large heavy pot with a lid, along with a ½ cup of water and the ground seasoning mixture. Rinse out the blender container with a little more water and add that, too, along with the salt. Stir to mix, cover the pot, and heat on high heat, then reduce to medium to steam the poultry for 10 to 20 minutes.

Prepare tomatoes:

4. If using fresh tomatoes, first drop in boiling water for a couple of minutes, then in cold water (this loosens the skins). Remove the skins and then puree the tomatoes in a blender. If using canned tomatoes, simply drain and puree, adding about half a cup of the juice from the can as well.

(continued on next page)

Sesame Soup with Poultry (continued)

Assemble soup:

5. Once the poultry is steamed, place a strainer over the soup, and add the pureed tomatoes, straining out the seeds. Add 2 cups of water, pouring it through the strainer, too, to get the last bit of tomato in the soup. Add an additional 2 cups of water, bring to a boil, then lower the heat to simmer the soup while preparing the sesame paste.

6. Mix the tahini (sesame paste) with 2 cups of the soup's hot broth in a small saucepan. Cook on medium heat, stirring occasionally, until the oil begins to separate. Pour mixture into a blender, using a spatula if necessary.

7. Remove the poultry pieces to another pot and strain the broth into the new pot with them.

8. Blend the sesame mixture in the blender with a little more broth if needed. Stir the sesame paste into the soup, rinsing the blender with broth from the pot, and scraping the dregs in with a spatula. Adjust the seasonings to taste.

Variations:

Use tomato sauce or paste in place of fresh or canned tomatoes.

Substitute vegetables for the fowl (use mushrooms, eggplant, etc.).

Use less tahini for a milder, lighter flavor.

Serve as a first course and garnish with parsley, grated hardboiled egg, or minced green onions.

Instead of using tahini, toast and grind sesame seeds and blend them with 1½ cups water in a smoothie maker.

Akuapem Amanokrom Odwira harvest festival in the Eastern Region of Ghana

Larambanga mosque, Northern Ghana. The oldest mosque in Ghana and one of the oldest in West Africa.

A buffet being served at Barbara Baëta's Flair Catering in Accra

Above: Preparing plantain strips/chips (page 49)
Below: Preparing *Ga Kenkey* (page 187)

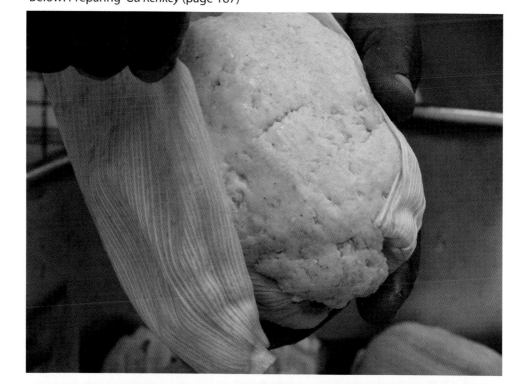

Top: Ingredients for grilling fish
Bottom: Grilling tilapia (page 134)

Selling *tubaani* (black-eyed pea steamed pudding, page 76)
at a market in Northern Ghana

Vintage photo of Palm Nut Soup / *Abɛ Nkwan* (page 107) and
Fufu (page 191) from Barbara Baëta's private collection

Palaver sauce garnished with fresh crabs (page 128)

Stewed Bambara Beans / *Aboboe* (page 142)
Savory Plantain Pancakes / *Tatale* (page 50)

Two varieties of palm nuts/fruit (*abɛ*)

Peanut Toffee / *Nkatie Cakes* (page 212)
Coconut Toffee (page 213 *var.*)

Varieties of chili peppers and nuts, spices, seeds and other dried ingredients used in Ghana

Fante Kenkey and *Ga Kenkey* (Steamed Fermented Corn Dough, page 187) and *Kenam* (Fried Fish, pages 138 and 139) served with Fresh Pepper Sauces (page 168) and *Shito* (page 170) in an *asanka*

Sesame Soup with Poultry (page 111) and Stiff Millet Porridge / *Tuo Zaafi* / *TZ* (page 182)

African Yam Balls / *Yɛlɛ Kakro* (page 80)

Tropical Fruit Salad (page 217)

Twisted Cakes / *Atwemo* formed in two different ways (page 222)

Grilled Prawns (page 136)

Statue of an okra farmer standing over Okra Soup with
Gboma Leaves and Crab / *Fetri Ma* (page 98)

Dancing during the Ewe Hogbetsotso (Festival of Exodus) in the Volta Region

Spicy Fried Plantain Cubes / *Kelewele* (page 52) served with peanuts

Authors Barbara Baëta and Fran Osseo-Asare in Barbara's kitchen, 2004

Barbara Baëta's classic image of Ɔtɔ (Mashed African Yams with Palm Oil and Eggs; pages 164-165)

STEWS

Fresh Fish Stew
Fante Fante

Fante Fante is a red sauce/stew made with very fresh fish. When I asked people in Ghana how to make this dish, which originated among the coastal Fante people of the Western Region, I was given multiple answers: we prepared a version at Flair Catering that was similar to a stew where some of the ingredients were first fried; another time I was instructed to use similar ingredients as Flair's, but without frying them first ("but you *never* fry the fish"); finally, I was told it could be made like a simple fish light soup without any palm oil. Some people said to grind the ingredients, others to grate them; some to add ground shrimp, others not to; some to season and steam the fish first separately in a little salted water and onion; some used ginger, many did not; some people said to use seasoning cubes, but others only to use fresh sea salt; most insisted on fresh red chili peppers . . . it was somewhat confusing.

After sifting through all of the information, I have included two versions in this book. This first one involves no frying; the second one (opposite page) is Barbara's version at Flair and does involve some frying. Both these stews include only a little water and are more like a sauce.

Ingredients

1 to 1½ pounds whole fresh fish (red snapper, grouper, or cassava fish)

1 lemon

2 large tomatoes, peeled and seeded, if desired (to get 2 cups when pureed)

1 onion, coarsely chopped

1 fresh red chili pepper of choice, seeded and with membranes removed, if desired (a habanero for very hot; part of a jalapeno for moderately hot)

1 tablespoon tomato paste (or to taste)

3 tablespoons grated or ground fresh ginger

1 or 2 cloves garlic, minced (optional)

Salt or seasoned salt, to taste

Additional seasonings to taste

4 tablespoons good quality palm oil (spiced *dzomi* oil if available)

Directions

1. Scale (if necessary) and clean the fish, cut into 4 pieces (or in halves if using 2 fish), and wash with a little water with lemon juice squeezed into it. (Optional: put the fish in a saucepan with a little chopped onion, some salt, and a little water and steam it for about 3 minutes.)

2. Puree the tomatoes, onion, chili pepper, tomato paste, and ginger in a blender along with the garlic, if using.

3. Put ¾ cup of water in a soup pot (use part of the water the fish was steamed in, if steamed). Add the fish pieces to the pot in a single layer, sprinkle them with salt, and pour the pureed ingredients over the fish, using another ¼ cup of water to rinse out your blender container. Bring to a boil, then lower the heat and simmer for 4 minutes.

4. Add 4 tablespoons of palm oil (Ghanaians might use twice that much) and shake the pan gently to mix everything without breaking the fish apart. Let simmer, covered, for about 15 minutes and adjust seasonings. Continue cooking, if needed, until the fish flakes easily.

To serve: *Fante Fante* goes well with *Fante kenkey, Banku* (page 186), yams, rice, potatoes, etc.

Flair's Fresh Fish Stew
Flair's Fante Fante

Makes 4 servings

This is the version of *Fante Fante* served at Flair. When preparing this dish at Flair Catering, we used basically the same ingredients as other recipes for **Fante Fante**, but in different amounts and using different techniques to prepare a Ghana-style tomato gravy/sauce.

Ingredients

1 to 1½ pounds whole fresh fish (red snapper, grouper, or cassava fish)

1 lemon

½ cup palm oil

½ cup well-packed grated onion plus a few extra slices

2 tablespoons tomato paste

Some slices fresh chili pepper to taste (see chart, page 37)

1 teaspoon grated fresh ginger

½ large shrimp-flavored seasoning cube (or substitute ground dried shrimp/crayfish)

Ground dried red chili pepper to taste

Pre-Seasoning for fish

1 clove garlic, crushed

1 heaping teaspoon grated onion

1 heaping teaspoon grated fresh ginger

½ large shrimp-flavored seasoning cube (or substitute ground dried shrimp/crayfish)

1 fresh chili pepper, chopped, seeded and with membranes removed, if desired (part of or a whole habanero for very hot; a jalapeno for moderately hot)

Directions

1. Scale (if necessary) and clean the fish, cut into 4 pieces (or in halves if using 2 fish), and wash with a little water with lemon juice squeezed into it and then shake off the extra water. Season the fish with the pre-seasoning ingredients and let marinate.
2. While the fish marinates, heat ½ cup of palm oil in a frying pan along with a few slices of onion to season it. Once the oil is hot, remove the onion slices and add the grated onion, tomato paste, and a few slices chili pepper, as desired, and sauté for about 5 minutes.
3. Add grated ginger and the half of the seasoning cube, and adjust the seasoning by adding more salt and some ground dried red pepper to taste.
4. Place the marinated fish in a single layer in the pan, add ⅓ cup of water and shake the pan to stir it, adding a few more slices of fresh chili pepper and another ½ teaspoon salt if desired.
5. Cover pan and simmer until the fish is cooked, about 15 minutes. Check during the cooking and add a little more water if needed.

To serve: *Fante Fante* goes well with *Fante kenkey*, *Banku* (page 186), yams, rice, potatoes, etc. Flair favors serving it with boiled African yam.

Variations: Include a little white pepper or a slight dash of nutmeg (⅛ teaspoon or less).

Sardine Stew in a Flash

Makes 4 to 5 servings

Sardines have been rediscovered in the West. Years ago, our Victorian ancestors considered them haute cuisine, and served them at dinner parties in fancy crystal and silver sardine servers. More recently, they have gained favor because they are filled with protein, minerals, vitamins, and heart-healthy omega-3 fatty acids. Yet they remain inexpensive, and can be conveniently stored in cans on the shelf next to cans of tuna fish. They are already cooked, and have a mild, pleasant flavor.

My Norwegian grandfather used to eat sardines, but I never ate them until I worked in Ghana and learned to favor them accompanied by a ball of *kenkey* and some fiery *shito*, or in this simple and satisfying stew. My grandfather ate the tiny sardines in oil in the flat tin box that you open with a key. Those can be used, but more common are the larger sardines that are canned with chili sauce or tomato sauce. This recipe features those marketed by Goya in 15-ounce cans or the smaller 3.5-ounce "tinapa" size. When I first went to Ghana my future sister-in-law always wrote "tinapa" on our shopping list and I thought that was a Ghanaian type of fish.

Sardine stew can be cooked in a flash after a busy day or when company arrives unexpectedly. It takes about twenty minutes, and goes well with plain boiled rice, so for a quick meal, put 2 cups of long-grain rice on to cook in an electric rice cooker before beginning the stew.

Ingredients

2 to 4 tablespoons peanut or other vegetable oil

1 medium onion, chopped or sliced

¼ teaspoon dried ground red pepper (or more to taste)

2 tablespoons tomato paste (optional)

2 eggs, beaten (optional)

1 (15-ounce) can Goya sardines in tomato (or chili) sauce; or 3 (5½-ounce) cans Goya tinapa sardines in tomato sauce or hot tomato sauce

Salt to taste

Directions

1. Heat oil on medium heat in a heavy 10-inch skillet, then add the onion and sauté on medium heat for a few minutes until translucent and just beginning to brown.

2. Stir in the ground red pepper, tomato paste, if using, and ¼ cup of water. (Optional: Add the eggs when adding the water to make a richer, thicker sauce. It is fine if the eggs solidify and curdle in the sauce, but to prevent that, lower the heat to cook.)

3. Gently empty the cans of sardines into the pan, leaving the sardines whole or allowing them to break up into small pieces. Use ¼ cup water to rinse out the sardine can, and stir into the stew.

4. Add salt to taste (or none), turn the heat to low and allow the stew to simmer for 10 to 15 minutes. Add a little more water if necessary.

To serve: If serving with rice, ladle a generous spoonful of rice onto a plate and cover with a spoonful of stew. If another vegetable is desired, cook up some fresh or frozen veggies in the microwave, or sauté some cabbage or other greens while the stew simmers. My family members automatically spoon some *Shito* (page 170) onto the side of the plate alongside the stew (or use any hot sauce). Top the meal off with seasonal fresh fruit.

Okra, Eggplant and Fish Stew

Makes 4 servings

Banku (a fermented corn dough) is often eaten with a stew made from okra or slightly bitter garden eggs (a type of eggplant), and smoked and/or fresh fish. Smoked fish imparts a lovely flavor, but for a low-salt version like this one, fresh fish alone may be used. Also, while salmon offers a contemporary twist, any firm-fleshed fish fillets may be used.

Ingredients

1 medium eggplant, peeled and cut into cubes (2 to 3 cups)

18 fresh or frozen okra

1 tablespoon coarsely chopped fresh ginger (or to taste)

2 large garlic cloves, coarsely chopped

1 jalapeno pepper (or more to taste; or a hotter variety pepper, if desired, see page 37)

2 or 3 large fresh or canned tomatoes, peeled and quartered

2 tablespoons red palm oil (*dzomi*, if available) or other vegetable oil

1 large onion, chopped

4 salmon fillets or other firm-fleshed fish fillet (about 4 ounces each)

1½ teaspoons salt (or to taste)

⅛ to ¼ teaspoon dried ground red pepper (optional)

1 tablespoon tomato paste (optional)

Variations:

This stew also works nicely made with just okra or just eggplant.

The eggplant may be added cubed without pureeing first.

Replace the fresh fish with 8 ounces of smoked fish.

Substitute tuna, tilapia, red snapper, or cod for the salmon.

Directions

Prepare vegetables:

1. Put the eggplant in a saucepan and cover with water. Cover the pan, bring the water to a boil, lower the heat, and simmer for 10 minutes to soften. When the eggplant is soft, remove it with a slotted spoon and puree in an electric blender or food processor. Pour into a bowl and set aside.

2. If using fresh okra, rinse and trim both ends. Then slice them into rounds, chop finely, or leave whole. Do not cut whole frozen okra. Set aside until needed.

3. Put the ginger, garlic, chili pepper, and tomatoes (seeded, if desired) in the blender or food processor and puree with a little water.

Prepare the stew:

4. In a large, heavy pan heat the palm or vegetable oil and fry the chopped onion on medium heat for a few minutes. Add the pureed tomato mixture and pureed eggplant.

5. Add the fish, turning the fillets to coat them with the spices and vegetables, then add the okra and salt and stir. Add a little water if the sauce seems too thick, cover and lower the heat and simmer until the fish and okra are cooked.

6. Adjust the seasonings. If it is not spicy enough, add a little dried red chili pepper (beginning with ⅛ to ¼ teaspoon). For more tomato flavor, stir in the tomato paste.

To serve: This stew can be accompanied by *Banku* (page 186), plain rice, or *Ampesi* (page 185). It also goes well with spicy *Shito* (page 170), any chili sauce, or dried red pepper flakes.

Eggplant Stew with Meat, Shrimp and Smoked Fish

Makes 6 to 8 servings

This recipe is adapted from a rich stew we cooked at Flair. It includes that common blending of meat and fresh and smoked seafood, laced together with exciting spiciness, fresh vegetables, and the distinctive flavor of palm oil. This is a more complex version of Okra, Eggplant, and Fish Stew (page 117) and is perfect for a special occasion.

We have made some adjustments to the Ghana recipe to make it easier to reproduce in the U.S.: Garden eggs (small egg-shaped eggplants) are replaced by purple eggplant; fresh crabs by tiger shrimp; the *momoni* (fermented fish with a pungent flavor and odor, especially beloved among many Ashanti in Ghana) by salted cod; the *kpakpo shito* peppers by jalapeno or habanero peppers; and the palm oil is lightened by mixing it with half canola oil; the amount of both salt and oil are reduced from the original Ghanaian version. Some people attempt to re-create the distinctive color (but not the flavor) of palm oil by mixing non-spicy paprika into a neutral oil like canola.

Ingredients

Meat and Seasonings

8 ounces stewing beef (or other meat, like lamb or goat), cut into 1/2-inch cubes

2 teaspoons grated fresh ginger

1 teaspoon minced, crushed, or ground fresh garlic

½ to 1 teaspoon dried ground red pepper (or to taste)

1 to 2 teaspoons seasoned salt or no-salt seasoning mixture of your choice

¼ cup sliced or chopped onion

1 jalapeno pepper (or more to taste; or a hotter variety pepper like habanero, if desired, see page 37), coarsely chopped (optional)

Stew

1 1-inch piece salted cod (optional)

1 pound fresh tomatoes

1 large eggplant, peeled and cubed

¼ cup vegetable oil (such as peanut or canola)

Directions

Season the meat:

1. Put the cut meat into a heavy pot. Sprinkle the ginger, garlic, ground red pepper, and seasoned salt over it, mixing to coat it well. Sprinkle ¼ cup of sliced or chopped onion and the coarsely chopped fresh chili pepper over the meat, along with ½ cup of water.

2. Heat the water to boiling, cover the pot and reduce the heat to allow the meat to simmer until almost tender, about 20 minutes, depending on the cut of meat. Add a little more water as it cooks if necessary to keep it from scorching. After the meat has steamed, remove from the heat until ready to proceed. (Remove the chopped peppers and the onion slices in the pot, if desired.)

Prepare other ingredients:

3. If using salted cod, soak in hot water for 10 minutes and then rinse.

4. Seed and grate the tomatoes. Yield should be about 2 cups of tomato pulp and juice.

5. Place the cubed eggplant in a saucepan and cover with water. Bring to a boil and then lower heat and simmer for about 10 minutes or until it is soft. Remove the eggplant with a slotted spoon and puree in an electric blender or food processor. Set aside until needed.

¼ cup palm oil (*dzomi* if available)

1 heaping teaspoon tomato paste

8 ounces onions or shallots, sliced or grated on a medium grater (about 1 cup grated, more if sliced)

4 tablespoons ground dried shrimp (or to taste; optional)

Additional hot fresh chili pepper (such as habanero) to taste or additional dried ground red pepper to taste (optional)

8 ounces smoked fish, rinsed and bones and skin removed, or 6 ounces boneless

1½ teaspoons ground or grated fresh ginger

1 teaspoon crushed fresh garlic

1 teaspoon fish seasoning (such as a packaged fish masala or curry powder)

1 teaspoon salt or seasoned salt (or to taste)

6 to 8 large shrimps, tailed and deveined with shells left on

Prepare the stew:

6. Put ¼ cup of vegetable oil and ¼ cup of palm oil into a heavy skillet or pot and sauté the salted cod and tomato paste for a couple of minutes.

7. Add the grated or sliced onions and sauté 2 minutes.

8. Add the meat and the broth from cooking it (about ⅓ cup), the grated tomatoes with juice, the pureed eggplant, and the ground dried shrimp, if using. Mix well.

9. Optional: For more heat, slice a habanero pepper partway through once or twice, and add it to the mixture. To increase the heat, push against the pepper as it cooks.

10. Stir in the smoked fish, ground or grated fresh ginger, crushed garlic, fish seasoning, and salt. Simmer the stew for 15 minutes for the flavors to blend.

11. Add the shrimp. Let simmer until the shrimp are cooked, and then check and adjust the seasonings, especially the spiciness and salt.

To serve: This stew goes with just about anything, especially yams, plantains, any kind of *Ampesi* (page 185), potatoes, *gari* (page 175), *Eba* (page 176), rice, *Akple* (page 189), *Ga Kenkey* (page 187). Offer the habanero in the stew (if using it) to anyone who wants it, or press it against the side of the pan to spice up the stew before removing it.

Make ahead: This stew is delicious made ahead and reheated.

Variations:

Omit the smoked fish and shrimp, or the meat, or substitute pig's feet.

Substitute 4 to 6 small soft-shelled fresh cleaned crabs for the shrimp: clean the crabs, whack off the sharp edges of their shells, remove the underside where the mouth is, and trim the ends of the claws before adding.

Instead of softening and blending the eggplant, cut it into small pieces and add directly to the stew.

Beef Stew with Browned Flour

Makes 4 to 5 servings

This easy, tasty stew uses familiar ingredients in familiar ways, but with a twist. While wheat flour is an imported ingredient, it has found its way into many classic Ghanaian dishes, such as this stew my sister-in-law taught me how to make years ago. The secret is to begin by browning the dry flour in a heavy pan. I am partial to cast iron for this.

Ingredients

2 tablespoons all-purpose white flour or whole wheat flour

2 tablespoons vegetable oil

1 medium onion, chopped or sliced

1 pound beef (like chuck roast or top round), sliced into medium strips (not as thin as for a stir-fry, but not as thick as for regular beef stew)

2 cloves garlic, minced or pressed

A little minced fresh chili pepper: part of a seeded jalapeno for mild, 1 green cayenne for hot, or ½ a seeded green or red habanero for very hot (optional)

1 (8-ounce) can tomato sauce

1 teaspoon salt or to taste

¼ to ½ teaspoon dried ground red pepper

Directions

Brown the flour:

1. Begin with a clean, dry, heavy frying pan. Heat the pan on medium for several minutes, then put the flour into the pan. Stir or gently shake the pan until the white flour turns brown, about 10 to 15 minutes. (Watch it carefully to keep from burning it. Compare it to the original color of the flour. When it is noticeably browner but not dark brown, remove the pan from the heat.) Empty the flour into a small bowl to prevent it from continuing to cook, and set aside.

Prepare stew:

2. Heat the oil in the same frying pan over medium heat, add a little of the chopped onion and sauté for a minute or two. Add the meat and raise the heat a little so that it browns on all sides, adding a little more oil if necessary to keep everything from sticking.

3. Once the meat is browned, add the rest of the chopped onion, the garlic, and minced chili pepper, if using, and stir well. Add the tomato sauce, salt, ground red pepper, and 1 cup of water and stir well.

4. Sprinkle the browned flour over the stew and stir again. Lower the heat to simmer, cover the pan and cook the stew until the meat is tender, about 20 minutes. Add a little more water if necessary. Check and adjust the seasonings (salt and red pepper) before serving.

To serve: Serve this stew with *Shito* (page 170) or any chili sauce as a condiment on the side and let everyone add his or her own at the table. This stew pairs well with rice, but it would go fine with other starches, such as mashed or boiled potatoes or yam slices.

Variations:
To create a one-pot meal, wash and chop a green of your choice (kale, spinach, etc.) and add it when the meat is almost cooked.

Liver Stew with Browned Flour

Follow the instructions for Meat Stew with Browned Flour replacing the meat with liver of your choice (beef, pork, mutton, chicken). Cooking times vary according to the type of liver, so adjust the time to avoid over- or under-cooking the liver. Liver should be cooked to 160 degrees F.

Corned Beef Stew

Makes 4 to 6 servings

This recipe, a household standby for unexpected guests, is also one of the first recipes I taught all my children. Historically, when folks in Ghana returned to their hometowns for holidays, they often carried "tinned" goods from the urban areas to give as gifts, such as tinned milk, sardines, mackerel, and Exeter corned beef. This stew, like a hash or chowder without the milk or potatoes, still carries a sense of being special, and reminds me of Christmas in Ghana.

Ingredients

⅓ cup peanut or other vegetable oil

1 large onion, sliced or chopped

1-inch piece fresh ginger, grated

2 or 3 cloves garlic, crushed or minced (optional)

¼ to ½ teaspoon dried ground red pepper to begin and/or a couple of teaspoons seeded and minced fresh chili peppers of your choice (jalapeno for mild, cayenne for medium, or habanero for hot)

½ to 1 teaspoon curry powder (or more for a zestier flavor)

½ teaspoon salt or to taste

1 (12-ounce) can corned beef (do not substitute any other type of corned beef), cut into chunks

4 to 5 medium fresh tomatoes, peeled, seeded and chopped or pureed; or canned tomatoes, chopped or pureed

2 tablespoons tomato paste (optional)

2 eggs, beaten

Directions

1. Heat the oil in a heavy pan, then add the chopped onion and cook for a few minutes on medium heat. Add the ginger, garlic, and fresh chili peppers, if using, and cook for a few more minutes.
2. Add the ground red pepper, curry powder, and salt and cook a few more minutes.
3. Add the corned beef and chopped or pureed tomatoes. Stir well, and allow the stew to simmer for 2 minutes. The meat will begin to break up evenly.
4. Lower the heat and stir the beaten eggs into the stew. Let the mixture simmer for 10 minutes. Most of the liquid should evaporate so the stew is not runny. If it is too dry, add a little water to keep it from sticking.

To serve: This stew goes well with plain rice, Rice and Beans (*Waakye*, page 160), or *Ampesi* (page 185). Garnish with some sliced onion and fresh bell pepper that were sautéed in a little oil, other fresh steamed or sautéed vegetables, or beans.

Variations:

You can use ground dried ginger (½ teaspoon) in place of fresh ginger; and/or an 8-ounce can of tomato sauce in place of tomatoes, but I find fresh seasonings and tomatoes taste better here.

Those who do not like spiciness may substitute ½ cup chopped green bell pepper for the chili pepper.

Canned mackerel or a similar ingredient could substitute for the corned beef.

Easy Adzuki Bean Stew with Smoked Fish

Asedua

Makes 4 to 6 servings

In Ghana, bean (or "beans") stew is commonly prepared with cowpeas, especially black-eyed peas or a small red type. Adzuki beans can be substituted, as in this version. This is a great "everyday" stew: easy to make, freezes well, and tastes even better the next day.

Ingredients

¼ to ⅓ cup palm oil, if available, or substitute peanut or other vegetable oil (*if you are new to palm oil, use half palm oil and half another vegetable oil*)

1 medium onion, chopped or sliced

2 cloves garlic, minced or crushed (optional)

½ to 1-inch piece fresh ginger, grated (optional)

¼ to ½ teaspoon dried ground red pepper, and/or some minced fresh chili pepper (1 seeded jalapeno for mild, 1 green cayenne for hot, or ½ a seeded green or red habanero for very hot)

1 (8-ounce) can tomato sauce

½ pound smoked fish with skin and bones removed (mackerel, whiting haddock, whitefish, trout, etc.)

1 cup adzuki beans, washed, soaked, and cooked till tender

½ teaspoon salt or seasoned salt (or to taste)

Directions

1. Heat oil in a heavy skillet on medium heat. Add the onion and cook until translucent.

2. If using fresh garlic, ginger, and/or chili peppers, add them and stir and cook for 2 minutes. Add the tomato sauce.

3. Break the fish into pieces and add to the stew, along with the drained adzuki beans, 1 cup of water, the dried red pepper, if using. (Smoked fish is salty and will take a few minutes to flavor the stew, so add any additional salt after stew simmers 10 minutes.) Stir well and allow to simmer while the flavors blend and the sauce thickens. After 15 minutes, taste and adjust salt and red pepper if necessary.

To serve: This stew is wonderful with Savory Plantain Pancakes (*Tatale*, page 50), and also pairs well with Spicy Fried Plantains (*Kelewele*, page 52), Simple *Gari* (page 175), or boiled rice.

Variations:

Use 1 pound fresh or frozen fish fillets in place of smoked fish.

Use smoked ham cubes or ham hocks in place of smoked fish.

Use mushrooms in place of fish for a vegetarian version, maybe flavored with a little soy sauce.

Add additional vegetables, such as chopped okra, eggplant, or zucchini.

Mash a portion of the beans before adding them for a thicker stew.

Substitute ½ cup of chopped bell pepper for the fresh chili peppers for less heat.

Bean Stew with Fried Ripe Plantains
Red-Red

Makes 10 to 12 servings

Any visitor to Ghana will likely be introduced to a recipe popular with foreigners: "*Red-Red*," the name of a stew served with ripe plantains. The "*red*" refers to the palm oil used to pre-pare the stew. Tomatoes and tomato paste further enhance its color. *Red-Red* is commonly made with black-eyed peas or other cowpeas.

This meal needs advance planning so nicely ripened but still firm plantains are available. Allow at least 1 large or 2 small ripe plantains per person.

> The name "*Red-Red*" is an example of the delightful African use of reduplication or "echo words" also evident in many of the Ghanaian recipe names.

Ingredients

- 2 cups uncooked dried black-eyed peas; or 6 cups cooked, canned, or frozen
- ½ cup red palm oil (*dzomi*, if avail-able) or other vegetable oil
- 2 cups chopped onions
- ½ teaspoon dried ground red pepper and/or a little minced fresh chili pepper (part of a seeded jalapeno for mild, a green cayenne for hot, and half a seeded green or red habanero for very hot)
- 2 teaspoons grated fresh ginger (or to taste)
- 3 cloves garlic, crushed or minced
- 2 teaspoons dried shrimp powder (or to taste)
- 2 cups pureed fresh (peeled and seeded) or canned tomatoes (do not use canned tomato puree)
- 2 tablespoons tomato paste (optional)
- ½ to 1 pound smoked fish, depend-ing on whether or not they are boned (e.g., whiting, mackerel,

Directions

Prepare dried peas (if using):

1. Rinse and pick over the black-eyed peas, removing any stones or discolored ones, then soak the peas in a pot in water for several hours or overnight. Drain and put fresh water in, bring to a boil, cover, and cook until tender, about an hour or so. Drain.

Prepare the stew:

2. Heat the palm oil in a frying pan, add the onion and sauté for about 10 minutes.
3. Add ground red pepper and/or fresh chili pep-per, ginger, garlic, and shrimp powder, and fry a few more minutes on medium heat.
4. Add the pureed tomatoes and fry together for a few minutes. Add tomato paste, if using.
5. Break fish into pieces and add to the stew. Add the drained cooked beans and simmer 10 min-utes, breaking the fish up as the stew cooks. Add a little more water if the stew cooks down too much. Check seasonings (especially the salt and pepper) and adjust to taste.
6. Let simmer or remove from heat while prepar-ing the plantains.

haddock, tuna, salmon, whitefish, but avoid herring), skinned and boned

1 large or 2 small ripe plantains per person

Vegetable oil for frying the plantains

½ cup dry gari (optional)

Cook the plantains:

7. Peel the ripe plantains and remove any stringy fibers on them. Cut them in half lengthwise, and then into several pieces cut on the diagonal. Put enough vegetable oil in the bottom of a large frying pan to cover it well (about ¼ to ½ inch deep). Heat on medium to medium-high heat.

8. Place the plantain pieces into the pan without crowding them (cook in batches, if necessary), using a turner to turn them over when they are well-browned on one side. Remove them to drain on paper towels in a basket or on a platter.

To serve: Serve the stew with warm fried plantains on the side. Gari is often sprinkled on top of the bean stew as a condiment (similar to the way Parmesan cheese is sprinkled on Italian food) or on the side, moistened with hot water. Also, the stew may be served with a cooked vegetable (spinach, okra, cabbage, etc.) as a side dish.

Variations:

Instead of frying the ripe plantains, boil them as for *Ampesi* (page 185), or roast them in a hot oven.

Simply cook the beans and then add some chopped onion, tomato, chili pepper, etc., into the same pot without frying anything. Boil, and add a few fresh or frozen okra that have been tailed or sliced.

For a low-salt version, either omit the smoked fish or substitute fresh fish.

Those who do not like spicy foods may substitute ½ cup of chopped bell pepper for the fresh chili pepper.

Vegetarian Peanut Stew

Makes 4 to 6 servings

Ingredients

2 tablespoons peanut or other oil

2 cups chopped onion

3 cloves garlic, crushed

1 tablespoon grated fresh ginger

1 fresh chili pepper, minced or added whole and removed at the end (a small seeded green jalapeno for mild; a green seeded cayenne for hot; or a green or red habanero for hottest)

3 to 4 cups vegetable stock or water

1 (8-ounce) can tomato sauce

2 tablespoons tomato paste (optional)

½ to 1 cup creamy natural-style peanut butter (no sugar added)

Vegetable choices:

A few fresh mushrooms, sliced or whole

1 cup peeled and coarsely chopped eggplant

1 medium sweet potato, peeled and cut into chunks

6 fresh or frozen okra, chopped or whole

2 cups greens of choice (e.g., kale, chard, spinach), washed and torn up

1 to 2 cups coarsely chopped tomato (Note: if using omit the tomato sauce)

Directions

1. Heat the oil in a large saucepan. Add the onions and sauté over medium heat for about 5 minutes. Add the garlic, ginger, and chili pepper and sauté for a few more minutes.
2. Add the vegetable stock or water, tomato sauce, tomato paste, if using, and salt to taste and stir well.
3. Add your vegetables of choice and bring to a simmer.
4. Remove 2 cups of soup broth and mix with ½ to 1 cup peanut butter in a small saucepan (the more peanut butter, the creamier the stew). Cook, stirring constantly, on medium heat until the oil separates out, then stir the mixture into the stew.
5. Cover and simmer the stew until flavors have blended and stew is thick.

To serve: The stew can be served over rice like a curry, with small bowls of condiments served alongside:

Condiments suggestions:
Chopped unsalted dry roasted peanuts, chopped bananas, chopped pineapple, orange segments, chopped tomatoes, chopped red or green sweet bell peppers, coconut, chopped hardboiled egg, chopped onions (raw or sautéed), cooked chopped okra.

Chicken or Meat Peanut Stew
For a delicious Chicken Peanut Stew, make the recipe for Chicken Peanut Soup on page 104 using less water. You can also replace the chicken with a pound of meat of your choice cut into cubes to make a Meat Peanut Stew. Stewing beef will take longer to soften than chicken. The smaller the cubes, the faster they will cook.

Mushroom Stew
Mmire Abom

Mushrooms are only available seasonally in Ghana, and are picked in the wild and usually add-ed to soups or stews to enhance the flavor. They have not been cultivated commercially, and people in the rural areas who pick them generally keep a little for themselves, but sell most of them along the roadsides or to wholesalers and use the cash they receive to buy meat or fish. There are a number of varieties growing wild in Ghana, often near termite mounds. In recent times, mushrooms have become an expensive luxury food item. There are currently numerous projects being initiated in Ghana by nonprofits in the hopes of introducing mushroom cultiva-tion as a money-making venture that can also help improve nutrition.

Ingredients

4 ounces mushrooms, any type (I commonly use white button, portabella, or baby bella)

1 heaping tablespoon all-purpose flour

¼ teaspoon salt or seasoned salt

¼ teaspoon dried ground red pepper

½ pound meat, any type (e.g., beef such as chuck or top round), chopped or sliced into small pieces

¼ cup vegetable oil

1 onion, chopped or sliced

4 medium tomatoes, chopped, sliced, or pureed

Other seasonings to taste (e.g., fresh minced chili pepper, grated fresh ginger, minced fresh garlic, additional seasoned salt, etc.)

Directions

1. Quickly rinse the mushrooms and pat dry with a paper towel, trim the stem edge, and break or cut mushrooms into pieces. Set on a plate.
2. On another plate, mix the flour with the salt or seasoned salt and dried ground red pepper.
3. Dredge the mushrooms in the flour. Dredge the meat pieces in the flour and put on a separate plate.
4. Pour some of the vegetable oil into a small bowl. Dip the mushrooms and/or meat in the oil to coat, and use a slotted spoon to remove them and set them back onto their original plates.
5. Pour the remaining oil into a skillet and heat on medium. Sauté the onion in the oil for 2 minutes on medium heat, stirring constantly. Add the tomatoes. Sprinkle any remaining seasoned flour over the mixture and stir well.
6. Add the mushrooms and meat, any other desired seasonings, and ¾ cup of water.
7. Simmer for about 30 minutes on medium heat, uncovered, until the stew thickens and the liquid cooks down. Stir occasionally and add additional water a tablespoon at a time as necessary. (If the meat is tough, you may have to cook it a little longer.) Adjust any seasonings before serving.

To serve: Serve the stew hot with boiled rice, *Ampesi* (page 185), or *Ga Kenkey* (page 187).

Palaver Sauce 2 Ways

Makes 6 servings

"Palaver Sauce" is sometimes called *kontomire* stew or "spinach stew." This is confusing, since "palaver sauce" often contains both beef and (usually smoked) fish and *agushi* (a Ghanaian melon seed), whereas *kontomire* stew (see Spinach Stew, page 130) is a less complicated version.

Here we give you two ways to make Palaver Sauce. Feel free to adapt either, including creating vegetarian versions, but just be sure to include plenty of greens. True-blue Ghanaians will see that both versions unabashedly omit the seasoning *momoni* (a pungent fermented fish). Using either version, the resulting stew provides a friendly mix where a lot of interesting ingredients get along very well together without any "*palaver*."

> There are many stories of how this stew came to be called "palaver" sauce. My bet is that it comes from the Portuguese word meaning "word," or "speech," or "talk," *palavra*. While today's meaning of the word in West Africa is that there has been some kind of trouble arising from an argument, in earlier days it meant "a parley between European explorers and representatives of local populations, especially in Africa."

Ingredients

2 (10-ounce) packages frozen greens (spinach, kontomire/cocoyam, collard, kale, etc.) or 2 pounds fresh greens

½ pound stewing beef, fat trimmed and cut into ½-inch cubes

Salt or seasoned salt (begin with ½ teaspoon and adjust at the end)

2 cups chopped onion or scallions (or a mix of both)

3 cloves garlic, crushed or minced

1 teaspoon dried ground red pepper (or to taste)

1 cup grated fresh tomatoes, juices reserved, or 1 (16-ounce) can chopped tomatoes

¼ cup tomato paste

½ pound fresh or frozen fish fillets (e.g., cod or haddock), cut into chunks

Directions for Easy Palaver Sauce

1. If using fresh greens, wash the leaves. Remove the tough central stems of kontomire, mustard greens, or chard. Layer several leaves together and roll them up very tightly, and slice very thinly. If using frozen greens, defrost and drain excess water. Set aside.

2. Put the meat cubes in a large pot with a scant ½ teaspoon salt and 1 cup water. Sprinkle ¼ cup of the onions, the garlic, and ¼ teaspoon of the ground red pepper over the meat. Bring to a boil, lower the heat, cover, and steam for 10 minutes to tenderize and flavor the beef.

3. After 10 minutes, add the rest of the onion, the rest of the ground red pepper, the tomatoes, tomato paste, fresh or frozen fish, and salted cod, if using, and let it cook together for a few minutes. The fish will break up as it cooks.

4. Add the chopped greens, stir well, and let the mixture simmer on medium to low heat, covered, for 15 minutes.

5. While the sauce simmers, remove the head, skin, and bones from the smoked fish. Stir the fish into the pot, and let it simmer, uncovered, while preparing the *agushi* or pumpkin seeds.

128 The GHANA Cookbook

1 square inch salted cod (optional)

8 ounces smoked/dried fish (such as smoked whiting or mackerel)

½ to 1 cup ground *agushi* or dehulled pumpkin seeds

½ cup palm oil (traditional *dzomi* if available); or other vegetable oil like peanut or canola; or a blend of palm oil with another oil

A few onion slices or 2 bay leaves for flavoring the oil

1 tablespoon dried ground shrimp (optional) (*Ghanaians would likely use this more liberally*)

Variations:

Smoked ham cubes or turkey may substitute for the smoked fish.

When preparing Palaver Sauce at Flair we include 4 soft-shelled crabs. If you find them in season, add them or substitute shrimp in their shells.

To thicken the sauce without *agushi* or pumpkin seeds, add 2 beaten eggs or 1 cup canned refried beans or 1 cup cooked pureed eggplant.

6. Grind the seeds in an electric blender mixed with an equal amount of water. Scoop the mixture into the sauce all at once (don't stir) and let the pot simmer covered for 10 minutes without stirring.
7. Uncover pot and mix the sauce and taste and adjust the seasonings as needed. Continue to simmer on low heat until most of the liquid is gone.

Directions for Flair's Classic Palaver Sauce

1. Begin as for Step 1 of the first version, but cook the greens separately in a ½ cup of boiling water for 5 minutes, then drain the greens and keep the cooking water to use later as needed. Set aside.
2. Season and steam the meat as in step 2 above but then remove and discard the onions you have used, if desired. Set aside.
3. Add the oil to a large frying pan or pot, along with a few slices of onion or a couple of bay leaves and fry them on medium until they are brown to season the oil, then remove the bay leaves or onion slices.
4. Stir in the chopped onion, ground red pepper, fresh or frozen fish, and salted cod, if using, and cook for 10 minutes on medium heat. Stir in the tomato paste and ¼ cup of water (use the water from cooking the greens) and cook, stirring constantly, for 3 minutes.
5. Add the fresh tomatoes. Add the meat that was steamed, along with any juices remaining in the pan. Add the ground dried shrimp if using. Remove the head, skin and bones from the smoked fish and break into pieces and stir in.
6. Mix the ground seeds with an equal amount of water, add to the stew, and cover. Allow it to set for 10 minutes, then stir and adjust any seasonings.

To serve: This stew goes well with plain rice or boiled yams, plantains (green or ripe), or potatoes.

Make ahead: This stew is also good reheated and can be frozen, too.

Spinach Stew
Kontomire Stew

Makes 4 servings

Ghanaians abroad commonly say they are making "spinach" stew. Actually in Ghana the stew likely features beloved *kontomire*/cocoyam/taro leaves, easily available wild or cultivated. *Kontomire's* flavor and texture differs from that of spinach—the leaves are thicker and hardier, more like kale or collard greens.

Ingredients

1 pound fresh cocoyam/taro/kontomire leaves or spinach or other greens (collard, mustard, chard, etc.)

6 to 8 ounces smoked fish

1-inch cube salted cod (optional)

¼ cup palm oil or other vegetable oil

1 or 2 onions, sliced or chopped

2 medium tomatoes, chopped or sliced

¼ to ½ teaspoon salt (or to taste—remember that the fish and cod will make the stew saltier)

Dried ground red pepper to taste (¼ to ½ teaspoon to begin)

Directions

Prepare greens:

1. Wash the leaves. Remove the tough central stem of the cocoyam leaves (or mustard greens or chard) by holding the end of the leaf by the stem with one hand and with the other hand pull firmly downwards, using your thumb and index finger to release the stem (alternatively, just cut it out). Layer several leaves together, roll them up very tightly, and slice very thin. Set aside.

Prepare fish:

2. Remove any skin and bones from the smoked fish. (HINT: if using salted herring, simmer them separately in a little water before adding them to the stew to remove some of their saltiness.)

3. If using salted cod, desalt it by soaking it in hot water for 10 minutes.

Make stew:

4. Heat the palm or vegetable oil and fry the onions for a few minutes,. Then add the tomatoes, salt, dried ground red pepper and fish and cook, stirring, for 2 or 3 minutes.

Already familiar with *kontomire*, slaves from West Africa readily embraced the collards and mustard greens they met in the Southern U.S. as they were prolific and cheap. Another name for *kontomire* is "elephant's ears." In Belo Horizonte, Brazil, I noticed people cutting up collard greens to accompany *feijoada* exactly the same way people cut *kontomire* in Ghana: washing well, removing the center stalk, rolling several leaves tightly together, and slicing them thinly.

5. Add the sliced greens along with ¼ cup water, mix well, cover and simmer on low heat until the greens are cooked and the flavors are mixed, about 20 minutes if using cocoyam leaves, less time if using spinach. Check frequently, adding more water as necessary to keep the stew from scorching.

To serve: This stew is classically served with boiled small green plantains, but it goes equally well with boiled yam, potatoes, white sweet potatoes, ripe plantains, cassava, Boiled Starchy Vegetables (*Ampesi*, page 185), or any other starch of your choice.

Variation:
Cook the whole leaves separately in boiling water and then drain and mash or puree them before adding to the stew. In this case, the stew will be ready about 10 minutes after adding them.

GARNISHING

Traditionally, many meals in Ghana were common one-pots or served with ingredients mixed together. More and more often today dishes are plated individually, with meats or fish separated from vegetables, which are also separated from the main starch. When bringing a platter to the table, Ghanaians are fond of garnishing savory foods with sliced tomatoes and onions and/or green peppers sprinkled over fish or casseroles. Sometimes tomato or lemon wedges decorate edges of the plates.

Lettuce or herbs may form a bed or a side garnish for salads or seafood.

A tomato gravy and/or plain boiled pasta are a common garnish for rice and beans.

Fruits are often sliced attractively to garnish desserts, and crushed nuts or coconut may also be sprinkled over dishes.

FISH & SHELLFISH

Grilled Tilapia

Makes 4 servings

Grilling over wood or charcoal is a basic cooking technique in much of sub-Saharan Africa, and Ghana is no exception. Ghana's most common freshwater fish is tilapia, and Ghanaians have also practiced small-scale fish farming for many decades, harvesting fish from streams, rivers, lagoons, and fish farms. Tilapia consumption has also been growing in popularity in the United States.

Ingredients

2 tablespoons grated shallots or onion

1 teaspoon salt (or to taste)

½ teaspoon dried ground red pepper or to taste

½ teaspoon grated fresh ginger (or to taste)

1 to 4 tablespoons minced fresh chili pepper (*kpakpo shito* if available, or a pepper of similar heat, see chart page 37)

4 tablespoons vegetable oil, like canola, divided

4 medium whole tilapia (8 ounces each)

Directions

1. If using a charcoal grill: Before making the seasoning and preparing and seasoning the fish, light charcoal and allow it to burn down for about 30 minutes.

Marinate fish:

2. Combine the shallots or onions, salt, dried ground red pepper, ginger, desired amount fresh chili pepper (add some and then taste marinade before adding more), and 1 table-spoon of the oil in a small bowl and set aside.
3. Clean and wash the fish, removing gills and fins (leave the heads on). (This is not as easy as Ghanaian women make it look. It requires a very sharp knife, patience, and care.) Cut 2 diagonal slits on each side of each of the fish.
4. If you have "strong" hands, use them to stuff and rub the seasoning mixture all over the fish, rubbing it into the slits and also inside the fish. Otherwise use a spoon or gloves. Do not discard any dregs left in the bowl. Leave the marinade on the fish for at least 15 minutes.

Grill fish:

5. When ready to grill, brush the grill rack with oil, and place it about an inch above the coals. Place the fish on the rack and baste them with a little oil to keep them soft and moist. After 3 to 5 minutes, turn over the fish and baste the other side.
6. Put 2 tablespoons of oil into the bowl that held the seasoning mixture and swirl. Using your hands or the brush, shake the seasoned oil over the fish until all the seasoning mixture is used (do not try to brush it on). Continue

You can remove the head and/or tail before grilling the tilapia but, as Barbara Baëta explains: "Ghanaians feel cheated if you don't leave the head on ... We eat *all* bones—fish bones, chicken bones, meat bones. Maybe that's why we have such healthy teeth."

turning the fish every few minutes. Depending on the thickness of the fish and fire's heat it will cook in 10 to 15 minutes. If the fish tails are in danger of burning, cover them with foil. Voila! Ghana-style grilled fish.

To serve: Grilled tilapia is often garnished with onion and tomato slices, and served with a Fresh Pepper Sauce (page 168) or *Shito* (page 170) or any tomato or hot sauce.

Variations:

Bake the fish in a moderately hot oven (400 degrees F) for 25 minutes.

People in Ghana often add a crushed shrimp-flavored seasoning cube. If they aren"t available you could substitute a little extra seasoned salt and spice mixture (e.g., some dried ground shrimp/crayfish and/or garlic).

Substitute one large tilapia, and make 3 slits instead of 2 and grill longer.

Grilled Prawns/Shrimp

Makes 6 to 8 servings

Many delicious crustaceans are found along West Africa's coast and in its rivers, including Ghana's. Grilling is a favored way of preparing them, as in this recipe, which is reminiscent of southern Africa's *peri-peri* (or *piri piri*) prawns or shrimp. One sees grilled prawns frequently being sold as a snack along the roadside near the coast in Ghana. They are also served at buffets with other dishes, or as an upscale party appetizer.

Fresh prawns are plentiful in Ghana, but frozen tiger shrimp can be substituted. If possible, choose those with heads and tails intact. If the shrimp are beheaded, they work, but it detracts a bit from the fabulous presentation. Allow two large shrimp per serving/skewer.

Ingredients

2 pounds large tiger shrimp or
  prawns (6 to 8 per pound)

Juice of 1 lemon

Marinade

¼ cup grated shallots or onion

1 heaping teaspoon ground or
  grated fresh ginger

1 teaspoon ground/grated/crushed
  fresh garlic

1 teaspoon salt or seasoned salt (or
  more to taste)

2 teaspoons dried ground red
  pepper (more or less to taste)

1 heaping teaspoon fish masala
  powder or curry powder or similar

4 tablespoons vegetable oil (canola
  or similar), plus a little extra to
  drizzle over shrimp while grilling

Special Equipment

8 wooden skewers, soaked in water
  for at least 30 minutes before
  using

Directions

Prepare shrimp:

1. Devein the shrimp by making a cut along the back and removing the thick vein (and devein the underside as well if desired). Leave the head on if possible. Remove the rest of the shell, but leave the last piece of shell next to the tail so that the tail stays attached. If the head falls off while grilling, it can be slipped back on. (Alternatively, butterfly some or all of the shrimp which increases the surface coated by the spicy seasonings.)

2. Put 3 cups of water into a bowl and add the lemon juice. Put the shrimp into the water, mixing well to coat all parts of them. Drain and put on paper towels to drain further.

Marinate shrimp:

3. Mix together all the marinade ingredients in a bowl large enough to hold the shrimp and taste for heat and adjust seasonings if needed. Stir the marinade and add the shrimp, tossing to coat them well. Marinate for at least 10 minutes.

Grill shrimp:

4. Thread 2 shrimp onto each skewer by inserting the skewer at the tail and working it up to the head, keeping each shrimp in a straight line. (This prevents the shrimp from curling up as they cook.)

6. When your coals have cooked down to medium hot, brush the grill rack with oil and set it close to the coals. Drizzle a little oil over each shrimp, turning the skewers so both sides are coated. Place the shrimp skewers on the grill and turn the skewers every couple of minutes to prevent burning, adding more oil if necessary. They should cook in 5 to 8 minutes, depending on the size of the prawns and the heat of the fire.

To serve: Grilled shrimp/prawns can be eaten with plain boiled rice or Coconut Rice (page 180), a Ghanaian tomato gravy (page 38), vegetables, or yams, or they can be served as an appetizer.

Variation: Broil instead of grill the shrimp/prawns.

In Ghana, fish and shellfish are often preserved by drying, salting, and smoking, and provide a distinctive flavor to soups and stews. If you are unable to obtain ingredients such as dried shrimp or smoked or salted fish, it will be necessary to experiment with ways of duplicating these flavors. Fortunately, smoked, salted, or dried fish and seafood are usually available in African or Asian markets.

Ghana Fried Fish
Kenam / Kyenam

The first time I traveled to Ghana in1971 I lived in Nungua along the coast and taught school. There I grew to love Ga *kenkey* (page 187), spicy *shito* (page 170), and fried fish. Though *kenam* and its accompaniments are easily obtained in Ghana, all three must be home-prepared when outside that environment. This classic meal was one of the first birthday dinners my adopted nephews requested when they came to live with us in 2002.

Here I am giving you two versions of Ghana's fried fish. For the first one, on this page, the fish is rubbed with salt before cooking as the Ga people living on Ghana's coast traditionally do. On the opposite page is Flair's version, Stuffed Fried Fish.

Ingredients
1 to 2 whole fish per person, e.g., red snapper, croakers, porgies (allow about 8 ounces fish per serving)

Juice of 1 lemon

2 to 3 cups vegetable oil for frying

Salt for rubbing (sea salt, if available)

> Vendors in Ghana usually use smallish fish. They often cook the fish longer, until it is very hard, which keeps it from spoiling quickly, but the fish can also be cooked so that the inside is still soft.

Directions
1. Clean and scale the fish, removing fins and gills (Ghanaians keep the heads on). Shorten the tail. Cut larger fish into 2 or 3 pieces. Put 2 or 3 cups water in a bowl and mix with the lemon juice. Rinse the fish in the water. Cut a diagonal slit or two in each side of each fish. Let the fish drain in a colander for a few minutes.
2. Heat about ½ inch of oil in a large heavy pan, such as a cast iron frying pan, on medium to medium-high heat.
3. Blot the fish dry if necessary with a paper towel, then season it by rubbing it with salt— the amount will vary according to the size and amount of the fish, but probably 1 to 2 teaspoons per fish.
4. Carefully place the fish in the hot oil to avoid splattering and without crowding them in the pan. Cook about 5 minutes on each side, care- fully turning the fish so that the skin does not tear.
5. Remove and drain on paper towels.

To serve: This simple method of cooking fish is wonderful with *Kenkey* (page 187), and Fresh Pepper Sauce (page 168) or *Shito* (page 170) or simply sliced onion and tomato.

Variation: Use filleted whole fish.

Stuffed Fried Fish
Kenam / Kyenam

This is the more common way to make contemporary *kenam*. It follows the same procedure for cleaning and preparing the fish as for Ghana Fried Fish (opposite page). However, the fish is left whole and the slits cut in the side are filled with a spicy seasoning.

Ingredients

1 to 2 whole fish per person, e.g., red snapper, croakers, porgies (allow about 8 ounces fish per serving)

Juice of 1 lemon

Sea salt, if available

2 to 3 cups vegetable oil for frying

Seasoning paste *(for 1 serving)*

2 tablespoons minced shallots or onion

1½ teaspoons grated fresh ginger

1 teaspoon minced fresh red chili pepper of choice (see chart page 37), or ½ teaspoon dried ground red pepper (or to taste)

Directions

1. Clean and scale the fish, removing fins and gills (Ghanaians keep the head on). Shorten the tail. Put 2 or 3 cups water in a bowl and mix with the lemon juice. Rinse the fish in the water. Let the fish drain in a colander for a few minutes and then blot dry with paper towels. Cut two diagonal slits in each side of the fish.
2. Using an electric blender, food processor, or a small mortar, grind the seasoning ingredients together to make a paste.
3. Sprinkle a little salt over both sides of the fish and rub it in. Stuff the slits with the spice mixture and push the slits together to close them up.
4. Heat about ½ inch of oil in a large heavy pan, such as a cast iron frying pan, on medium to medium-high heat. Carefully place the fish in the hot oil to avoid splattering and without crowding them in the pan. Cook about 5 minutes on each side, carefully turning the fish so that the skin does not tear.
5. Remove and drain on paper towels.

To serve: This fried fish is wonderful with *Kenkey* (page 187), and Fresh Pepper Sauce (page 168) or *Shito* (page 170) or simply sliced onion and tomato. It is also delicious served with Ghanaian Basic Tomato Gravy (page 38).

Variation: Crumble a seasoning cube into the spice mixture.

VEGETARIAN MAIN DISHES

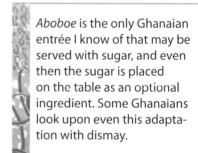

Stewed Bambara Beans
Aboboe

Makes 6 to 8 servings

The Ewe people are found in parts of Togo and Benin and especially in the Volta Region in Ghana. Stewed Bambara Beans is a simple, everyday kind of dish that the Ewe and other Ghanaians enjoy. It is called *azinogoe bobɔ* in Ewe, a version of "*aboboe*" in Twi and Ga. It is also known simply as stewed beans, boiled beans, or *bobo*.

The "beans" here are bambara beans or bambara groundnuts (*Vigna subterranean*) indigenous to West Africa. They lend themselves easily to crockpot cooking.

> *Aboboe* is the only Ghanaian entrée I know of that may be served with sugar, and even then the sugar is placed on the table as an optional ingredient. Some Ghanaians look upon even this adaptation with dismay.

Ingredients

2 cups (a little less than 1 pound) dried bambara beans or garbanzo beans

1 onion or 2 shallots

2 teaspoons tomato paste

1 fresh tomato

¼ to ½ teaspoon dried ground red pepper, or 1 small seeded jalapeno (mild); or 1 green cayenne, seeds and membranes removed (hotter); or ½ green or red habanero (hottest)

1 teaspoon salt (or to taste)

1 cup dry gari for serving (optional)

Directions

1. Rinse and pick over the bambara or garbanzo beans. Put them in a slow cooker (crockpot) with 6 cups of water. Peel the onion or shallots and add them whole, along with the tomato paste, whole tomato, and dried ground red pepper or whole fresh chili. Cover and cook for several hours on high or overnight on low. Check occasionally and add additional water if necessary as the beans cook.

2. Half an hour before serving, remove the whole vegetables with a slotted spoon and grind them in an electric blender or *asanka*. If using a whole chili pepper, add it a little at a time to the other blended vegetables until you have desired heat. Add the salt and adjust the other seasonings as well. Stir the mixture back into the beans.

3. The stew should be thick. Remove the cover on the slow cooker if there is too much liquid remaining and let it cook down.

To serve: The beans are good simply served with a couple of tablespoons of dry *gari* sprinkled over the top. They are the traditional accompaniment to Savory Plantain Pancakes (*Tatale*, page 50). They also go well with Fried or Grilled Ripe Plantain (pages 52, 56) or Spicy Plantain Balls (*Kaklo*, page 54).

Pureed Black-eyed Peas
Adayi

Boiled black-eyed peas are also known as "*aboboe*" (page 142). When black-eyed peas are cooked and then mashed or pureed, as here, the dish is called "*adayi*." When served with moistened *gari* and heated in coconut oil, it makes a simple, humble, but soothing and satisfying meal.

Ingredients
2 cups dried black-eyed peas or
    other cowpeas

Salt to taste

Directions
1. Rinse and pick over the dried black-eyed peas or other cowpeas, removing any stones or damaged peas. Soak the peas in water to cover in a large pot for a few hours or overnight. (Or use the quick-soak method: put them in a large pot, cover well with water, bring to a boil and boil for a few minutes, then leave them to sit for an hour.)
2. Drain off the water from the peas and add fresh water to cover. Bring to a boil and simmer for 45 minutes or until the peas are cooked and most of the water has cooked away.
3. Add salt to taste, then mash the peas well (using a spoon or potato masher) or puree them in an electric blender.

To serve: *Adayi* makes an easy meal when eaten with *gari* (page 175). Heat a little coconut or other vegetable oil, and dampen the gari with warm water and the heated oil and serve with the pureed beans.

Variations:
Cook in a slow cooker: Omit the presoaking, and cook them on low heat for several hours or overnight.

Use dehulled black-eyed peas (see page 25), soak them and grind them in a blender, then cook.

Add a whole onion or ¼ to ½ teaspoon of dried ground red pepper or a whole seeded jalapeno to the pot when cooking.

Savory African Yam with Onion Omelet

Makes 4 servings

This is a good use for leftover boiled African yams. Barbara playfully calls it "African French Toast"—savory, not sweet, and using African yams, not bread. Fresh African yams are available in West African, Caribbean, or Latin American markets, and are sometimes sold in major grocery stores as "*name*" (American yams are not a good substitute).

Ingredients

1 pound African yams

1 teaspoon salt or seasoned salt (or to taste)

8 eggs

½ teaspoon ground white or black pepper (or if you like a little heat substitute ¼ to ½ teaspoon dried ground red pepper)

1 tablespoon vegetable oil (or as needed)

½ cup thinly sliced onion

To serve: This dish looks lovely when half a serving plate or platter holds the yam slices, the other half the omelet, and the platter is garnished with sliced tomato, bell pepper, etc. Or it can be served with ketchup or any pepper sauce (page 168) or *Shito* (page 170) drizzled over it or served on the side.

Directions

1. Peel the African yams and cut into rounds about ½-inch thick. Cut each round slice in half, put into a saucepan with 2 cups water and ½ teaspoon of salt. Bring to a boil, cover the pan, lower the heat to medium-low and cook for 10 to 15 minutes, until tender. Remove from heat, drain off the water (it can be saved for soup for another day), and set yams aside.

2. Break 6 of the eggs into a bowl, add ¼ teaspoon of salt and the pepper, mixing with a fork or whisk. Dip the yam slices a few at a time into the bowl of beaten egg, turning once to coat. Set them on a plate.

3. In a medium skillet, add 1 tablespoon of vegetable oil to coat the bottom of the pan and heat on medium heat for several minutes.

4. Fry the yam slices in a single layer in batches on medium heat, drizzling about ½ teaspoon of the egg mixture on top of each slice, but not enough to make them "wet." Brown well on one side and repeat the process on the other side. (There will still be some of the egg mixture remaining, set it aside.) Remove the cooked yam slices as they are done to a warm plate or keep in a low oven.

6. Add 1 teaspoon of oil to the skillet (or enough to prevent sticking) and sauté the onions in the pan, adding a pinch of salt.

7. Break 2 more eggs into the remaining egg mixture and beat together. Pour the egg mixture over the sautéed onions and cook on medium heat until set. Turn the egg mixture over, then fold it in half to make an omelet.

MEAT & POULTRY

Ga Roast Pork
Domedu

Makes 12 to 18 servings

Traditionally this Ga roast pork would be baked in a clay oven and cooked over low heat to infuse it with a special flavor. The Ewes prepare a similar dish. While Barbara suggests one could actually create a clay oven by taking clay and shaping it over a big pan turned upside down and letting it dry, this recipe substitutes a regular oven and also adapts some of the seasonings.

Ingredients

1 boneless leg of pork (about 6 pounds)

⅔ cup grated onion with juices

2 teaspoons grated fresh ginger

1 teaspoon minced fresh garlic

1 teaspoon crushed aniseed

2 to 3 teaspoons salt or seasoned salt of choice (use less if using seasoning cubes)

2 to 3 teaspoons dried ground red pepper

3 small shrimp-flavored or other seasoning cubes, crumbled (optional)

3 tablespoons vegetable oil

Directions

Marinate pork:

1. Pierce the pork roast with a knife in several places to enable seasonings to penetrate thoroughly. Score the skin in a criss-cross pattern.
2. Mix together the onion, ginger, garlic, aniseed, seasoned salt, ground red pepper, seasoning cubes, and oil to make a seasoning paste.
3. Thoroughly coat the entire pork leg, making sure that the seasoning penetrates as much as possible to the inside: use a knife to cut through between the skin and the flesh, pulling the skin back and pushing the seasonings as far in as possible. Some of the seasoning may also be pushed inside the actual roast where the bones originally were. Spread any remaining seasoning mixture over the outside of the pork leg.
4. Allow the pork to marinate at least 1 to 2 hours, or overnight in the refrigerator.

Roast pork:

5. Preheat the oven to 450 degrees F. If the pork roast marinated in the refrigerator, allow it to come to room temperature before roasting. Put the pork leg in a roasting pan and cover with foil or a lid.
6. Roast the pork for 20 minutes, then turn the pan 180 degrees and lower the heat to 350 degrees F and continue roasting for about 2 hours, or until the internal heat reaches 145 degrees F. Baste the roast with the juices in the pan occasionally and remove the cover or foil the last hour. Let roast sit for a few minutes before serving.

To serve: Use the drippings in the pan to make a Ghana-style gravy (either a plain gravy or a gravy with flour, see page 38). Along with gravy and hot sauces, this roast pairs well with Seasoned Gari (*Pino*, page 177), *Ga Kenkey* (page 187), rice, or yams.

Variation: To barbecue in a grill with a hinged cover, use indirect heat with the cover closed for about 2 to 3 hours, opening the lid and removing the foil to crisp the roast the last hour so that the skin gets crackly. Baste with oil during the last hour.

Ashanti Chicken

Makes about 8 servings

"Ashanti fowl" is a legendary Ghanaian recipe. The dish is essentially a combination galantine/ballontine—it is made from a whole deboned chicken that is stuffed and roasted, and eaten with Ghanaian gravy. It is special largely because it looks like a regular roasted chicken until it is cut. The printed recipes first appeared in *Gold Coast Nutrition and Cookery* (*GCNC*) published in 1953, and later in Alice Dede's 1969 *Ghanaian Favourite Dishes*. The original recipe used bread for the stuffing, but later versions substitute African yam. Barbara Baëta's 1972 version uses cooked mashed yams or potatoes in the stuffing. A starchy potato, like a russet, with a bit of flour added is one substitution for African yams. Or bread can be substituted.

What follows is a slightly adapted version of the recipe we prepared at Flair. Ashanti chicken is definitely a special occasion dish.

Ingredients

Chicken
1 whole chicken, any size (roaster preferred)

½ teaspoon salt or seasoned salt

1 teaspoon dried ground red pepper

1 seasoning cube, crumbled (optional)

Vegetable oil for basting (optional)

Chicken stock
Bones and giblets from deboned chicken

Seasonings of choice: onion, garlic, ginger

Salt and pepper

Stuffing
2 pounds African yams, or 2 pounds russet potatoes and 2 tablespoons flour

1 onion, chopped

3 cloves garlic, crushed

Several pureed fresh tomatoes, seeded and peeled if desired

Salt to taste

Directions

Prepare chicken:
1. The first task is to debone the chicken. There are several ways to complete this task. The goal is to remove the bones, leaving the meat and skin intact. If you want to try to do this on your own there are numerous online video tutorials that can provide guidance. Save the giblets and heart from the chicken for use in making stock. Remove as much excess fat as possible while working through the deboning process. If this is too daunting, ask your butcher to do it for you, asking him to keep the whole chicken intact with as much of the skin intact as possible and to give you the bones and giblets for making the stock.

2. Once the chicken is deboned, season the inside of the chicken with the salt, ground red pepper, and seasoning cube, if using. Fold the skin over the chicken and let it marinate, refrigerating the chicken while preparing the stock and stuffing.

Make the stock:
3. Put the chicken bones and giblets in a stockpot with some water, onions, garlic, salt, ginger, pepper, etc. (whatever seasonings desired) and simmer to make stock while making the stuffing and the chicken is roasting. Once the bits of chicken left clinging to the bones and giblets are cooked, they can be removed and

Dried ground red pepper to taste

3 to 4 tablespoons creamy natural-style peanut butter (no sugar added) or butter

½ cup bits of cooked chicken from the stock (optional)

Ghanaian Basic Tomato Gravy (page 38) for serving

Special equipment
Small sharp deboning knife (if doing deboning yourself)

Twine and needle (for sewing up the stuffed chicken)

Variations:
Experiment with the stuffing by chopping, not mashing, the potatoes or yams, or by including chopped okra, mushrooms, nuts, etc.

Spicy Ashanti Chicken

For an optional spicy coating, mix together 1½ teaspoons ground fresh ginger, 2 tablespoons tomato paste, 2 cloves crushed garlic, ½ teaspoon dried ground red pepper, and 1 medium grated onion and rub the mixture on the chicken skin before roasting.

added to the stuffing. Use some of the stock to make the Ghanaian Tomato Gravy and reserve the rest for another use.

Make stuffing:
4. Peel and cut the yams into thick slices and then cut them in half (or peel and quarter potatoes, if using). Boil in salted water until just cooked, about 15 to 20 minutes.
5. Very lightly mash the yams or potatoes with a fork or masher (do not whip). If using potatoes, add 2 tablespoons of flour. Mix in the onion, garlic, pureed tomatoes, salt, dried ground red pepper (a little at a time until desired heat), and peanut butter or butter. Add some of the bits of leftover cooked chicken from making the broth.

Stuff and roast chicken:
6. Preheat oven to 375 degrees F. Remove the chicken from the refrigerator, open it up, skin side down, and spread the stuffing evenly over it, pushing some extra into the drumstick and wing sections. Sew the chicken closed with some kitchen twine and a needle.
7. Brush the outside of the stuffed chicken with a little vegetable oil and sprinkle with some salt or any desired optional seasonings.
8. Place in a roasting pan and roast at 375 degrees F for about 75 to 90 minutes, until a thermometer pushed into the thickest part of the chicken reaches 185 degrees F. Use the juices in the bottom of the pan to baste the chicken several times while it is cooking (add a cup of water to the roasting pan if there are no juices). If the chicken browns too quickly, cover the drumstick/wing/breast sections as needed with aluminum foil to protect them.
9. Make Ghanaian Basic Tomato Gravy (page 39) using some of the chicken stock.

To serve: Serve the chicken with the tomato gravy on the side.

ONE-POT MEALS

Gari One-Pot
Gari Foto

Makes 6 servings

Gari, made from soaked, fermented, and dried cassava roots, is a converneience food reminiscent of couscous (see page 174). *Gari Foto* is a satisfying one-pot dish that is easy to prepare and inexpensive. *Gari Foto* combines scrambled eggs, a basic Ghanaian tomato gravy, a protein source such as leftover meat, fish, or canned meat like the corned beef used here, and *gari*. It was originally viewed as a quick end-of-the-week recipe to be made with leftovers. Barbara was largely responsible for popularizing *Gari Foto* as a respectable "company dish" via her television cooking shows in the 1960s and by serving it at her restaurant. Today it may be served to guests, or as a family-friendly quick meal.

Ingredients

¼ teaspoon salt

2 cups dry *gari*

6 tablespoons peanut or other vegetable oil, divided

1 onion, chopped

2 eggs, beaten

2 tablespoons red palm oil (or other vegetable oil if not available)

½ tin (6 ounces) canned corned beef (*don't use any other type of corned beef*)

2 cloves garlic, minced

2 cups chopped fresh tomatoes (peeled and seeded, if desired)

1 teaspoon grated fresh ginger

¼ teaspoon dried ground red pepper

Directions

1. Measure out ¾ cup of water and add ¼ teaspoon salt. Put the *gari* in a bowl and gradually sprinkle the water over the *gari* a tablespoon at a time, mixing it in using your fingers to judge how damp it is. Use up to 8 tablespoons. The gari should be dampened, but not thoroughly wet. If it still seems dry, add a little more of the water.

2. Heat 1 tablespoon of peanut or other oil in a large heavy skillet on medium heat. Add 1 tablespoon of the chopped onion to the hot oil and sauté for a minute. Pour in the beaten eggs and scramble. When cooked, turn them out of the pan onto a plate and set aside.

3. After removing the eggs from the pan, add 2 tablespoons red palm oil and 5 tablespoons of peanut or other oil to the skillet and heat on medium.

4. When the oil in the pan is hot, add remainder of the chopped onion and sauté for 2 minutes. Stir in the corned beef (it will break up as it cooks).

5. After a minute, add the garlic, tomatoes, ginger, and dried ground red pepper and stir well.

6. Cut up the scrambled eggs and add to the stew.

7. Turn the heat to low and mix in the moistened *gari*, using a fork or your fingers to break up any lumps of *gari*. Keep stirring until the stew saturates the *gari* and there are no dry lumps of the *gari*. Taste and add salt if needed.

To serve: Garnish the finished dish as desired (e.g., using any combination of decorative egg strips, sliced peppers, onions, tomatoes, parsley, etc.). *Gari Foto* may be eaten alone or with a vegetable side dish, with a pepper sauce, or with a red bean stew. It is normally mildly spiced, and may be served warm or at room temperature. Leftovers heat up nicely in a microwave.

Variations:

Substitute canned tomatoes for the fresh tomatoes.

Substitute 1 cup of any leftover meat, fish, or poultry cut in chunks for the corned beef.

Substitute ½ teaspoon dried ground ginger for the fresh ginger.

Add minced fresh chili pepper, keeping the spiciness mild (see page 37 for pepper heat chart).

Stir in 2 teaspoons dried ground shrimp with the other seasonings.

Special Occasion Gari Foto

For a special, more formal version of *Gari Foto*: In Step 2, mix 1 tablespoon of tomato sauce (or 1 teaspoon of tomato paste mixed with 2 teaspoons water) into the eggs before adding them to the skillet. Instead of scrambling the egg, fry as for an omelet. Then cut the omelet in half. Cut one half into thin strips to garnish the final *gari foto* when serving. Break up the other half and add to the stew just before adding the dampened *gari*.

Vegetarian Gari Foto

Omit the corned beef and either substitute a cup of canned beans of choice or increase the number of eggs. Chop and add vegetables of your choice to the stew, e.g., carrots, mushrooms, green beans, peas, sweet bell peppers.

Coconut-Bean One-Pot
Ayikple

Makes 4 generous servings

This porridge is best eaten immediately after it is prepared. Barbara insists it is no good once it cools, and unlike many dishes, is not as good reheated. *Ayikple* has an amazing flavor and texture. The crayfish and herring provide a magical umami flavor. The delicate but rich coconut milk is reminiscent of the cooking of the Bahia region of Brazil.

Ingredients
1 cup dried adzuki beans

1 can coconut milk plus 2 cups water

2 teaspoons grated or ground fresh ginger (or to taste)

Sliced fresh chili peppers to taste: e.g., ⅛ to ¼ cup seeded green jalapeno peppers for mild; ⅛ cup fresh cayenne peppers, seeds and membranes removed for hot; or ⅛ to ¼ teaspoon dried ground red pepper (add more after cooking if a spicier flavor is desired)

⅓ cup smoked herring, ground or pounded

¼ cup dried ground (or pounded) crayfish

1 teaspoon salt or seasoned salt (or to taste)

Up to 2 cups Toasted Corn Flour (*Ablemamu*, page 29); or substitute stone-ground white corn flour toasted in a fry pan over medium heat until light brown (do not use cornmeal)

Ghanaian Basic Tomato Gravy
See ingredients and instructions on page 39

Directions
Prepare beans:
1. Rinse and pick through the beans, cover with water, and soak overnight. (Or use the quick method: cover the beans with water in a pot, boil for a few minutes, and remove from heat and let sit covered for an hour.)
2. When ready to begin cooking, drain the soaking water off the beans and add 8 cups of fresh water. Simmer them, covered, until tender. This may take several hours.

Prepare tomato gravy:
3. While the beans cook, make the tomato gravy following the instructions on page 39.

Assemble one-pot:
4. When the beans are cooked, drain and add the coconut milk and water (4 cups total). Add 1⅓ to 1½ cups tomato gravy, the ginger, chili pepper, herrings, dried crayfish, and salt. Simmer on medium for a few minutes to allow the flavors to blend, making sure the mixture does not scorch. Taste the mixture as it cooks and remove the sliced chili peppers if worried about it becoming too spicy.
5. The tricky part is right at the end, when adding the toasted corn flour: Sprinkle half of the flour in quickly, stirring like crazy with a strong wooden spoon or a stirring stick to make sure it does not get lumpy. Repeat with most of the remaining flour until the porridge is very thick.

To serve: *Shito* (page 170), Fresh Pepper Sauce (page 168), or any chili sambal are nice on the side. I have garnished it with grilled tiger shrimp. At Flair, we ate this meal with a hearty red Slavic wine. Ghanaians do not always have the same ideas about which wines "go" with which foods as North Americans. Round out a fabulous meal with some fresh watermelon, papaya, or pineapple.

Cocoyam/Taro One-Pot
Nyoma / Mpotompoto

Makes 3 to 4 servings

I first thought "nyoma" and "mpotompoto" were two different dishes, and later began to suspect they were the same. Several Ghanaians confirmed this. Barbara once told me that when it is made with yams, the Ewes call it *teba* ("yam mud") and that it is also known in Ewe as *dablui*, which means "cook it and mix it up." She describes it as a kind of Ghanaian goulash. In Twi, *poto* means "to mash/grind." ("*mpotompoto*"—note that lovely reduplication again). However, the root vegetable used is not necessarily mashed, just cooked in broth until the starch, whether cocoyam, African yam, white sweet potato, or cassava, disintegrates. This dish is also recommended as a weaning food for young children. It makes a light, comforting, one-pot meal.

There are many variations of this dish. This is a simple one using dried ground red pepper, cocoyam, palm oil, salt, tomatoes, and dried shrimp. If cocoyams/taro are not available at your local grocery store, try an Asian market.

Ingredients

¼ cup dried smoked shrimps

3 cocoyams/taro, peeled and cut in ½-inch cubes (1 pound after peeling)

1 medium onion, peeled

2 medium tomatoes

½ teaspoon salt (or to taste)

¼ teaspoon dried ground red pepper (or to taste)

¼ cup good quality palm oil

Substitutions

African yam or white sweet potato in place of the cocoyam

Shrimp-flavored seasoning cubes or dried herrings in place of the dried smoked shrimp

Another vegetable oil in place of the palm oil

Directions

1. Pound the dried shrimp, if whole, in a mortar and pestle (If desired, break off the head and end of the tail first).
2. Put the diced cocoyam, whole onion, and whole tomatoes in a pot with 5 cups of water. Bring to a boil, then lower the heat and cook until the cocoyam is soft, about 20 minutes.
3. Using a slotted spoon, remove the tomatoes and onion. Discard the tomato peels if desired, and grind the tomatoes and onion in a blender, food processor, or *asanka*. Return them to the pot.
4. Add the pounded shrimp, salt, ground red pepper, and red palm oil. Let the mixture simmer briefly to blend the flavors. Taste and adjust seasoning, if necessary.

Variations:

Perhaps the most common variation: Omit pre-cooking the cocoyam and simply make the gravy, then add additional water and cook the cocoyam in it.

Boil the cocoyam separately. Make a gravy: using ½ cup palm or other vegetable oil, fry the onion a few minutes, then add sliced tomatoes (and other seasonings as desired, such as ginger, garlic, etc.). Mix everything together after the cocoyam is tender.

Party-Perfect Jollof Rice with Chicken

Jollof Rice / Jolof / Djolof / Benachin

Makes 8 to 10 servings

"*Jollof* rice" is one of the better-known classic West African dishes. It is amusing to read that this is the "national dish" of any specific West African country, since it belongs to the entire region, with many variations in name and ingredients. It is sometimes credited with originating among the Wolof people of Senegal and Gambia, but is now claimed by many other West African nations, including Ghana, Nigeria, Liberia, and Sierra Leone. Senegal's famous "*ceebu jen*" (from Wolof words for "rice" and "fish," aka *thiebou djenne*) is a similar rice paella, but is not the same. Ghana's *jollof* rice has a distinctive red color from the tomatoes and tomato paste used, not red palm oil as versions from Nigeria might. It is somewhat reminiscent of Spanish rice. Sometimes another one-pot in Ghana, "*Gari Foto*" (page 152), is called *Gari Jollof*.

Jollof has infinite variations. In this section we give you recipes for chicken, meat, vegetable, and seafood versions but in West Africa distinctions are not always meaningful, and meat, poultry, and seafood can also be combined in the same recipe. In Ghana of the 1970s, the protein source was cooked with the rice. Increasingly, unless being served in a buffet, the rice is cooked separately, with the protein served on the side. This may reflect Western influence and ideas of proper plating of food and protein serving sizes, but my preference continues to be with pieces of meat/poultry mixed into the rice.

Traditionally in Ghana chicken bones are chewed and provide welcome calcium to the diet. However, outside of Ghana, boneless chicken proves less messy and is easier to eat and cook. While in today's Ghana it is difficult to imagine being served *jollof* without Maggi or Royco seasoning cubes used, I prefer stock and seasonings such as fresh garlic, fresh chili pepper, fresh ginger, etc. I also remove the chicken skin. One challenge when making *jollof* rice is preventing mushiness. Cooking it in the oven where the heat is evenly distributed eliminates that problem.

Ingredients

- 2 pounds boneless skinless chicken, cubed; or 3 pounds skinless pieces with bones, cut into pieces with a heavy cleaver (for example, cut a thigh or drumstick into 2 pieces) (free range or roasting chickens are recommended)
- 1 cup finely chopped onion
- 1 tablespoon minced or crushed fresh garlic
- 1 tablespoon grated fresh ginger
- 2 teaspoons salt or seasoned salt

Directions

Prepare chicken:

1. In a large bowl, mix together ¼ cup of the onion, 1 teaspoon of the garlic, 1 teaspoon of the ginger, ½ teaspoon salt, ⅛ teaspoon black (or white) pepper, and ⅛ teaspoon of the red pepper. Add the chicken pieces, toss to coat, and let marinate for 5 to 10 minutes.

2. Heat 4 tablespoons of oil in a heavy skillet, add 2 tablespoons of the onion and sauté for 1 minute. Add half of the chicken pieces or enough to fill the pan without crowding, and brown on medium to medium-high heat. Remove the chicken pieces as they brown

½ teaspoon ground black or white pepper (optional)

½ teaspoon dried ground red pepper

5 tablespoons peanut or other vegetable oil

3 to 4 cups water or broth, or a combination (including up to 1 cup of drained juice from tomatoes)

1 bay leaf (optional)

1 teaspoon curry powder or ½ teaspoon dried thyme (or to taste)

2 cups grated or chopped fresh tomatoes, seeded and juices saved

4 to 5 tablespoons tomato paste

2 cups long grain white rice (not parboiled)

2 to 3 cups fresh chopped vegetables (such as carrots, green peas, bell peppers, green beans, corn) or frozen mixed vegetables

and put in a roaster or casserole dish (with a cover) large enough to hold the chicken, rice, and stock or water. Repeat the process with the remaining chicken, adding 2 more table-spoons of onion and 1 more tablespoon of oil if needed.

Prepare casserole:

3. While browning the chicken, put the 4 cups of stock/water/tomato juice into a saucepan with a bay leaf (if using) and heat to a boil, then keep warm until needed.

4. Preheat the oven to 350 degrees F, and make sure the oven rack is low enough to fit the covered roasting pan on it.

5. After all the chicken is browned and in the roaster, add the remaining 1 tablespoon oil to the skillet and add the remaining onion, garlic, ginger, and the curry powder or thyme, if us-ing, and stir-fry for a few minutes. Stir in the tomatoes, tomato paste, and remaining pepper and salt. Add 3½ cups (reserving remaining ½ cup) of the heated liquid and stir to loosen the onion from the pan.

6. Pour the rice into the roasting pan with the browned chicken. Then pour the tomato mixture into the roasting pan and stir.

7. Cover pan and place in the oven. Bake for 15 to 20 minutes. Remove from the oven and check rice for doneness and to determine if more liq-uid is needed. Add reserved ½ cup of liquid, reheated, if needed. Stir the rice gently from the outside in as the outside edges will cook more quickly. Return to the oven for another 10 to 15 minutes while preparing the vegetables.

8. Cook the vegetables separately, either in a microwave or on the stovetop.

(continued on next page)

9. When the rice is tender, remove the pan from the oven and gently toss in the vegetables (stirring too much will make it mushy) and allow to rest, covered, for a few minutes before serving.

Troubleshooting: If there is still liquid in the roaster once the rice is tender, uncover and let roaster sit in the oven for a few minutes to evaporate.

To serve: Serve with braised cabbage or other greens on the side and/or Ghanaian Basic Tomato Gravy (page 38) or *Shito* (page 170).

Make ahead: This recipe tastes good reheated the next day and also freezes nicely. It is easily doubled or tripled for a party.

Variations:

Add additional spices of choice, or increase amount of curry powder.

Alternatively, this may all be cooked in a large pot on the stovetop, avoiding burning the bottom but not stirring too often which would make the rice mushy.

The vegetables may be added directly to the rice while it is cooking, or stirred in during the final minutes of cooking.

Jollof Rice with Meat

Follow the chicken recipe, substituting 2 pounds of cubed boneless lean meat (beef, goat, lamb, etc.) for the chicken. Tough meat, such as goat or stewing beef, requires a longer time precooking than chicken. If so, after seasoning and browning it, add a ¼ to ½ cup of water and steam it on low heat, covered, until it is almost tender. It will continue cooking in the roasting pan while the rice cooks.

Vegetarian Jollof Rice

You can make *jollof* rice without the meat to be served as a side dish. Before sautéing the seasonings, put the onions, garlic, and ginger in a blender and grind to make a paste. Then follow the directions for making the Chicken Jollof Rice, sautéing the paste first for about 5 minutes, stirring, then adding the seasonings and tomatoes, etc.

Jollof Rice with Fish or Shrimp

Jollof rice may also be made with shrimp or fish. Caution must be taken not to overcook the seafood, however. Fish could be pan-fried like the chicken but then left out of the pan while the rice is cooking and placed on top of the rice near the end.

Rice and Beans
Waakye

Makes 6 servings

Africa is home to both the legumes known as "cowpeas," the most famous of which is the "black-eyed pea," and a type of indigenous rice (*Oryza glaberrima*). The (Nigerian) Hausa word for "cowpea" is "*wáákéé*" or "*wake*," and Hausa is spoken widely in northern Ghana. When rice is combined with *wáákéé* one has Ghana's "*waakye*" (pronounced "WAAtchy"), a classic rice and beans dish that has spread throughout the country and beyond. It makes a great vegetarian meal by itself, and can be eaten for breakfast or lunch. In Ghana it is often sold at roadside stands, and is a filling, healthful, and relatively inexpensive meal.

    Waakye is simple to make. In Ghana one often uses fresh or dried millet leaves (stalks), and *kanwa* (a mineral used to soften the beans), but baking soda (sodium bicarbonate) can be substituted to give the *waakye* its characteristic color.

Ingredients

1 (15.5-ounce) can black-eyed peas, drained and lightly rinsed or 1½ cups cooked black-eyed peas (*for rice cooker recipe*); or 1 cup dried black-eyed peas (*for everyday recipe*)

1 cup white rice (washed if necessary)

1 tablespoon vegetable oil

½ cup chopped onion

½ to 1 teaspoon baking soda (a full teaspoon will make it darker)

½ teaspoon salt

Directions for Rice Cooker

1. Put the black-eyed peas, rice, oil, onion, baking soda, salt and 2 cups water in a rice cooker. Stir, cover, and cook until rice is tender, about 30 minutes (cooker will automatically stop when done). If the rice is still wet after it is cooked, remove the lid to release steam.

Directions for Everyday Waakye

1. Rinse and pick over the black-eyed peas, then soak them for 4 hours covered with water. (Or use the quick method: bring black-eyed peas to a boil in a saucepan, let them boil for a couple of minutes and then sit covered for an hour, then proceed.)

2. Drain off the water from the peas and add 2½ cups of fresh water to the saucepan, along with all the other ingredients. Bring the water to a boil, lower the heat and simmer, covered, until the rice and beans are tender, about 45 minutes. Be careful not to burn the rice, and add a little more water if necessary as it cooks. If the rice and beans are tender, but water remains, remove the lid the last few minutes to allow the extra water to cook away.

To serve: *See next page.*

Rice and Beans Deluxe
Waakye Deluxe

Ingredients
1 cup dried black-eyed peas

1 cup white rice (washed if necessary)

1 to 2 tablespoons coconut cream plus enough coconut milk to make 1 cup

½ cup chopped onion

½ to 1 teaspoon baking soda (a full teaspoon will make it darker)

½ teaspoon salt

¼ to ½ teaspoon dried herb of choice (e.g., thyme, oregano)

Directions
1. Pick over the black-eyed peas and rinse well. Put them into a saucepan with 3 cups water, bring to a boil, lower the heat and simmer for 30 to 40 minutes.
2. Add remaining ingredients. Return the water to a boil, lower the heat and cook, covered, until the rice and beans are tender, about 30 minutes. Check during cooking to make sure it does not scorch, and remove lid, if necessary, to cook off any excess water when the rice and beans are tender.

To serve: Either *Waakye* can be served simply, with a little Ghanaian Basic Tomato Gravy (page 38), *Shito* (page 170), or any chili sauce on the side. It also pairs well with greens and/or a meat, fish, or poultry stew. In an interesting bit of culinary fusion, Ghanaians today commonly garnish *Waakye* with a little plain boiled spaghetti.

Time-saving hint: Cook a pound or two of black-eyed peas and freeze them in batches to make *waakye* faster.

If available, try a locally grown Ghanaian rice. Most of the rice sold in Ghana today is imported, especially from Thailand, Vietnam, and the United States. People have come to prefer the quality and taste of white rice. My preference is long-grain rice, especially basmati, but any will work.

Toasted Cornmeal One-Pot with Crab

Aprapransa

Makes 6 servings

This dish has several names. I first met it in the Eastern Region as its Twi name, *aprapransa*. It is also called *akpledzi* (Ga or Ewe), *apragyaa* (Fante), or *akplijii*.

When my husband recalls his grandmother's version, garnished with Ghana's wonderful freshwater crabs, his eyes still glaze over. *Aprapransa* has an interesting texture and unusual flavor. The cream of palm fruit used means that it is a very rich dish reserved for special occasions. It also requires some time and effort, and for those outside of Ghana, several adaptations. There is really no substitute for the cream of palm fruit or the smoked/dried shrimp/crayfish. Also, try to find authentic *ablemamu*, if possible, or make your own.

Though this dish is served as a "one pot," it has two components. The first is a bean and palm fruit soup that is thickened with toasted corn flour. Secondly, a thick gravy or "dressing" is served on top and/or the side.

Ingredients

Bean and Palm Fruit Soup

⅔ cup dried adzuki beans

1 tablespoon salted cod (optional)

1¼ cups finely chopped shallots or onions

8 to 10 ounces smoked whiting or other smoked fish, skin and bones removed and flaked

3 or 4 medium tomatoes, peeled if desired and chopped

1 small slice Scotch bonnet pepper (hot) or larger slice jalapeno pepper (mild), or more to taste

2 tablespoons powdered shrimp/ crayfish

1 can (800-gram) cream of palm fruit

Salt or seasoned salt to taste

2 to 2¼ cups toasted corn flour (*ablemamu*, page 29)

Directions

Prepare the beans:

1. Rinse and pick over the beans for stones. Cover with water and presoak the beans overnight. (Or use the quick method: cover the beans with water, boil for 3 minutes, let them sit about an hour.) Drain the beans and put in a large pot with fresh water to cover. Cook the beans several hours until almost tender. Drain.

Prepare the salted cod *(if using)*:

2. Simmer the piece of salted cod in water in a small pan for a few minutes or soak it for 30 minutes in warm water, then rinse well.

Prepare soup:

3. Put into a large pot the 1¼ cup finely chopped shallots or onions, smoked fish, tomatoes, chili pepper, powdered crayfish, ¾ of the can of cream of palm fruit, 2 cups of water, and half of the cooked and drained beans (the rest to be added near the end). Bring to a simmer. As the soup simmers, skim off the palm oil that rises to the top (1½ to 2 cups of oil). Save ½ cup to use in making the stew and store the rest for another recipe. Taste and adjust salt and pepper as desired.

Crab

2 King crab legs or 4 fresh cleaned crabs

1 tablespoon finely chopped onion

Gravy/Dressing

1 cup chopped onion

Small slice to one-half seeded chili pepper of choice (see heat chart on page 37)

½ cup palm oil (from soup)

½ teaspoon salt

¼ teaspoon dried ground red pepper (optional)

1 to 2 medium tomatoes, sliced

Prepare crab:

4. While the soup simmers, cook the crab legs or crabs separately in a pot with salted water and the tablespoon of chopped onion, then set them aside to garnish the final dish.

Prepare gravy/dressing:

5. Put half the onion and ¼ of a seeded chili pepper (or to taste) in an electric blender with just enough water to grind. Grind to a paste. Heat ½ cup of the palm oil from the soup on medium and fry the ground onion mixture, ½ teaspoon salt, and a little dried ground red pepper, if desired, for several minutes. Add the remaining onion and the tomatoes to the oil and fry together to make the gravy. Set the gravy aside.

Finish the soup:

6. Remove 2 cups of soup from the pot and set aside in a bowl. Slowly stir the toasted corn flour into the remaining soup in the pot, stirring constantly to prevent lumps forming. Once all the corn flour is added, stir in the reserved soup and continue to cook and stir on low-to-medium heat until the mixture just pulls away from the side. If the *aprapransa* is very wet, try cooking it a bit longer or adding a little more toasted corn flour. The final mixture should be soft, but not runny.

7. Stir in the rest of the cooked beans.

To serve: *Aprapransa* is lovely served on a large oval platter with some of the gravy/dressing spread over it and crab on top (if using king crab legs, break them into six pieces), and with a smaller bowl of gravy on the side.

Variation: Add some meat to the soup.

ƆTƆ'S SPECIAL RELEVANCE

As I once explained in an article in *Gastronomica*:[1]

Oto is commonly served at the naming ceremony for a new baby (an "outdooring") or the purification of the mother after birth; at puberty ceremonies for girls; at festivals associated with twins, whom the Akan and Ga people consider sacred; at special occasions after the birth of the third, seventh, or tenth child of the same sex (sacred numbers in the Akan and Ga cultures); at harvest celebrations; after the first and third weeks of deaths in a family, when not only family members eat ɔtɔ, but the house is sprinkled with ɔtɔ to satisfy the dead; and on special days in the Akan calendar known as "Bad Days" or "*Dabone*."[2] *Dabone* is based on the belief that on particular days the spirits inhabiting forest or farmland will be offended if anyone invades their territory, so people stay home and away from their farms to avoid meeting or offending the spirits. Thus, ɔtɔ is served to both the living and the dead. In addition, on other special occasions in normal adult life, e.g., recovery from illness, escape from accidents, birthdays, ɔtɔ is the customary dish prepared to thank the *nsamanfo* (spirits) by sharing a meal with them. The *nsamanfo* are believed to dislike food that is highly seasoned. Hence ɔtɔ is given without salt or pepper.

---

[1] "We Eat First With Our Eyes," *Gastronomica*, Spring 2002. Quoted by permission.
[2] E. Chapman Nyaho, E. Amarteifio, and J. Asare, *Ghana Recipe Book* (Accra-Tema: Ghana Publishing Corporation, 1970), pp. 118-9.

Mashed African Yam with Palm Oil and Egg

Ɔtɔ

Makes 2 to 4 servings

I am especially pleased to present this recipe for yam *ɔtɔ*. Three decades ago, I was thrilled to discover my first postcard of food in Ghana—a postcard celebrating *ɔtɔ* with a photo of this traditional Ghanaian dish. The back simply said in English (and also in French): "African Gourmet," and gave very simple directions on preparing it. Many years later I received a card from Barbara, and discovered she was the source, and that same photo was part of her personal stationery. Here is Flair Catering's version of yam *ɔtɔ*.

The first day we made this at Flair, Barbara mentioned she had recently had *ɔtɔ* at a celebration in Accra for the 70th birthday of a Fante friend. To thank God they first went to a church service in the morning, then began their breakfast at 8:30 a.m. with *ɔtɔ*, topped with a hardboiled egg for each person. The *ɔtɔ* was followed by an extensive banquet of Ghanaian and Western dishes that continued on until lunch.

Ingredients

1 piece African yam (about 1 pound), peeled (*do not substitute American yams*)

1 teaspoon salt (or to taste)

½ cup good quality palm oil (preferably *dzomi*)

An onion slice or piece of ginger or bay leaf for flavoring the oil

1 onion, finely chopped (about ¾ cup)

2 to 4 hardboiled eggs, peeled (1 per person)

Directions

1. Slice the yam in half lengthwise, then slice it into slices about ½ inch thick. Put the slices in a medium pot and cover them with water. Add the salt, cover the pot, bring to a boil, then lower the heat and cook for about 15 minutes, depending on the thickness of the yam slices.

2. Heat the palm oil in a pan. Add a slice of onion, ginger, or a bay leaf first and fry briefly to season the oil, then remove it. Add the chopped onion to the oil and fry briefly. Remove from heat.

3. Drain the yams and put in an *asanka* or other bowl and mash with a wooden masher or potato masher, then mix it with a wooden spoon. (Do not mash the yam as thoroughly as you would potatoes. One does not want a paste or a smooth "whipped" mass, but a denser, more textured one.)

4. Continue to mix the yams as you add the onion mixture with the oil into the bowl. Switching to a fork may make it easier to blend without smashing it.

5. Garnish with a whole hardboiled egg for each person. (*See sidebar on page 166.*)

EGGS

One cannot truly understand ɔtɔ (page 165) without understanding eggs and the role of eggs in Ghanaian society:

"Ɔtɔ is always accompanied by hard-boiled eggs. Eggs, a key symbol in Ghanaian culture, are often used for sacrifices, at purification rites, as pacification fees, gifts, for thanksgiving after illness, and at numerous other occasions.

   The very oval form of the egg is the symbol of female beauty and, at the same time, bears an element of 'cleansing power.' The egg is laid by the hen with what the Ghanaian considers to be amazing ease; it is therefore made to symbolize easy labour and fecundity.

   When eggs are carved on the staff of a "linguist" (the king's spokesperson), they proclaim that the king "wants peace with everyone (for there is no bone or any hard substance in an egg) and that he is a careful, patient, and prudent person (for an egg is so fragile that without these qualities it would be broken)." *

In Ghana one often sees wooden carvings of a hand holding an egg. The message is "Power is like an egg: if you hold it too tightly it breaks, and if you hold it too loosely, it drops and breaks."

---

*Sarpong, *Ghana in Retrospect : Some Aspects of Ghanaian Culture* (Ghana Publishing Company, 1974), pp. 104, 106, 109.

CONDIMENTS

Fresh Pepper Sauce

This is Ghana's salsa. It needs wonderful fresh tomatoes and chili peppers to do it justice—the good soup (or sauce) truly comes from the good earth. The "proper" (and easiest and most efficient) way to make the sauce is using an *asanka* and the wooden mashing tool (*apotoyewa* or *apotoriwa*). It can be prepared without them but remember the texture is very important: one does not want a watery, bland, uninteresting mess. When using a clay *asanka*, scald the *asanka* with boiling water before and after use. Barbara Baëta cleans hers using a little lemon juice as well.

For a "red" sauce use red chili peppers, for a "green" sauce use green chili peppers. Read "Cooking with Peppers" on page 36 before beginning and use proper precautions when working with chili peppers. The proportions are flexible. Adjust according to personal preference.

Ingredients
- 2 tablespoons minced red or green chili pepper of your choice (*kpakpo shito* are used in Ghana; see pepper heat chart, page 37), with or without seeds and membranes
- 1 large onion, chopped
- 1½ cups chopped fresh plum or other variety tomatoes
- 1 teaspoon salt or to taste

To serve: Fresh pepper sauces go well with Ghana-style Grilled Tilapia (page 134), Ghana Fried Fish (*Kenam*, page 138). or eggs. If not eaten immediately, refrigerate and use within a day or two.

Variation: Substitute red or green sweet bell peppers for part of the chili peppers if you like less heat.

Directions using an *asanka*
1. Put the chopped ingredients in the *asanka* with salt. Using a rocking motion, crush a little of the ingredients at a time, and continue working around the bowl until everything is well mashed, but small pieces still exist, about 10 to 15 minutes. (A Ghanaian friend/spouse would likely be glad to assist—it is not as easy as it looks.) Adjust the seasonings to taste.
2. The sauce can now be eaten, but Barbara advises simmering it over low heat for 15 to 20 minutes to make it less watery and raw tasting.

Directions using a blender
1. Use the same ingredients, but grate rather than chop a portion of the onions and tomatoes and set them aside with a little of the minced chili pepper.
2. Very briefly pulse the rest of the ingredients in a food processor or electric blender, then remove and combine with the grated ingredients. Adjust seasonings and simmer over low heat for 15 or 20 minutes if desired.

Flavored Oils

Flavored oils are used in Ghana as a condiment that can be drizzled over starches, stews, or cooked cowpeas. It is similar to the way Fulbe cattle herders in Mauritania, Mali, and Northern Senegal use the oil butter *nebam sirme*. This spicy condiment can be made with a light-colored oil (like canola, safflower, or peanut) or the classic carotene-rich red palm oil. It reminds me of Asian chili oil made with sesame oil (sesame is originally from Africa) but with an African touch. Easy and quick to make, this might be just the perfect holiday gift for that African gourmand on your list.

Ingredients

Several hot chili peppers of your choice (in Ghana I use my favored *kpakpo shito* peppers; see pepper heat chart on page 37)

½ cup vegetable oil of your choice

½ cup sliced or coarsely chopped onion, plus a few extra slices

1 teaspoon ground or grated fresh ginger (or to taste)

1 teaspoon dried ground red pepper (or to taste)

Directions

1. Wash the chili peppers, slice off the stem ends, then cut them up or make slits in them. It is not necessary to remove the seeds.
2. Heat a small skillet on the stove for 2 minutes, add the oil and a few slices of onion and cook, stirring, for 2 or 3 minutes. Remove the browned onion.
3. Add the ½ cup sliced or coarsely chopped onion, the fresh chili peppers, ginger, and dried ground red pepper. Lower the heat and simmer the mixture for 15 minutes, pressing down on the chili peppers as they cook to help release their oils, and stirring occasionally.
4. Strain the mixture twice into a measuring cup or bowl—once to remove the large pieces of pepper and ginger, and then a second time with a fine tea strainer to remove the dregs.
5. Store in a glass jar.

To serve: These oils are nice drizzled over cooked cowpeas Pureed Black-eyed Peas (*Adayi*, page 143), Stewed Bambara Beans (*Aboboe*, page 142), Ghanaian Basic Tomato Gravy (page 38), and almost any Ghanaian starch, from *gari* to *ampesi*.

Chili Pepper and Shrimp Sambal
Shito / Shitɔ / Shitor / Shito Din / Mako Tuntum

Traditionally *shito* (SHE-toe) was as ubiquitous in Ghana as ketchup is in the U.S. *Shito* literally means "pepper" in the Ga language, and can refer to hot peppers or the hot sauce/condiment itself made from dried peppers, dried shrimps, and sometimes small dried herrings as well as onion, tomato, and other seasonings.

When I taught in Nungua, a Ga area, Ga *Kenkey* (aka *komi*, page 187) was commonly eaten with *shito* and fried fish (*Kenam*, page 138). I have always assumed that *shito* is a Ga invention. It is popular with boarding school students throughout the country, likely because it pairs well with both *kenkey* and *gari*, filling and inexpensive foods that do not require refrigeration, along with canned corned beef or sardines. In Twi, the word for "chili pepper" is *mako*, so *shito* is also called *mako tuntum* (black or dark pepper).

The recipe for *shito* has largely been an oral tradition until the past 20 years when it started appearing in some cookbooks. There are now a number of online recipes also. However, it deeply saddens me to see imported tabasco sauce frequently replacing *shito* on restaurant tables in Ghana.

Making *shito* is generally a complicated and time-consuming process, and also produces a strong "fishy" odor while cooking. Friend and colleague Gloria Mensah, a no-nonsense, efficient single mom and trained culinary professional skilled at adapting traditional recipes to the 21st century, sometimes bakes *shito* in large batches in her oven and substitutes readily available canned mackerel for the dried herrings. She has also adapted the recipe for a slow cooker. A slow cooker has the added advantage that in nice weather or a covered area it can sit outside for a day or a day-and-a-half while cooking so the powerful odor does not permeate the house. Along with substituting canned mackerel, Gloria also uses ginger paste and garlic paste from an Indian market to eliminate making them from scratch. Another time saver is the ability to purchase dried shrimp from a local international market rather than drying them in the oven before grinding them. This is a simplified step-by-step crockpot *shito* recipe adapted from Gloria Mensah's version.

Ingredients
1 cup dried shrimp (from a 3.5-ounce/100-gram package)

2 cups canned mackerel (from a 15-ounce/425-gram can)

¼ cup dried ground red pepper (for medium-heat)

2 cups canned Italian plum tomatoes

2 large onions, cut into chunks

¼ cup ginger paste (from pureed fresh ginger or bought)

Directions
Optional Step:
1. Rinse the dried shrimp, blot them dry with a paper towel, then spread them out on a baking sheet in a 200 degree F oven for an hour while completing the other prep work. (Note: I imagine Gloria omits this step.)

Prepare the mackerel:
2. A crucial requirement in making *shito* is to remove all water. Dry and blot the drained canned mackerel with paper towels before flaking it with your fingers. Put the flaked mackerel in a large bowl and add the ground red pepper.

If you know any students in North America from Ghana, a small jar of *shito* and a little bag of *gari* would likely make a far more welcome gift over the holidays than any candy canes or chocolate chip cookies.

¼ cup garlic paste (from pureed fresh garlic or bought)

1 tablespoon tomato paste (optional)

1 to 2 cups vegetable oil, such as canola or peanut (not red palm oil)

Prepare tomatoes:

3. Crush the Italian plum tomatoes by lifting the tomatoes out of the liquid first and then squeezing them through your fingers into a small bowl. If using already crushed canned tomatoes, drain off most of the liquid.

Assemble *shito*:

4. Mix 1 cup of the crushed tomatoes with the mackerel.

5. Blend the second cup of tomatoes with the onions in a small blender or food processor and add to the mackerel mixture.

6. Grind the dried shrimps in the electric blender and add them to the mixture. Stir in the ginger paste, garlic paste, and tomato paste, if using, and finally 1 cup of oil. Add up to 1 cup more oil for a moister, longer lasting *shito*.

Cook *shito*:

7. Put everything in a crockpot, cover and cook on low for 12 to 18 hours, stirring every few hours. The *shito* is ready when it is dark brown, but not burned (constant stirring and pressing is another trick to making *shito*), and all the water has cooked out. (This may not always work in the crockpot: some slow cookers may take longer, or it may need to be finished in a cast iron or nonstick heavy skillet on a stovetop. To finish on the stovetop, heat a skillet on medium heat, then lower to low and stir constantly for 30 to 45 minutes. It will continue to cook a little in the pan even after it is taken off the heat.)

(continued on next page)

Chili Pepper and Shrimp Sambal (continued)
Shito / Shitor / Shito Din / Mako Tuntum

8. Allow the *shito* to cool completely and store in glass jars. When cooked very dry and covered with a generous coating of oil, *shito* keeps well at room temperature.

Variations:

Some Ghanaians skip the mackerel altogether and make *shito* using only flaked dried shrimp from Thailand. This is even easier, but the Thai version has 2 percent sugar added to the dried shrimp.

A vegetarian family locally makes a great *shito* using seaweed in place of the dried shrimp and fish.

Many Ghanaians nowadays add shrimp-flavored or other seasoning cubes to their *shito*.

If dried shrimp aren't available, substitute fresh shelled and deveined shrimp, dried in a slow oven.

Shito can also be cooked uncovered in a slow oven.

Substitute tuna for the mackerel.

GRAINS, ROOTS & OTHER STARCHES

GARI

Gari (aka *gali* or *garri*) is Ghana's original convenience food. It is a pro-cessed form of cassava (*manioc, mandioca, yucca, yuca, singkong, ketela,* or *ubi kayu* around the world) similar to Brazil's *farinha de mandioca.* But unlike Brazil's version, *gari* is fermented. In Nigeria and Ghana, especially, *gari* is a popular and growing urban convenience food: it is inexpensive, has a long shelf life, is quick and simple to prepare, and is very filling.

North Americans have traditionally only known the root "cassava" as "tapioca," a starch commonly used to make puddings and thicken sauces. There is much more to the cassava than that. It is a staff of life to many people in tropical places, and especially in West Africa. With the popularity of gluten-free cooking rising, there has been increased awareness of cassava in the U.S.

Processing cassava to make *gari* involves washing, peeling, grating, soaking, pressing, drying, and toasting. The net result is a kind of cassa-va "couscous," that can be served simply by adding lightly salted water. I prefer to boil the water before sprinkling/pouring it on the *gari. Gari* is quite filling. It swells up to three times its size when water is added, and can be eaten as a side accompaniment to a stew. There is a wonderful tangy smell from the fermentation of the cassava that releases when the water hits the *gari.*

Gari has a very accessible flavor, even to those who have never tasted it before. It is mild, and a good accompaniment for a variety of stews, or when cooked into a one-pot like *Gari Foto* (page 152). We give you three recipes for it here. Dry *gari* is likely only available in the U.S. at African or international markets or online. There is no substitute.

Simple Gari

This is the easiest way to serve *gari*. Simply boil the water separately and then bring it to the table in a pitcher and let each person serve him or herself individually.

Ingredients

¼ cup dry *gari* per person

Directions

1. Heat about ½ to ¾ cup water per person to boiling and pour into a pitcher.
2. Spoon or pour about ¼ cup of dry *gari* on each individual plate.
3. Sprinkle each serving of the *gari* with ½ to ¾ cup boiling or hot water (more or less to taste). Stir the water and *gari* on the plate and allow to rest for a couple of minutes until it swells to about 3 times its size. Add additional water if it seems too thick, or additional *gari* if it seems too watery.

To serve: Eat with a stew or sauce on top or to the side of the *gari*.

Variation: Mix the *gari* and water together in a serving bowl first, allow the *gari* to absorb the water, and serve directly to the plate.

Nigerian-style Gari
Eba

Makes 5 servings

Not all *gari* has the same texture. There are a variety of types of *gari*, and Nigerians seem to prefer a coarser dry cassava meal than Ghanaians and commonly cook it with more water to make their beloved *eba*. Their culinary influence has permeated Ghana and *eba* is now frequently found in restaurants and chop bars there as well.

Ingredients
1½ cups dry *gari*

Directions
1. Bring 4 cups of water to a boil in a saucepan. Set 1 cup of the hot water aside in case too much dry *gari* gets added. Remove the pan from the heat.
2. Begin sprinkling the dry *gari* into the water by hand until it mostly covers the top of the water. Use a strong spoon (like a Ghanaian wooden stirring stick) to stir the *gari*, turning it and mixing it well and pressing it against the sides of the bowl or pan, until it becomes a thick paste. Add a little more of the reserved hot water if necessary. After several minutes of stirring, spoon the *eba* out into desired serving sizes.

To serve: *Eba* is commonly eaten with thick soups/stews. (In Nigeria, there is less distinction between soups and stews than in Ghana.)

Variations: Sometimes in restaurants the *eba* is formed into balls and placed in small plastic bags. The plastic bags also serve to keep flies off and thus are more hygienic.

Seasoned Gari
Pino

Makes 2 to 3 servings

This dish, like seasoned couscous, provides a delicious quick side starch for a meal. *Pino* is similar to, but lighter than, Nigerian *eba*, where the *gari* is much denser.

Ingredients

1 tablespoon peanut or other vegetable oil

3 tablespoons finely chopped onion

2 cups chicken stock

2 teaspoons tomato paste (or to taste)

¼ teaspoon seasoned salt (or to taste)

⅛ to ¼ teaspoon dried ground red pepper (or to taste)

1 cup dry *gari*

Directions

1. Heat oil in a skillet on medium and quickly fry the chopped onion for 2 minutes. Add the stock, tomato paste, salt, and ground red pepper and heat to almost boiling. Taste and adjust seasonings if necessary.
2. Place the gari in a bowl and pour the hot liquid over it, stirring it quickly and gently with a fork or spoon, being careful to keep it from clumping or becoming lumpy.
3. Wet a small dome-shaped bowl and lightly press the *pino* into it. Place a plate on top of the bowl and turn it upside down to release the molded *pino*.

To serve: *Pino* makes a lovely light but satisfying and sophisticated meal, especially when paired with Ghana-style Kebabs (*Chichinga*, page 74), some fresh vegetables, and a bottle of chilled chardonnay. Garnish as desired, e.g., a little parsley, basil, green pepper, and/or tomato.

Variation: Some leftover Ghanaian Basic Tomato Gravy (page 38) mixed with water or a seasoning cube and water may replace the 2 cups of chicken stock.

Cassava Couscous
Attiéké / Acheke

Makes 2 to 2½ cups

Attiéké is similar to *gari* (page 175) but is composed of steamed cassava granules and is more couscous-like. Also, *attiéké* is only slightly fermented and has a more delicate quality. Originally from Côte d'Ivoire, it has spread throughout much of West Africa. The only type available in North America (at international or African markets or online) is generally a dried version easily prepared in either a microwave or a steamer.

Ingredients
1 cup dry *attiéké*

Directions for microwave
Mix 1 cup of water and the dry *attiéké* in a microwave-safe bowl and allow to sit for about 15 minutes so the *attiéké* absorbs the water. Stir and heat in a microwave oven 2 to 3 minutes. (Optional: Cover with a damp paper towel.) Fluff with a fork and serve.

Directions for steamer:
Mix 1 cup of water and the dry *attiéké* and allow to sit for about 15 minutes so the *attiéké* absorbs the water. After all the water has been absorbed, put into the top of a steamer insert and place over boiling water and steam, covered, for several minutes, fluffing with a fork once or twice during the steaming process.

To serve: *Attiéké* may be eaten warm or at room temperature, and can replace rice with any stew. It pairs especially well with Grilled Tilapia (page 134) served with Ghanaian Basic Tomato Gravy (page 38), and/or Fresh Pepper Sauce (page 168).

Ivorians feel about dry *attiéké* the way many North Americans feel about instant mashed potatoes: not the real thing. My daughter Masi, married to an Ivorian and living in New York City, explains her solution: "The *acheke* we eat comes from family members who bring it here from Abidjan. We keep the balls of *acheke* in the freezer so they last longer. When defrosted, you break it up with your fingers so it's not clumpy and sprinkle some water on top and microwave with a moist paper towel over. Once you take it out of the microwave you should eat it right away or it will get crusty."

Rice Balls
Omo Tuo

Makes 3 to 4 servings (2 balls each)

These are oh-so-easy-to-make and go well with almost any West African soup, but especially Chicken Peanut Soup (page 104).

Ingredients

1 cup any white rice (short-grain rice is preferred)

½ teaspoon salt

Directions

1. Bring the rice, 3 to 4 cups of water, and salt to a boil in a large heavy pot. Turn down the heat to low, cover, and allow the rice to cook 15 to 20 minutes. If necessary, take off the lid and let it cook down another 5 to 10 minutes. When the rice is cooked but not completely dry, turn off the heat and let it sit until it is cool enough to handle.
2. Using a potato masher, a strong wooden spoon, a heavy glass, or an *apotoriwa* (a wooden mashing tool wonderfully easy to hold and use), mash the rice until it is fairly smooth.
3. Fill a cup with cold water and place next to the pan. Wet hands with the cold water, then dip an ice cream scoop or spoon into the water and scoop up enough rice to shape into a ball, like a snowball. Squeeze the ball tightly with your hands to pack the rice together well. If the ball will not stick together, put the rice back on the stove to dry it out slightly.

Variations:

To make these using an electric rice cooker, decrease the water to 2½ to 3 cups and turn off the cooker when the rice is cooked and most of the water is gone.

Make the rice balls using brown rice. Brown rice balls are somewhat heavier. Use more water and allow a longer cooking time.

To serve: Small balls may replace bread when served as a first course (e.g., with a light soup). Use a small spoon or melon baller (dipped in water first) to scoop out the rice and then shape tiny balls and serve 2 or 3 in each bowl of soup.

Make ahead: Rice balls can be made ahead of time and warmed in the oven or microwave (covered with a damp paper towel) or a steamer just before serving. They are also easily frozen.

Coconut Rice

Makes 6 to 8 servings

Cooking rice with coconut milk and/or coconut cream elevates humble rice to something special. This is a foolproof way to cook a quantity of rice in the oven, but works equally well made in a rice cooker for the family or a small group of guests. A convenient alternative is to use a canned unsweetened coconut milk. An electric rice cooker is my preferred way to cook rice, especially when guests are around, since it frees up the stovetop and needs no attention while cooking.

Ingredients

3 cups white rice (any type, prefer-ably long grain, such as basmati or jasmine)

1½ cups coconut milk with cream, canned or homemade (see page 28 for directions for making coconut milk)

3½ to 4 cups water (a little more if cooking on the stovetop)

1 teaspoon salt (optional)

Directions for rice-cooker

Rinse the rice, if necessary. Put all the ingredients in the rice cooker, cover, turn on and leave until cooked. Many rice cookers will keep the rice warm for up to 2 hours without burning it.

Directions for stovetop

Rinse the rice, if necessary. Place all ingredients in a large cooking pot. Turn the heat on to high and bring to a boil. Immediately turn the heat down to low and cover, making sure the rice does not boil over as the heat lowers. Allow to simmer about 20 minutes, or until cooked. Avoid lifting the lid too soon, but add a little water near the end if the rice becomes too dry before the grains are tender.

To serve: Fluff rice with a fork before serving. Serve with any stew as a side dish.

Variations:

To dress the rice up, increase the proportion of coconut milk and/or coconut cream; add ½ to 1 teaspoon of turmeric or a few strands of saffron to give it a lovely golden tint and add a delicate flavor

Substitute brown rice, but increase the water and cooking times.

Coconut Rice for a Crowd

Makes 96 ½-cup servings

This recipe makes enough for two large 18-inch oval enameled roasting pans with covers and serves up to 96 people. The recipe can easily be halved. This is the only way I am able to successfully prepare large quantities of rice without having it go mushy on me as it does when cooked on a stovetop.

Ingredients

16 cups any long-grain white rice, washed, if necessary

2 teaspoons turmeric for a faint yellow tint (or more if a more pronounced color is desired)

2 (13- to 15-ounce) cans coconut milk with cream (or milk and cream from 2 coconuts, see page 28)

1½ tablespoons salt

Directions

1. Preheat oven to 375 degrees F. Bring 32 cups of water to a boil on the stovetop in one or two large pots (if using turmeric, add to the water at this point).
2. Add the coconut milk/cream and salt to the water on the stove and stir.
3. Put half of the rice in each of 2 large roasting pans.
4. Open the preheated oven, pull out the racks and place the pans on them. Pour 14 to 15 cups of the hot water mixture into each pan, reserving the rest. Stir and cover immediately with lids, gently push in the racks and close the oven.
5. After 30 minutes, reheat any water mixture still in the pan on the stove. Open the oven door, pull out the rack, and carefully lift the roasting pan lids (tilting them away from you to avoid the steam) and stir. Add more water mixture if necessary. Replace the lids and allow the rice to finish cooking, about 15 to 30 more minutes (total cooking time is 45 to 60 minutes).
6. Once the rice is tender, if it is too wet, remove the lids near the end of the cooking to allow it to dry some.

Stiff Millet Porridge American-style
Tuo Zaafi (TZ)

Makes 3 ½-cup servings

Tuo Zaafi, commonly called "*TZ*" ("tee zed," said to mean "very hot" in Hausa and Dagbani) is a classic dish from Northern Ghana. This staple starch is to many northern Ghanaians what *fufu* is to many Akans, or *kenkey* is to many Ga people. Along with *Omo Tuo* (Rice Balls, page 179), it is a preferred standard carbohydrate-based accompaniment that goes with many of the soups and sauces of Northern Ghana. *TZ* is a thick porridge with many variations: it can be made from millet, "guinea corn" (sorghum), maize, and/or cassava mixtures. The grain can be fermented or not. It tends to be less elastic than *fufu*, and ranges in consistency from soft like *banku* to loaf-like that can be cut with a knife. It is very creamy and smooth, with a mild flavor.

During a visit to Tamale, Mrs. Comfort Awu Akor and her daughter Amadu George Shetu demonstrated making both this dish and a sesame soup to accompany it (see page 111). We made our *TZ* from *fonio* but this adapted recipe is made with gluten-free millet flour which is more easily available in the U.S.

Ingredients
1 cup millet flour

¼ to ½ teaspoon salt (optional)

Directions
1. In a saucepan with a handle, using a whisk mix 2 cups water and 1 cup millet flour and the salt, if desired, until there are no lumps.
2. On medium heat, cook the millet mixture, stirring constantly with the whisk for about 5 minutes, or until it thickens. Switch to a stirring stick or sturdy wooden spoon and cook another 5 minutes over medium heat, stirring and turning the porridge constantly.
3. Lower the heat to low, cover the pan, and let the mixture cook another 10 to 15 minutes without stirring. Do check to see that it is not burning though it will likely scorch slightly. If worried, heat ⅓ cup water in a microwave and pour the water around the outside edge of the porridge without stirring it in.
4. After the porridge has been on the heat about 20 minutes, it should form a soft, somewhat sticky mass, but should keep its shape. It will harden as it cools.

To serve:
There are a variety of options:

Wet the inside of a serving bowl, along with a large spoon, the stirring stick, and/or your hands. Spoon the mixture into the bowl, press it down slightly to mold it into a multi-portion size (or shape it into individual servings in small bowls). Wet a knife or spoon before cutting or serving.

In Ghana cooks often shape *TZ* into individual balls that are wrapped in plastic bags (as with *Banku*, page 186).

The *TZ* can be ladled into individual serving bowls along with a soup.

Make ahead: If the *TZ* will not be eaten immediately, cover it with plastic wrap to prevent it from drying out and forming a crust. While *fufu* is not served as a leftover, *TZ* definitely may be. In Tamale we ate ours cut into slices the next day.

Variations: For a fresher, possibly less bitter flavor, grind your own whole millet into flour, or grind and substitute whole sorghum. Use corn flour and or cassava flour in place of some or all of the millet flour. Any millet flour may be used.

Much traditional cooking in Ghana is completed seated on stools low to the ground to cook on fires from charcoal or wood, and Ghanaians have developed an ingenious way to hold the cooking pot steady over a fire using iron rods held in place by their feet.

African Yam Fries
Yɛlɛ Ni Ashi

Ironically, these days in restaurants in Accra it often seems easier to buy "potato chips"—what are known as "French fries" in the U.S.—than it is to get freshly made, superb, and tasty indigenous African yam fries. Warning: If making these for a Ghanaian male away from home he might become your friend for life.

Ingredients
Fresh African yams*

Vegetable oil for frying

* Be sure to use African yams NOT American sweet potatoes; they can be found in West African or Caribbean or Latin American markets and are sometimes available in regular supermarkets under the name "name."

Directions
1. Peel and cut the yams as for French fries (as thick or thin as desired), and sprinkle them with salt. (One 1970 Ghanaian cookbook advises cutting the yam into pieces 1-inch square and ½-inch thick.)
2. Fill a deep fryer or cooking pot with enough vegetable oil to cover the yam pieces and heat to about 360 to 375 degrees F. Do not fill the pot over half full to prevent it boiling over when the yams are added.
3. Fry the yam pieces in batches for about 5 minutes (depending on the size of the pieces) or until they are a light creamy yellow and just crisp but cooked through. Remove with a slotted spoon, or lift the basket if using a fryer. Note: If left in the oil even a few minutes longer, they will become increasingly bitter.
4. Drain excess oil on paper towels.

To serve: In Ghana these are served with some *Shito* (page 170), Fresh Pepper Sauce (page 168), or a tasty Ghanaian stew.

BOILED STARCHY VEGETABLES
Ampesi

Frying is a popular cooking method in Ghana, but healthful and simple peeled and boiled starchy vegetables are more commonly served. *Ampesi* is said to have originally been an Akan dish, especially beloved in the Brong-Ahafo region. It consists of a number of cut-up starchy vegetables being boiled together in a large pot. In Ghana I was taught to put the heavier vegetables that take longer to cook on the bottom of the cooking pot, and the faster-cooking ones on top. Then they may be cooked together, removing them as they become tender. The vegetables commonly included are African yams, green plantains, ripe plantains, white sweet potatoes, cassava (manioc), and cocoyam (taro). North Americans may add to this potatoes or American yams. *Ampesi* is usually eaten as an accompaniment to stews.

Stirred Fermented Corn Dough
Banku

Makes 4 servings

Fermented corn dough can either be homemade, bought frozen, or prepared from a powder mix. If using powdered "instant" *banku*, first add water to make the dough, then proceed as with already prepared dough.

Ingredients

1½ cups homemade fermented corn dough (page 31) with any mold scraped off, or frozen packaged *banku* dough (corn and cassava), defrosted

1 teaspoon salt

Banku is commonly shaped into balls using plastic wrap (placing the plastic wrap over a bowl, adding a large spoonful of dough, wrapping one side of the plastic wrap over a side and then folding over the other side, holding and twisting both edges and rotating the packet to make a smooth ball). While this is common practice in Ghana to keep the balls sanitary, my materials scientist husband believes it to be an unhealthy practice, so I recommend forming the balls without plastic wrap. Instead, form the balls by wetting a calabash or flat bowl, add the cooked *banku* and shape it into a smooth rounded loaf by shaking and turning the bowl.

Directions

1. In a 3-quart saucepan with a handle, mix the dough with 1½ cups water by hand or with a wire whisk to make a smooth paste. Mix in the salt.
2. Put on the stove to heat on medium-high, stirring constantly with the whisk or with a stirring stick or very strong wooden spoon. After 5 minutes the mixture should begin to thicken. Lower the heat to medium and switch over to a stirring stick or wooden spoon if previously using a whisk.
3. Continue to cook, stirring constantly to keep it from forming lumps, scraping the bottom of the pan and turning the dough as it cooks, also pressing it against the sides of the pan. After another 5 minutes, turn the heat to low and continue stirring and turning. Scrape the spoon against the side of the saucepan occasionally and mix the scrapings into the dough. If necessary, add a little water around the edges of the pan to keep it from scorching, and/or turn down the heat.
4. The *banku* should be quite stiff within 15 to 20 minutes on the stove. Remove it from the heat and let it sit a few minutes. When it is cool enough to handle, wet your hands and shape the *banku* into one large or several small loaves for individual servings.

To serve: *Banku* is usually eaten warm or luke-warm. It is a classic accompaniment to eggplant and okra stews (pages 117 and 118), as well as Grilled Tilapia (page 134). It is also eaten with Pepper Sauce (page 168) and/or *Shito* (page 170).

Steamed Fermented Corn Dough
Ga Kenkey

Makes about 4 servings (4 balls)

Ghana's popular steamed fermented corn dough ball is commonly called *kenkey* (or *dokono, dokon, kokui, tim,* or *komi.*) *Kenkey* is Ghana's challenge to polenta and comes in numerous versions. Most common are the Ga and Fante styles. I first lived in Nungua along the coast of Ghana where Ga *kenkey* predominates, so that is my preference. In contrast, Fante *kenkey* is unsalted, steamed in plantain leaves rather than cornhusks, and shaped differently. Ga *kenkey* is made from a starter dough like that used for *banku*. However, while *banku* is very soft, *kenkey* is steamed (or sometimes boiled) to make a much firmer ball that can be sliced or served whole.

Ingredients

3 cups of corn flour fermented into corn dough (see page 31)

1 teaspoon salt

8 to 16 (depending on size) dried corn husks for wrapping the dough (available where Latin ingredients are sold)

> Ghanaians abroad often substitute aluminum foil or plastic wrap for the corn husks, but the foil and wrap do not allow the balls to steam properly and you lose the wonderful delicate flavor imparted by the corn husks.

Directions

Prepare corn husks:

1. Before preparing the dough for steaming, put the dried cornhusks in a bowl of warm water to soften for about 30 minutes or until they are pliable. Push them under the water to make sure they are covered.

Prepare the "aflata":

2. In a 3-quart saucepan mix 2 cups of water with half of the dough and the salt. Cook the mixture over medium heat for about 10 minutes, stirring constantly with a heavy wooden spoon or paddle, being careful not to scorch or burn it. The dough will thicken in about 5 minutes, and by 10 minutes will be quite thick. If it gets too thick and hard to stir, add a little water around the outside of the pan to warm, and then stir it into the dough. Remove the pan from the heat and stir in the uncooked portion of the corn dough, mixing them together well.

Shape and wrap the balls:

3. To form the balls of dough, Ghanaians would just hold the dough (about ¼ of it) in one hand and expertly shape it into a ball by repeatedly tossing it up a little and turning it in moistened hands. For the rest of us it is easier and safer to wet one's hands and use both to shape the ball.
4. Place the dough ball on top of a good-sized softened corn husk with no tears or holes, with the "fat" end facing the bottom. Holding

(continued on next page)

Steamed Fermented Corn Dough (continued)
Ga Kenkey

the dough ball and softened corn husk in one hand, place another corn husk over the uncovered part of the dough ball, making sure that it overlaps at least ¼ inch over the previous husk. Repeat the process with additional corn husks if necessary until the ball is covered.

5. Twist the narrow ends (at the top) of the corn husks together tightly and poke a hole in the topside of the dough by pushing the corn husks apart at a place where they overlap, then push the twisted end into the ball of dough and cover it with the soft dough and return the corn husks to the overlapped position. Do the same thing for the other end (this is trickier because the husks are thicker). Repeat with remaining dough and corn husks to make four *kenkey* balls..

Steam the *kenkey*:

6. Put a steamer insert into a stainless steel pot with boiling water beneath it and place the balls in the steamer. Steam them for about 60 minutes, adding a little water as necessary. When removing the balls from the pot let them cool slightly before unwrapping them, to avoid scalding yourself.

To serve: *Kenkey* is best served warm. Classic accompaniments include Stuffed Fried Fish (*Kenam*, page 139), Fresh Pepper Sauce (page 168), and/or the classic *Shito* (page 170). *Kenkey* and a stew or fried fish and pepper sauce is a great meal to eat with your hands, but *kenkey* is also served sliced as a side accompaniment to a stew. It is also used to make Iced *Kenkey* (page 199).

Make ahead: *Kenkey* can be steamed and stored in the refrigerator or frozen and thawed.

Cooked Corn and Cassava Dough
Akple

The only difficulty in preparing *akple* is obtaining corn dough and cassava dough. A recipe for making the cassava dough is found on page 31 and instructions for preparing unfermented corn dough are included here. The proportions for making *akple* are one-third cassava dough to two-thirds corn dough. Here is a small recipe to try before increasing the amounts.

Ingredients

1 cup white stone-ground cornmeal

1 teaspoon cornstarch

½ cup cassava dough (page 31)

A rounded ⅛ teaspoon salt

Note: As more and more frozen foods from Ghana are imported, it may now be possible to find frozen versions of both corn and cassava dough in specialty West African or international markets.

Directions
Make the corn dough:

1. Blend the cornmeal in an electric blender to make it a little finer. Mix the cornmeal in a bowl with the cornstarch. Mix ½ cup of water into the cornmeal.

Prepare the *akple*:

2. Mix together the ½ cup of cassava dough with 1 cup of corn dough in a saucepan along with ½ cup of water and the salt to get a smooth creamy mixture. A nice heavy wooden spoon or stirring stick works well.
3. Put the mixture on the stove on medium heat and stir as it heats. Add another ½ cup of water all at once and continue stirring until it forms a solid mass, 10 to 15 minutes. Do not allow the dough to become lumpy or scorch on the bottom. Turn it while stirring.
4. When the mixture is fairly solid and no longer "wet" looking, take a calabash or bowl, wet it thoroughly and put a spoonful of the dough into the calabash/bowl and shaking it vigorously roll the dough inside into a circle or oval shape. Repeat with the rest of the dough.

To serve: Originally, *Akple* was eaten mainly with soup like *Fetri Detsi* (Ewe-style Light Okra Soup with Chicken, page 96) but it goes well with many other dishes, such as Ghana Fried Fish (*Kenam*, page 138) served with Fresh Pepper Sauce (page 168) and/or *Shito* (page 170), Palaver Sauce (page 128), or an eggplant stew (pages 117 and 118).

FUFU

"Fufu" is an iconic West African carbohydrate dish. Images of two women (or a woman and a child)—one standing upright and holding a long wooden pestle while she pounds, with a woman seated on a low stool who turns something in the mortar—are often used to epitomize the food culture of places throughout the region. But what is in the mortar varies widely, and what is called *fufu* and the preparation techniques also vary from place to place and country to country. Even within Ghana, *fufu* varies. Throughout much of southern Ghana it is prepared from individual starches or combinations of plantain/cassava/cocoyam/yam peeled, boiled, and then pounded into heavy elastic dumplings. In Northern Ghana it may be made solely from African yams, and using a differently shaped wooden mortar, with not one person, as in other parts of Ghana, but several people pounding together. In Fante regions, the plantains may be ripe, not green. However, in parts of Central Africa, *fufu* is prepared from white corn flour, cassava corn flour, or a combination. Nigeria has an "oatmeal" *fufu*. In Ghana there is no substitute for freshly pounded *fufu*. Some say it is an acquired taste, particularly because one does not chew the *fufu*, and it is generally eaten with the hands. With me, it was love at first swallow. *Fufu* is perceived as a "heavy" meal and allows a Ghanaian to reach satiety, which is why rich desserts are so seldom considered necessary to a meal. Also, "soup and *fufu*" seems more often to be eaten at the afternoon meal than the evenings in contemporary society, likely because it is deemed too heavy to digest just before sleeping.

Ghana-style Dumplings
Fufu

Makes 2 to 3 servings

I have never succeeded in preparing "real" *fufu* in the U.S., despite once bringing a Ghanaian mortar and pestle with me. Experiments with blenders, food processors, microwaves, and "make-do" mortars and pestles also failed. So in the U.S., Ghana-style *fufu* is usually made from boxed *fufu* powder, readily available in many international or African markets. There are various versions, generally called plantain and cocoyam flour, yam and plantain flour, or plain yam *fufu* flour. All I have seen also include potato granules. While *fufu* may be prepared on a stovetop, the easiest way is to use a microwave, except for large batches. Note that serving sizes in Ghana are much larger than recommended for North Americans.

Ingredients

1 cup Ghanaian boxed *fufu* flour, any type

To form the *fufu* into balls, Ghanaians sometimes wet a calabash or a bowl, put a lump of *fufu* in the calabash and shake it around until it forms an oval ball. Sometimes working around the edges, they deftly pull the *fufu* from the outside into the center to make a smooth surface when it is turned out of the bowl or calabash. They make it look much easier than it actually is.

Directions for microwave

1. In a large, round glass or ceramic bowl, pitcher, or pan, mix the *fufu* flour with 2 cups water, stirring with your hand, a whisk, or a spoon to dissolve all the lumps. Microwave uncovered on high for 3 minutes.

2. Remove the container, using potholders if necessary. Stir the *fufu* with a strong wooden spoon or stirring stick for 1 to 2 minutes, smashing any lumps and mixing the *fufu* from the outside towards the center in a folding motion similar to the way one folds whipped cream into a batter, only the *fufu* is much thicker and harder to stir and turn.

3. Return the *fufu* to the microwave oven and cook on high for 3 minutes. Remove the bowl and repeat the stirring process. If the *fufu* seems dry, sprinkle up to ⅓ cup of water over it but do not mix it in. Return the *fufu* to the microwave oven for another 3 minutes. Allow the *fufu* to sit briefly, then pour off any extra water that remains on top (if added)—do not mix it into the *fufu*.

4. Wet a bowl, spoon, or your hands, and form *fufu* balls the desired size and place onto a moistened plate or platter to keep them from sticking. The *fufu* will be hot, so be careful if using your hands. (A good size is about ¾ of a cup for those familiar with *fufu*, smaller for those just trying it.)

(continued on next page)

Ghana-Style Dumplings (continued)
Fufu

Fufu should be eaten immediately after making it. People in Ghana would consider it an insult if they were offered "left-over" *fufu* the next day.

The traditional way to eat *fufu* is using your right hand only, tear off a small piece using your thumb, index finger, and one or two adjoining fingers. Next make a small indentation with your thumb, scoop up some of the soup and put the whole thing into your mouth and swallow it without chewing. The peristaltic motion as it slides down your throat is reminiscent of swallowing oysters.

Directions for stovetop

1. Mix the *fufu* powder with 2 cups of cold water in a saucepan. Put it on the stovetop on medium heat, stir constantly with a heavy wooden spoon or stirring stick as it heats and begins to thicken.
2. Continue turning the *fufu*, stirring from the inside to the outside. A little additional water may be added as necessary by pouring it around the outside edges of the pan, and lowering the heat, to keep the *fufu* from scorching. It will take a strong arm and about 20 minutes to reach the proper elasticity. Form into balls as described in Step 4 above.

Note: Different people prefer different textures to the *fufu*—some like it softer or and some like it harder. You can experiment with increasing the water, or cooking for another few minutes.

To serve:

After forming into balls, put the *fufu* into individual bowls and ladle a little soup over. Alternatively, people may help themselves to *fufu* and then have the soup served. (If you or the diners are cutting larger balls of *fufu* into smaller servings, have a spoon in a cup of water nearby to wet the spoon before cutting and serving the *fufu* to prevent it from sticking.) In restaurants, the soup and *fufu* are served together.

While "soup and *fufu*" is a common meal by itself, for a non-traditional twist one may serve two or three mini teaspoon-size balls of *fufu* in a light soup as a first course to a meal.

Variation: If you cannot find *fufu* flour, substitute 1 cup potato starch flour mixed with 2 cups instant mashed potatoes and 4 cups of water. Cook as described above.

BREAKFAST & BEVERAGES

Rice Water

Makes 2 to 4 servings

This is a light and easy-to-prepare/easy-to-digest Ghanaian gluten-free porridge/drink. It is just rice cooked with extra water. While rice water is an ordinary breakfast porridge for anyone, in Ghana it is especially recommended for children and invalids, especially when made thinner with even more water or richer with extra milk. The texture differs from North American "Cream of Rice" cereal, which is made from ground rice.

Ingredients
1 cup any white rice

½ teaspoon salt (or to taste)

Directions
Put 4 cups water, rice, and salt in a saucepan. Bring the water to a boil, lower the heat, and simmer until the rice is tender and begins to disintegrate, about 30 minutes. Add more water if necessary. The thickness varies according to taste, but should be easily pourable.

To serve: Rice water can be served in a bowl or a cup, with milk and sugar or honey added to taste. I first learned to drink it with canned evaporated milk. More recently people add powdered whole milk (like Nestle's NIDO) or fresh milk. Coconut milk or soy milk also works well. The amounts of each can be adjusted to taste. Rice water can be served hot, warm, at room temperature, or cold. Add flavorings (cinnamon, nutmeg, etc.) to taste, along with sugar, chopped nuts, and/or coconut.

Corn Porridge
Koko

Makes 4 servings

This simple and common porridge is made almost the same way as "Tom Brown" (page 197). Instead of toasted corn flour this version uses unfermented corn dough made (outside of Ghana) by simply adding a cup of water to a cup of white finely stoneground cornmeal. In busy urban areas of Ghana, a farseeing entrepreneur, Albert Osei, founded the popular "Koko King" company, pioneering the advent of portable cups of healthy, inexpensive but hygienically prepared breakfast porridges that people can purchase on their way to work or school. This porridge is on the menu.

Ingredients
1 cup white stoneground cornmeal, pulsed for a few minutes in electric blender to make finer

½ to 1 teaspoon salt (or to taste)

Directions
1. Bring 1½ cups water to a boil in a saucepan.
2. While it heats, in a mixing bowl mix the cornmeal with 2 cups of water. (For a finer texture, often appreciated in Ghana, pour the mixture through a fine strainer into another bowl to strain out the larger pieces of the chaff.)
3. Add the salt to the boiling water and slowly stir in the corn dough mixture, stirring until thickened.

To serve: Serve warm with desired flavorings, e.g. sugar, honey, chopped nuts, coconut, nutmeg, any milk, fresh lemongrass, etc.

Variation:
Koko is also made with Fermented Corn Dough (*Banku* Dough, page 31). The texture will be slightly different, though, since the fermented corn dough is not as finely ground as in Ghana.

Millet Porridge
Use millet flour instead of corn flour: first mix a cup of millet flour with 1½ to 2 cups of water and then proceed as above.

Hausa Spiced Porridge
Hausa Koko

Makes 2 to 3 servings

Porridge is a popular Ghanaian breakfast. While the basic *Koko* (page 195) is often made from finely ground white corn flour, there is a spiced version from the North called *Hausa koko,* which is classically made from fermented millet or sorghum, though it may also be made from fermented corn. In Ghana it is often made with early pearl millet. Millet flour may be purchased from an African market, or substitute millet available in health food or international markets.

The grain is soaked, ground with ginger, chili pepper, cloves, and *hwentia*, and fermented, then cooked with salt and enough water to make a clear, thin porridge. It is possible to soak and grind and ferment one's own millet and spices, but a simpler method is simply to buy millet flour and make an unfermented version using easily available spices. This is an American "make-do" version of *Hausa koko*.

Ingredients

1 (½-inch) piece fresh ginger, coarsely chopped

½ cup millet flour

¼ teaspoon ground cloves

⅛ teaspoon dried ground red pepper (or to taste)

⅛ to ¼ teaspoon finely ground black pepper or ground *hwentia* (or to taste)

¼ to ½ teaspoon salt

NOTE: As with *Fufu* (page 190), the time-consuming process of making this porridge has been replaced by a packaged powder now available online. The procedure with the powder is simply to add cold water to mix the powder and then mix with boiling water while stirring with a stirring stick.

Directions

1. Put the ginger in a small blender with ½ cup water and pulse to puree. Set aside.
2. Mix the millet flour in a saucepan with 1½ cups water using a whisk.
3. Strain the pureed ginger mixture into the millet through a tea strainer, pressing a spoon or your fingers against the ginger to remove as much liquid as possible. Discard the dregs.
4. Add the seasonings to the millet mixture and stir.
5. Bring 2 cups of water to a boil (in a microwave, if available) and set near the saucepan.
6. Over medium-high heat, bring the millet mixture to a boil, stirring a few times with a whisk to prevent lumps forming for the first 2 minutes, then reduce the heat to medium, and stir constantly. Within about 6 minutes, the porridge will come to a boil and thicken. Lower heat and continue stirring, and gradually add as much of the hot water as needed to achieve the desired consistency of porridge. *Hausa koko* is usually somewhat thin and very smooth.

Variation:

For a milder version, substitute ⅛ teaspoon of dried ginger for the fresh ginger and use just a pinch of the cloves and peppers.

To serve: This porridge is traditionally served with Ghanaian doughnuts (*bofrot*, pages 84 and 86) or Black-eyed Pea Fritters (*Akara*, page 78). While eaten as a breakfast food and served to invalids since it is easily digestible, this also makes a warming, satisfying afternoon snack. Add sweetener and evaporated or any milk as desired.

Toasted Corn Flour Porridge
"Tom Brown" / Ablemamu

Makes 2 servings

The basic "Tom Brown" porridge recipe is quite simple. While it can be made from various starches or combinations of ground grains, it is generally made from toasted corn flour. The hardest part is getting the right corn flour (see page 29 for an explanation and instructions for toasting). This is a favorite student breakfast food I remember fondly from my days teaching at a boarding school in Nungua, along the coast of Ghana.

Ingredients
½ cup Toasted Corn Flour
  (*Ablemamu*, page 29)

¼ teaspoon salt

Directions
1. Bring ½ cup of water to a boil in a saucepan.
2. While the water heats, put the toasted corn flour, salt, and ½ cup water in a bowl and mix thoroughly using a whisk.
3. When the water in the pan boils, reduce the heat to low and slowly stir in the batter. It will thicken and cook in a couple of minutes. Its consistency is creamier and lighter than oatmeal.

To serve: This porridge is great with honey or sugar, evaporated or any milk, and/or chopped peanuts on top.

Ewe Corn Porridge
Koklui

This makes a nice morning meal or evening snack.

Ingredients
Heaping ½ cup slightly fermented white corn dough (*Banku*, page 31)

½ teaspoon salt (or to taste; use less if the corn dough is very sour)

Directions
1. Rub the corn dough between your hands or through a coarse sieve into a bowl or pan, and then shake it in a circular motion until it is the size of dry couscous.
2. Bring 2 cups of water to a boil.
3. Stir the corn dough into the boiling water. If it is too thick, add about ½ cup of hot water. It is ready almost immediately. Stir in the salt.

Variations:
Add a few leaves of lemongrass.

Add some nutmeg, sugar, or honey.

Barbara makes her own "at home for myself" dessert by making the porridge thicker and adding sugar after the salt, then adding a little liquor such as sweet red wine, chilling it and folding in a little cream.

Iced Kenkey

Makes 1 to 2 servings

When I was a child growing up in California, my Tennessee-born mother sometimes snacked on graham crackers crumbled into a bowl and covered with milk. Similarly, a snack my late sister-in-law Afua used to enjoy when she attended the boarding school where I taught in Nungua was called "iced" or "ice" *kenkey*. She simply crumbled part of a ball of Ga *kenkey* with her fingers into a cup and added cold water and "plenty" of evaporated milk and sugar, stirred it well, and drank/ate it from a large mug. We had no refrigerator, and if we had I am sure she would have used ice water to prepare it.

I checked in with a couple of Ghanaians—my sister-in-law Theodora, and my friend Julia—to make sure of the recipe. Julia insists that "iced *kenkey*" made from Fante *kenkey* tastes superior to that from other types of *kenkey*. Iced *kenkey* is quick and easy to make when *kenkey* is on hand. It is also a popular inexpensive snack/street food. It can tide people over until they can have a more filling meal. Iced *kenkey* is also used as a weaning food for children.

Ingredients

1 cup *Ga Kenkey* (page 187)

½ cup cold water

⅓ cup evaporated or other milk (or to taste)

1 tablespoon sugar (or to taste)

Directions

1. Break off a cup of *kenkey* from a ball, crumbling it into pieces in a bowl using your fingers, or a fork to help break it up. Add the cold water and mix well.
2. Pour mixture into one or two mugs and add milk and sugar to taste, beginning with about ⅓ cup of evaporated milk or other milk and 1 tablespoon of sugar.

To serve: Iced *kenkey* is roughly the consistency of Rice Water (page 194), and can be drunk or eaten with a spoon. Sometimes unsalted roasted peanuts are sprinkled over it.

TROPICAL FRUIT SMOOTHIES

There is a treat that rarely fails to elicit enthusiasm in Ghana: the versatile, always-delicious, fruit smoothie. While this is not a traditional class of recipes, it is one easily embraced by Ghanaians—another example of their creativity and openness to experimentation. The country possesses a wealth of tropical fruits: pineapple, watermelon, banana, mango, avocado, papaya, guava, soursop, orange, lemon, lime, passion fruit, grapefruit, etc. and flavorings are abundant. A fruit smoothie is a healthful, satisfying, energizing, cooling drink.

Fruit smoothies are also user-friendly: any combination of fruits or vegetables, liquids, and flavorings can be mixed together in whatever proportions desired. The combination of fruits depends completely on one's own preferences. While fruit drinks can be blended completely from fresh, unfrozen fruit, nothing quite compares to a thirst-quenching smoothie made from frozen fruit and/or ice or fruit juice "ice" cubes.

Best served immediately after making, smoothies are commonly poured into a tall glass, sipped through a fat straw, or drunk from a glass. If very thick they can be eaten with a spoon, like a dessert. Smoothies go well at any time: as a power-packed way to start the day, a snack any time, or an end to a meal.

Gari Soaking
Gari-Potowye

This recipe is similar to Iced *Kenkey* (page 199). It is another snack/porridge-type food that is inexpensive, quick, and easy to make. I learned to call it "*gari soak*" or "*gari soaking*." My sister-in-law, Theodora, tells me its Fante name is "*gari-potowye*." People often use it to quickly quench their thirst or hunger until they can make or eat something more filling. In other words, it is another Ghanaian convenience food made from cassava meal.

Ingredients
¼ to ⅓ cup dry gari per serving (*Ghanaians might use up to twice that much*)

¼ to ½ cup cold or iced water

Milk and sweetener as desired

Directions
1. Rinse the *gari* in a bowl of water a couple of times, pouring the water, chaff, and impurities off each time.
2. After rinsing the *gari*, add the ¼ to ½ cup cold or iced water and let mixture sit to thicken. (If adding milk, use the lower amount of water. You can always add more milk or water if the mixture is too thick after it sits for a few minutes. Conversely, if it is too thin, a little more *gari* can always be sprinkled in.)

To serve: My sister-in-law likes her *gari-potowye* best after refrigerating it for about 30 minutes so it softens. As with iced *kenkey*, one may add roasted peanuts, milk, and sugar or other sweetener to taste. *Gari-potowye* is usually eaten with a spoon, not drunk. It can be prepared more or less thick, crisper or soggier, according to taste.

Ghana-Inspired Hot Chocolate

Makes 1 serving

Both cocoa and cassava are abundant in Ghana. The country is a world-class cocoa producer, and cassava is a dietary staple. The availability of the two, and a love of chocolate in all forms, inspired this recipe. While drinking "hot chocolate" was not a part of traditional culture, chocolate-flavored beverages and foods are making their way into the Ghanaian diet. Blending chocolate with cassava starch (tapioca) produces a wonderful mixture, thick enough to eat with a spoon, but thin enough to drink. Here is a simple recipe to prepare in a microwave oven that is luxuriously rich, smooth, creamy, and satisfying.

Ingredients

12 to 16 ounces any type milk (if using evaporated milk dilute with some water)

2 heaping teaspoons tapioca starch

1 ounce dark chocolate with a high percentage of cocoa

Sugar or sweetener to taste

Directions

1. Fill a generous mug with milk and use a fork or small whisk to mix in the tapioca starch until it is dissolved. Heat on high in a microwave for 2 minutes, stirring every 30 seconds to ensure no lumps form as it thickens.
2. Add the chocolate to the milk and whisk while it melts. Return mug to the microwave and heat on high for 30 seconds and then whisk again. Taste and add sweetener, if desired, and stir again.
3. Return it to the microwave for 30 seconds. If the mixture is not thick enough, heat for another 30 seconds.

To serve: For a special touch, garnish with a little whipped cream and grated chocolate.

Variations:

This can be made on a stovetop on medium heat (and quantities increased).

Try making with coconut milk/water, or flavorings like vanilla, mint, or lemongrass.

Taking a cue from Mexico's *atole*, one might also experiment with thickening the chocolate milk with cornstarch.

Ginger Beer

Makes 8 to 10 servings

Here is a simple recipe for a soft drink popular throughout sub-Saharan Africa. Ginger beer is often carbonated and made with yeast, but this version skips that step. For bubbles, use seltzer (carbonated) water to dilute the concentrate to taste. It is always delightful when folks outside of Ghana shake their heads and say with awe: "You made this from scratch?"

Ingredients

4 to 8 ounces peeled fresh ginger, amount depending on strength desired

2 cup hot/boiling water

½ to ¾ cup sugar (or to taste)

2 tablespoons lime or lemon juice

6 cloves

Small piece cinnamon stick (¼ of a short stick; optional)

Special equipment
Cheesecloth

Variations:

Increase or decrease the ginger or sugar or replace the sugar with honey.

Substitute fresh pineapple chunks for the cloves and cinnamon, and blend them with the original chopped ginger.

If an electric blender is not available, the ginger may be grated and mashed with a spoon or mashing tool, rather than blended.

Directions

1. Chop the peeled ginger into chunks, put into a blender with 1 cup of the hot water and blend for 1 to 2 minutes, pulsing until it is well pureed.
2. Pour the ginger mixture into a nonreactive bowl (e.g., stainless steel, glass, plastic) and pour 1 cup of boiling water over it, then cover the bowl loosely, and let sit for at least 2 hours.
3. Line a strainer or colander with a cheesecloth that has been folded at least twice, and set it over a large nonreactive metal bowl. Slowly pour the ginger mixture through the strainer. Pick up the cheesecloth by the four corners, then twist and squeeze it to remove as much of the water as possible. Discard the ginger "dregs" remaining in the cloth.
4. Add 2 cups of cold water to the liquid in the bowl. (At this point, you can add more water to the concentrate unless it will be diluted with seltzer or other water later.)
5. Add the sugar, stirring to dissolve. Add the lime or lemon juice, cloves, and cinnamon stick (if using) and let the mixture sit for an hour.
6. Remove the spices and carefully pour the ginger beer into a pitcher or covered container. Store, covered, in the refrigerator.

To serve: Serve the ginger beer well chilled (over ice cubes for North Americans) and diluted to taste with water or seltzer water. Plan on ½ cup of ginger beer per serving. Some folks mix in rum, vodka, or other alcohol.

Lemongrass Tea

The scientific name for lemongrass is *cymbopogon*, and the species commonly found in parts of Africa is called *cymbopogon citratus*. Lemongrass (and lemongrass oil) are important herbal remedies in Africa and have been widely studied: the grass is used medicinally to treat illnesses from colds to fever to acne to cancer. It is also said to be an insect and snake repellant. My husband's mother in Ghana always had fresh lemongrass growing in the garden for tea. He remembers loving it with milk and sugar.

Health considerations aside, it can be enjoyed just for its wonderful delicate citrus flavor. Though it pales in comparison to fresh lemongrass, tea can also be made from dried lemongrass available in health food stores.

Ingredients
1 fresh lemongrass stalk for 2 people or 1 tablespoon dried lemongrass per person*

Lemongrass may be found in local grocery stores, where it is likely pricey and may or may not be very fresh, or from online sources, but fresh lemongrass is generally available inexpensively in Asian markets.

Directions
1. If using fresh lemongrass, wash it and trim the ends, peeling away the outer leaves. With a sharp knife, chop the inner leaves and stalk into small pieces to get 2 tablespoons of loosely packed leaves (or more) for each cup. (After making it once, adjust the amount of leaves to taste.)
2. Pour boiling water over the leaves in a cup or teapot and leave it covered for several minutes to steep. Lemongrass tea does not get bitter if it steeps for a long time. If desired, strain out the tea leaves when serving.

To serve: Serve plain or add evaporated or other milk and/or sugar or honey to taste. Some people add a little fresh ginger when brewing it. This tea goes well with Twisted Cakes (page 222) or Ghana-style Doughnuts (*Togbei/Bofrot*, pages 84 and 86).

Variation: Some recipes suggest boiling the lemongrass in the pot with the water, as one would for chai.

In Ghana, lemongrass is also sometimes added as an herb to soups or stews to provide a mild citrusy flavor.

Hibiscus Iced Tea
Bissap / Zobo / Sobolo

Makes about 16 servings

Dried hibiscus flowers make a lovely deep red, refreshing tea popular in Ghana and other parts of West Africa. The smooth, sweet-tangy combination tends to draw rave reviews. Dried hibiscus flowers pair well with other flavorings, like pineapple and mango juices, as well as some alcohol, like rum. Recently, hibiscus has been touted in the West as an "African superfood." It is also claimed to help lower blood pressure. This means the dried flowers are becoming much more widely available. This is the first version I learned at Flair in Ghana, and still make most often. Enjoy! But be forewarned, *bissap* is addictive—not literally, but because it tastes so wonderful.

Ingredients

2 cups dried hibiscus flowers (*bissap* or *roselle*)

¼ cup chopped fresh lemongrass (optional)

1 to 2 cups sugar (to taste)

1 cup pineapple or mango juice

Juice of 1 lemon or lime (optional)

½ teaspoon vanilla extract

Special equipment
Cheesecloth

Directions

1. Bring 5 cups of water to a boil. While it heats, put the dried hibiscus flowers in a metal strainer in the sink and rinse them lightly with water to remove any sand or grit they might contain (the dried flowers bleed immediately, so keep the strainer in the sink).
2. Put the rinsed flowers and lemongrass, if using, into a large stainless steel, ceramic, or other nonreactive bowl, and pour the boiling water over all. Cover the bowl (I use a cheesecloth) and let it steep for at least 4 hours.
3. After 4 hours, bring another 2 cups of water to a boil. (NOTE: If the tea will not be diluted and served with sparkling water, increase this to 4 cups.)
4. Place a strainer over a second large bowl. Empty the hibiscus mixture into it to drain. Return the hibiscus solids to the original bowl and pour the just-boiled water over them. Stir the mixture well, and let it sit 10 minutes this time.
5. Line the strainer with a folded cheesecloth. Pour the hibiscus mixture through the strainer again to add to the previously strained liquid. Pick up the cheesecloth by the ends and twist it tightly to remove as much liquid as possible, being careful not to burn yourself. Discard the solids. (Immediately rinse the cheesecloth out well with cold water or it will stain.)

(continued on next page)

6. Stir in the sugar to taste and the mango or pineapple juice, lemon or lime juice, if using, and vanilla. After all of the sugar has dissolved, carefully pour the liquid into a pitcher or jar, leaving any sediment behind in the bowl. (A funnel works well to fill empty water or soda bottles, if desired.) Cover or cap and chill the *bissap* in the refrigerator.

To serve: Pour into a glass with ice and/or sparkling water, as desired. Garnish with fresh mint leaves, fruit slices, or sugarcane swizzle sticks (page 213).

Variations:

Omit the fruit juice and add additional water to replace it.

Use rum flavoring or a little fresh ginger instead of vanilla.

Substitute other sweetener of choice.

Shandy

Ingredients
Any lager beer (in Ghana, Club or Star), well chilled

Ginger ale or ginger beer (page 203) or other soft drink or carbonated citrus drink, well chilled

Directions
Simply mix together one part lager beer and one part ginger ale (or other carbonated drink). Make sure the drinks are very well chilled first, and use ice cubes if desired. Garnishes might include a slice of lemon or lime, or a sugarcane swizzle stick (page 213).

Chapman

Makes 2 servings

This red, refreshing drink comes by way of Nigeria. It appears the Chapman was popularized in Nigeria during the mid-1960s, and there was even a canned red "Fanta Chapman." Nigeria's influence continues to spread in Ghana, and the Chapman is a user-friendly drink that can make its home anywhere. The Chapman is a popular social drink among Muslim adults in Nigeria who abstain from alcohol. The bitters and cucumber add subtle but distinctive flavors to the drink, and the ice prevents it from excessive sweetness. A hallmark of the drink is its signature red color. The ingredients used to obtain that hue vary, ranging from black currant syrup to pomegranate juice to cranberry juice.

Ingredients

2 to 8 tablespoons grenadine syrup, black currant syrup, pomegranate juice, or cranberry juices

Enough ice cubes to fill 2 tall glasses or beer mugs at least halfway

1 cup chilled lemon-lime soda or similar soft drink

1 cup chilled orange soda

1 lemon (a slice for a garnish, and a good squeeze of juice, about 1 tablespoon, in each glass)

1 lime (a slice or two for garnish, and a good squeeze of juice, about 1 tablespoon, in each glass)

Several unpeeled cucumber slices for each glass

Few shakes of Angostura bitters (less than ⅛ teaspoon in each glass)

Directions

1. Chill all ingredients except for the bitters, and the two tall glasses or mugs.
2. Pour desired amount of grenadine syrup into each chilled glass (1 to 4 tablespoons per glass), then add at least half a glass of ice cubes to each, followed by both sodas and then a squeeze of lemon and/or lime juice (or use either alone).
3. Add the cucumber slices, and top it all off with a few good shakes of the Angostura bitters. Stir.

To serve: Garnish the drinks with lemon, lime, and/or cucumber slices. Along with lime or lemon slices, experiment garnishing with such ingredients as banana or orange slices, mint leaves, or a sugarcane swizzle stick (see page 213).

Variations:

To prevent the ice from melting and watering down the drink, make the ice cubes from additional Sprite, Fanta, or similar drink.

Adjust the proportions of any of the ingredients according to your taste preferences.

Omit either the lemon or lime, or substitute a few orange slices.

Vodka may be added with good success.

Tamarind Drink
Puha

Makes about 16 servings (½ gallon)

TAMARIND

The name of the capital of Senegal, "Dakar," comes from the Wolof word for "tamarind." Tamarind originated not in India but in Africa, even though its common English name comes from the Arabic *tamar-u'l-Hind,* meaning "the date of India." Tamarind is the "secret" ingredient in many barbecue sauces as well as Worcestershire sauce. It has a wonderful sweet-tart flavor that makes it a favorite for drinks throughout Africa.

In Ghana, the tamarind is processed into balls and sold in the outdoor markets, while in the U.S. it is possible to get imported plastic packages of "soft" or "wet" tamarind imported from places like Thailand and India. Not all tamarind has the same flavor, however.

I once spent a pleasant afternoon in Tamale, northern Ghana with the industrious Mrs. Comfort Awu Akor and her daughter, Amadu George Shetu, learning to make a popular tamarind drink known by the Hausa word "*puha.*" Comfort made it in commercial quantities (over 13 gallons) to sell from her home in little plastic bags chilled or frozen, but I have modified the recipe. She used Ashanti pepper but you can use other peppercorns if you cannot find it.

Ingredients

4 ounces (125 grams) packaged tamarind (without salt)

½ teaspoon whole black peppercorns (or 1 teaspoon Ashanti peppercorns/masoro, if available)

1 teaspoon whole cloves

3 tablespoons ground or grated fresh ginger (or to taste)

2 cups sugar (or to taste)

Directions

1. Bring 3 cups of water to a boil, turn off the heat, and add the tamarind. Stir to break it up and then let steep for 1 to 2 hours.
2. After the tamarind has steeped, use clean hands to squeeze it thoroughly to remove the pulp from the seeds.
3. Lightly toast the peppercorns on medium heat for a minute or two in a small frying pan. Crush the peppercorns and cloves using a mortar and pestle.
4. Set a large strainer over another bowl, and pour the tamarind mixture into it, shaking it and using your hand to squeeze as much liquid as possible out of the mixture. In several batches, pour 3 cups of fresh water through the strainer, pressing on the solids to extract juices. Discard the solids in the strainer.

5. Put 3 more cups of water into an empty bowl and add the crushed pepper and cloves and the ginger. Stir them and let them soak in the water for 10 minutes.
6. Using a tea strainer, strain the water with the spices into the tamarind mixture. Discard the spice mixture.
7. Strain the mixture one last time, then put a few cups of the tamarind mixture into a bowl and add about 1¾ cups of sugar (in Ghana they likely use more sugar to make a sweeter drink than I prefer, so add to your taste). Mix it until the sugar dissolves, then add it back into the bowl with the other tamarind mixture and taste for sweetness and adjust as needed.

To serve: Chilled *puha* makes a refreshing drink, which people claim has various health benefits. However, my favorite way to serve *puha* is to freeze it into small cubes and use it as a palate cleanser between dinner courses.

Variation: It is also possible to buy tamarind concentrate, which would eliminate the first two steps.

CANDY, DESSERTS & BAKED GOODS

Peanut Toffee
Nkatie Cake

Makes about 8 servings

Ghanaians use available ingredients to create simple candies or "toffees," sometimes called "cakes." Here is a version made with peanuts. This relative of peanut brittle requires only three simple ingredients: peanuts, sugar, and a little water. You need to watch the caramelizing sugar carefully as it can quickly burn. Also it hardens very quickly once off the heat so work quickly to stir in the peanuts and spread the toffee.

Ingredients

¾ cup dry roasted unsalted peanuts

½ cup sugar

Troubleshooting: If crystals form while heating the sugar the heat was probably too low.

Directions

1. Coarsely crush the peanuts between two pieces of waxed paper or in a plastic or paper bag using a rolling pin or other heavy object like a meat tenderizer. Set aside beside the stovetop.
2. Wet a glass cutting board with a little water or cover with parchment paper or rub with a little margarine or butter and set aside. Also rub a little margarine or butter on a spatula, spoon, and/or knife for spreading and set aside.
3. Put 2 tablespoons of water and the sugar in a heavy 2-quart saucepan and briefly stir to combine. Let it cook on medium heat WITH-OUT STIRRING until the mixture turns light golden brown, about 5 or 6 minutes. Swirl the pan gently once in a while if the burner browns unevenly. As soon as it is a nice light golden brown, *immediately* remove the pan from the heat, *quickly* stir in the peanuts, and *immediately* turn the toffee onto the wet cutting board and use the prepared spatula, knife, or spoon to press the toffee flat. (It will be VERY HOT so do not touch it.)
4. As the candy cools it will harden. Simply break it into pieces, or score it while it is still warm into squares, diamonds, or triangles and break them off after it hardens. Alternatively, take small spoonfuls of the warm, but not hot candy, and roll into balls.

To serve: This makes a delicious treat that also keeps well in an airtight container.

Variations:

Coconut Toffee

Substitute ¾ cup unsweetened fresh or dried grated coconut for the peanuts. Toast the coconut first by spreading out on a baking sheet and baking at 350 degrees F for about 10 to 15 minutes, shaking the pan every few minutes. Then proceed as with the above recipe.

Sesame Toffee

Substitute ¾ cup white sesame seeds for the peanuts. Toast them lightly first in a small skillet, stirring constantly, before proceeding as above.

SUGAR CANE

You are fortunate if you live in an area where fresh sugar cane is available. In Ghana, fresh pieces of sugar cane are chewed as a snack, or cut into small pieces to make a refreshing light natural dessert. The canes can also be peeled and cut into longer sticks to make drink stirrers (swizzle sticks). A delicious example of "more with less."

PAPAYAS (PAWPAWS)

Though papayas likely originated in the Americas, probably southern Mexico and adjacent Central America, they are found all over the tropical and subtropical world, and imported to grocery stores throughout North America and other countries. There are many types, but in Ghana I think of them as the small ones and the big ones. Both taste wonderful when ripe. And papayas (including their seeds) have numerous health benefits to recommend them, especially as a natural source of papain, which aids in digestion, but they also contain loads of vitamins C and E, fiber, potassium, and lycopene. Papayas are technically an herb, and are soft and sweet and juicy with a mild flavor. Their flesh looks somewhat like ripe cantaloupe, and has a similar texture, but the flavor is vivid and delicious.

Papayas are a wonderful addition cut up in fruit salads. But one of my favorite ways to eat them is for breakfast using this "recipe" for **Papayas with Lime**: slice the papaya and sprinkle with a little lime juice. It seems like cheating to offer this as a "recipe" but nature might just provide some of the most delicious desserts. The sweet tartness of the lime enhances the flavor of the papaya wonderfully. All that is needed is a ripe fruit. If one cannot step outside and pick it off a tree, it is possible to buy it green and let it ripen at home. Do not worry if it looks kind of blotchy. It should be mostly yellow and soft to the touch. Some people like the seeds' peppery flavor and sprinkle a few on top as a garnish, or you can just remove them.

Papaya Fool
Pawpaw Fool

Makes 3 to 4 servings

Ghana is not particularly big on desserts. However, a classic fruit-based one in Ghana and other parts of English-speaking countries of Africa is the "fool," which in North America nowadays usually means a mixture of whipped cream and crushed fruit. In Ghana, it means a custard mixed with crushed, and usually cooked, fresh fruit like mango, papaya, or soursop.

I was taught to make this fool using "Bird's custard powder," invented in 1837 by the English chemist Alfred Bird, and containing corn flour, salt, vanilla, and annatto (for color). At Flair we used evaporated milk, as in this recipe. It can also be made including eggs, and/or substituting coconut milk for cow's milk. This recipe is adapted from a papaya fool we made in Barbara's kitchen.

Ingredients
2 cups fresh (peeled and seeded), frozen (defrosted), or canned (drained) papaya chunks

2 tablespoons sugar (or to taste)

½ cup evaporated milk

3½ tablespoons Bird's custard powder

Directions
Prepare papaya:
1. Blend the papaya chunks with ½ cup water in a food processor or blender for a few seconds until pureed.
2. Pour the pureed fruit into a saucepan and stir in the sugar. Heat the papaya mixture and cook for a few minutes, stirring with a whisk. Briefly remove from the heat while preparing the custard.

Prepare custard:
3. Pour ¼ cup of the evaporated milk into a bowl and mix with ¼ cup water and the custard powder.
4. In a microwave, slightly heat the remaining ¼ cup of evaporated milk, about 1½ minutes. (If no microwave is available, heat it slightly in another saucepan on the stove.)
5. Gradually pour the heated milk into the custard mixture, stirring constantly with a whisk to prevent the custard from forming lumps.

Assemble fool:
6. Return the heated papaya puree to the stove on medium heat. Use the whisk to gradually mix the custard into the pureed fruit, stirring vigorously to prevent lumps. Remove a small amount, cool, and taste. Stir in additional sugar for a sweeter flavor, if desired. Bring just to a boil, stirring constantly with a whisk. For a

(continued on next page)

thinner custard, stir in additional water or milk a little at a time—remember the custard will thicken more as it cools. Remove from heat.

7. If there are lumps in the custard, or a smoother custard is desired, pour the mixture through a strainer into individual serving dishes or a serving bowl. When straining, use a spoon to force the pudding through the strainer, and scrape the bottom of the strainer repeatedly. If no straining is desired, spoon the custard directly into the bowl or bowls.

To serve: Serve warm, at room temperature, or chilled. Garnish as desired, e.g., fresh mango and/or papaya (pawpaw) slices, mint leaves, nuts, whipped cream, chopped peanuts or cashews, a little cinnamon, some mandarin orange slices, mango or cherry slices. Voila! Dessert is ready in just a few minutes. Barbara likes to soft freeze her fools sometimes. It is best made the same day it is served.

Variations:
If Bird's Custard Powder is not available, substitute 4 tablespoons of any vanilla cooked custard mix. Don't add any sugar until tasting near the end since American-style custard mixes have added sugar. The fruit could also simply be mixed in with whipped cream for another North American version.

Mango Fool
Follow the same directions as for the papaya fool but substitute mango for the papaya, and reduce the sugar by 1 tablespoon (more may be added near the end, if desired).

TROPICAL FRUIT SALAD

Probably my all-time favorite Ghanaian dessert is a pure, fresh, wonder-ful tropical fruit salad. It dresses up or down with ease, can be prepared and chilled ahead of time, and is a clean, refreshing finish to a meal. It is also basically foolproof. Plus, for those who do not like to spend much time prepping, takeout salad bars in North America mean one can often purchase fresh tropical fruits like melons or pineapple pre-sliced. It is basically a mix-and-match kind of salad. Here are some suggestions of fruits, which may or may not be available, depending on where you live: papaya, mango, pineapple, watermelon, bananas, oranges, tangerines, fresh coconut, soursop (seeded), guava.

Proportions depend upon personal preference. A nicely balanced example would be to use the following amounts of fruit: 1 cup cubed ripe papaya, 1 cup diced ripe mango, 2 seedless navel oranges or tangerines peeled and sectioned, 2 cups diced pineapple, 2 cups diced watermelon, ½ cup coconut water, and ¼ cup thinly sliced fresh coco-nut; add some banana slices just before serving (sprinkle them with lime or lemon juice to keep them from turning brown if necessary).

Some people like to keep the cut up fruit separate until just before serving (my preference); some people like to mix the fruits together to let the flavors blend. Either way is delicious. Best served chilled. this dessert or snack is wonderful by itself, or with "Twisted Cakes" (page 222). Whipped cream or plain or frozen yogurt also go well with it. A whole watermelon or pineapple can also make a "boat" or basket to use as a serving dish. Another lovely way to serve the fruit is to cut it into slices or wedges and arrange them attractively on a platter.

Tiger Nut Pudding

Atadwe Milkye / Ataanme Nmliche / Atagbe Meky

Makes 4 servings

Ghanaians favor tiger nut tubers raw as a snack food. That is one way to eat them—simply spitting out the fiber after chewing them and sucking out the wonderful sweet milky juice. There is also a wonderfully rich pudding in Ghana made from tiger nuts ground together with rice and sugar, then strained repeatedly, cooked, and chilled. Delightful for anyone, but especially a great choice for the lactose intolerant! When I asked Barbara to teach me to make it, she reminisced about serving this pudding to Hassanal Bolkiah, the Sultan of Brunei, and his family in 1999. She served it in crystal champagne glasses with fresh fruit.

Ingredients

1 cup tiger nuts*

¼ cup white rice flour or white rice

⅛ to ½ teaspoon salt (or to taste)

¼ cup sugar (or to taste)

A few drops of food coloring (optional)

Milk or cream for serving (optional)

Special equipment

Cheesecloth

---

* In the past it was necessary in the U.S. to import tiger nuts from Spain, but they are now available through U.S. distributors and can be ordered online

Directions

1. Remove any shriveled or discolored tiger nuts and rinse them well several times. If desired, let them soak in water in a nonreactive bowl (plastic, glass, ceramic, stainless steel) for a few hours in the refrigerator and then rinse and drain again. (If they are very fresh this extra soaking is not necessary.)

2. When ready to make the pudding, drain off the water from the tiger nuts, rinse once more, and drain again.

3. Put the tiger nuts and the white rice (if using; if using rice flour, do not add at this point) into a food processor and add 1 cup of water. Grind/pulse the nuts and rice several minutes until they are fine and powdery (similar to ground almonds). Use a spatula to push down the mixture a few times if necessary.

4. Scrape the ground mixture into a nonreactive bowl. Add another ½ cup water to the bowl of the food processor to rinse as much of the dregs out of the processor as possible. Mix the water into the tiger nut mixture. If using already ground rice flour, stir it in at this point.

5. Place a folded cheesecloth over a metal strainer that is over another bowl. Scrape the tiger nut mixture into the cheesecloth, then gather up the edges of the cheesecloth and twist and squeeze as much liquid as possible into the bowl. Open the cheesecloth (still over the strainer) and pour ⅔ cup of water into the cheesecloth, and then squeeze it again to force

TIGER NUTS

The grass-like sedge, *Cyperus esculentus*, is originally from ancient Egypt. Its nut-like fruits (actually small root vegetables or tubers) grow underground like peanuts/groundnuts and are known in Ghana as "tiger nuts." Though it grows throughout the Americas, including almost every state in the U.S., it has historically been considered an annoying weed or else used as feed or as fish bait. But the U.S. health food market has recently become aware of the many virtues and delights of tiger nuts, ranging from being gluten-free and lactose-free as well as paleo and non-GMO and raw foods diet friendly. They are now available in some supermarkets and health food stores, as well as online. In Ghana they are also said to be considered an aphrodisiac.

In Ghana we added another step after Step 5, using an undyed silk scarf to strain once more, we placed the silk scarf over the strainer and poured the tiger nut mixture through it a final time, squeezing out the liquid as done with the cheesecloth. It was like milking a cow to get all the liquid through the silk and there was very little chaff remaining in the scarf to discard. I have made it both ways and am not convinced this step makes much difference (plus silk scarves might have dyes that run) so this step is optional. Either way, the final product is definitely silky smooth!

as much "milk" as possible into the bowl again. Discard the "dregs" of the nuts.

6. After the final straining, pour the "milk" into a heavy nonreactive metal pot (e.g., stainless steel), and add a very little salt to taste (begin with $1/8$ teaspoon), and about $1/4$ cup sugar (also to taste—Ghanaians tend to prefer less sugar than North Americans). Heat the mixture over medium heat, stirring constantly, but do not let it boil. It will thicken in a few minutes. Immediately remove it from the heat and pour or ladle it into 4 serving dishes.

To serve: For a lovely presentation, use clear glass dishes that will show off three layers nicely. Then first divide the pudding into three other bowls and immediately stir a few drops of red food coloring in one, then a few drops of yellow food coloring in another, leaving one bowl the natural off-white color. Quickly layer the three colors into the glass dishes. Allow to cool, and serve topped with evaporated milk, whipped cream, and/or fresh fruit.

Variations: In Ghana this pudding is sometimes colored and flavored with "black jack," a licorice or aniseed flavoring.

Caramel Custard

Makes 4 to 5 servings

Ghanaians have embraced custards, likely a British influence from Gold Coast days. This classic baked custard dessert is commonly known in Ghana as "caramel custard," but it is also known in other places as caramel flan. It is a stunning, stylish dessert made memorable by the caramel coating the top. The main differences from U.S. versions of this custard include the use of evaporated milk and the greatly reduced amount of sugar. The recipe has two parts: making the caramel and preparing and baking the custard that tops it.

Ingredients
¾ cup sugar, divided

4 eggs

1 teaspoon ground nutmeg

2 teaspoons vanilla extract

1 cup evaporated milk

Directions
Prepare equipment:
1. Before making the custard, place 4 or 5 six-ounce custard cups or a larger soufflé pan (in Ghana we sometimes use small empty evaporated milk cans) near the stove so they are ready for the caramel. Also have ready a large pan in which to set the custard cups in a water bath. Preheat the oven to 315 degrees F, and place an oven rack in the center.

Prepare the caramel topping:
2. Put ½ cup of the sugar in a small heavy saucepan. Heat the sugar slowly over medium heat on the stovetop until it begins to melt, swirling the pan occasionally (depending on your stove, this may take 8 to 12 minutes). Watch it carefully. As the sugar begins to melt, lower the heat to low and stir gently a few times, moving lumps towards the center with a silicone spatula or a long-handled wooden spoon until it becomes evenly golden (once it starts to change color watch it carefully so it doesn't burn, which can happen quickly).
3. When the sugar is gold-to-brown remove it from the heat and *immediately* pour the caramel into the bottom of the custard cups or pan. Let sit while preparing the custard. (The caramel hardens quickly, so it is a good idea to put the saucepan and stirring spoon into hot water right away to soak and dissolve the sugar to make them easier to clean.)

Prepare the custard:

4. Beat the eggs and ¼ cup of sugar together in a bowl until well mixed but not frothy. Stir in the nutmeg, vanilla, evaporated milk, and 1½ cups water. Strain the mixture through a fine mesh strainer into another bowl (I was told this makes the custard smoother, plus it removes extra nutmeg).
5. Pour the custard into the individual cups with the caramel in them (or the large mold if making one large custard).

Bake the custard:

6. Set the pan that will hold the custard-filled containers on the stove top, put the container(s) in the pan and half-fill the pan with warm or hot water. Then carefully place it in the oven on the center rack. Bake the custard for about 60 minutes or until a knife put in one comes out clean.
7. Remove pan from oven carefully. Using pot holders, carefully take out the very hot individual custard container(s) from the water, replace the hot water with slightly warm water, and return the custard containers to the water to cool.

To serve: Serve the custard warm or cool. It can be chilled in a refrigerator. To remove the custard when serving, go around the edge of the custard with a clean finger or a knife to loosen it, then turn it upside down onto individual serving plates or a serving platter and remove the cup. Très élégante!

Variations:

Omit the caramel and bake without it to make a simple flan. Garnish with fresh fruit or toasted coconut or nuts, or sprinkle with nutmeg or cinnamon, or a sprig of mint on the side.

For a lighter version, use one 5-ounce can of evaporated milk and enough water to make 2½ cups liquid total.

Substitute another type of milk (soy or almond, etc.) for the liquid.

Coconut Caramel Custard

Sprinkle fresh or frozen grated unsweetened coconut onto the pudding just as it is going into the oven (about 2 tablespoons per serving) and stir slightly.

Twisted Cakes
Atwemo

Makes about 16 servings

Often in the U.S. when I make the deep-fried dough called *atwemo* or "twisted cakes," people say it reminds them of Pennsylvania Dutch "funnel cakes" and they want to sprinkle them with powdered sugar. That is definitely a North American idea. West Africans are traditionally more moderate in their sugar consumption. These crispy treats are a combination cracker/cookie. A hard savory version is called *Chin-chin* in Nigeria (page 82).

I was first taught to make these by my friend and neighbor Abenaa Owusu, from the Ashanti region, and later found printed recipes for them where they were called *atwemo* or *atwimo* (Twi and Fante), and *atsomo* (Ga and Ewe). The indigenous names are interesting since usually recipes using imported Western ingredients like wheat flour have European or European-derived names (e.g., "twisted cakes," "diamond cakes").

As in Ghana, *atwemo* is a standard holiday/birthday/special occasion treat at our house. However, in Ghana it is also a popular snack food packaged in clear plastic and sold in supermarkets, at kiosks, and marketed by street vendors. They are not always "twisted," but can be simply cut into small cubes or diamond shapes.

Along with plantain chips/strips, "twisted cakes" is one of the most requested recipes at my cooking demonstrations. This is also a fun recipe for assembly-line production with almost any age group. I have made them with nursery and kindergarten students through to adults, including nursing home residents. They cook very quickly, the frying kills any lingering germs from children's fingers, and, with a deep-fryer, they can be made any place with an electrical outlet. However, when preparing these with children it is important to have a designated adult to do the frying away from the preparation area, and to oversee rolling the dough out so it is thin enough. Cutting the dough into diamonds using plastic or dull table knives, and the twisting process are fun, and even very young helpers can carry plates of twisted dough to the fryer, or loosen the cut diamonds from the board so they can be twisted. The dough can easily be rolled into balls, frozen, and fried in smaller batches as needed. This is a richer, more tender version than many sold on the streets in Ghana.

Ingredients

4 cups all-purpose flour

½ teaspoon salt

½ teaspoon ground nutmeg

2 teaspoons baking powder

½ cup margarine or butter, cubed

½ cup sugar

1 egg

¾ cup milk (*in Ghana it is made with half evaporated milk and half water*)

1 teaspoon vanilla extract

Vegetable oil for deep-frying

Directions

Make dough:

1. Sift the flour, salt, nutmeg, and baking powder together in a large bowl. Use a pastry blender or your hands to rub or cut the margarine or butter into the sifted ingredients. Add the sugar and mix in with a spoon.

2. Break the egg into a small bowl and beat slightly with a fork. Add the milk and vanilla and mix together.

3. Add the liquid ingredients to the flour mixture and mix well (after stirring a little with a spoon, I dust my hands with flour and mix the dough together with my hands), knead it lightly but not enough to make it tough. Add a little more flour if it is sticky; a little more milk if it seems too dry and will not hold together. Divide the dough into 4 equal parts.

Form the cakes:

4. Sprinkle a few drops of water on the counter, then put a couple of sheets of waxed paper down, sprinkle some flour on top of that and a little on the rolling pin, then roll the dough out to between ⅛ and ¼ inch thick. (I like my *atwemo* on the crispy side, so I tend to go thin; the dough can also be rolled out on any flour-dusted work surface.)

5. Cut the dough into strips about 1 inch wide. Next, cut the dough strips diagonally to make diamond shapes about 1¼ inch long.

6. Cut a slit in the center of each diamond. Pick up one diamond, push one end through the slit in the middle and pull that end all the way through (that's the "twist"). If the dough is only pulled partway through the slit you end up with what my children used to call "birds." Those will taste fine, but it's better to learn to twist the dough properly and pull the pointed

(continued on next page)

Twisted Cakes (continued)
Atwemo

end all the way through. Repeat with the rest of the diamonds.

7. Continue rolling out the scraps of dough and repeating the process. To prevent the dough from becoming tough, or simply to simplify the process, just cut the excess dough into triangles or other shapes and skip the twisting (however, cook any untwisted ones separately since the cooking times will vary a bit).

Fry the cakes:

8. While cutting and twisting the *atwemo*, fill an electric deep fryer or pan with vegetable oil (never more than half full; it will bubble up when adding the *atwemo*) and heat it to about 365 degrees F.

9. Carefully but quickly slip a couple dozen or so *atwemo* into the hot oil, one by one. Do not drop them and splatter the oil. Stir them frequently while they are cooking, making sure to turn them over so they brown on both sides. It will only take a few minutes to cook each batch. They should be quite golden when they are ready; perhaps a little browner than you think at first.

10. Remove them with the slotted spoon as they cook, and place into a paper towel-lined colander (or directly onto paper towels) to cool and drain off excess oil. Store the pastries covered in an airtight container.

Troubleshooting: (If the oil is not hot enough the *atwemo* will fall to the bottom of the pan and stay there; if it is too hot they will bounce up immediately and brown before they are cooked all the way through.)

Make ahead: *Atwemo* freeze beautifully.

To serve: *Atwemo* work equally well as a snack or a dessert, alone or served with ice cream or a fruit salad. Even children who are more likely to say "yuck" to new foods seem to say "yum" from their first taste.

Variation: You can make smaller daintier *atwemo* by cutting the strips smaller in Step 5, about ½ inch by 1 inch works well.

Cassava Cookies
Gari Biscuits

Makes 2 to 3 dozen, depending on size

These crispy cookies have an uncluttered, fresh, pure taste. The coconut and *gari* deliver a crunchy texture with a mild, pleasing flavor. One would likely use evaporated milk and margarine in Ghana. North Americans, with our pronounced sweet tooth, may need to increase the sugar. For a vegan version, use margarine and substitute soy or almond milk.

Ingredients

½ cup finely sifted dry *gari*

½ cup plus 1 to 2 tablespoons sifted all-purpose flour

⅓ cup sugar

¼ teaspoon salt

1 teaspoon baking powder

¾ cup grated unsweetened fresh coconut; or about ⅔ cup frozen, defrosted

2 tablespoons margarine or butter

4 to 5 tablespoons evaporated milk (or regular, soy, or almond milk)

Directions

1. Preheat oven to 375 degrees F. Grease or oil a baking sheet.
2. In a bowl, sprinkle 1 teaspoon of water over the *gari*, and mix it in well with your fingers.
3. Add the flour, sugar, salt, baking powder and coconut to the bowl, and mix.
4. Using your fingers or knives, cut the margarine or butter into the mixture until it resembles cornmeal.
5. Stir in 3 tablespoons of the milk. If the mixture seems too dry to stick together, add more milk 1 tablespoon at a time until the batter will form small patties.
6. Shape cookies as desired. For example: hand-form them into small patties; or pat some of the dough onto a lightly floured board and cut out circles using a small jar or glass; or form small balls, set them on the cookie sheet, and press them with a fork as one would for peanut butter cookies—making tine marks first one way, then once again at right angles to the first.
7. Bake the cookies on cookie sheets in the preheated oven for about 12 to 15 minutes, until they turn very lightly golden—the tops are whiter, the bottoms browned. The longer they cook, the crisper they become.

Variations:
Sprinkle the cookies with coconut, sugar, or *gari*.

Add other flavorings like vanilla or lemon.

Ripe Plantain Loaf
Ofam

Makes 1 cake

Ofam is Ghana's challenge to Western holiday fruitcakes: a rich, heavy plantain loaf made from sweet, over-ripe plantains, spices, and red palm oil. It is not difficult to make, but does require some special ingredients—over-ripe plantains and palm oil.

Ingredients

2 pounds overripe (black) plantains

1 cup finely grated onion

3 tablespoons grated fresh ginger

1 to 3 fresh chili peppers (or to taste), seeded and ground or minced (to start try just a part of a jalapeno [mild], or cayenne [hot], or habanero [hottest])

1 to 2 teaspoons salt (or to taste)

¾ cup rice flour or all-purpose flour

Up to 1 cup good-quality red palm oil

Directions

1. Heat oven to 350 degrees F.
2. Peel the plantains and mash them. Traditionally a wooden mortar with a wooden pestle is used. If they are very ripe a fork will do fine, or use an *apotoyewa*, potato masher, ricer, glass, or similar. Remember, texture is important in Ghanaian dishes, so do not do this in a blender. You want 2½ to 2¾ cups of well-mashed plantains.
3. Put the mashed plantains in a large mixing bowl and add the grated onion and ginger. Add the chili pepper a little at a time, tasting the batter for spiciness as you go (the peppers may be seeded and ground in a blender or mini food processor with a couple of tablespoons of water).
4. Stir the batter gently, adding a little salt (in Ghana we used 2 teaspoons, but for North Americans 1 teaspoon is likely enough).
5. Stir in ½ cup of the flour. The mixture should be a thick batter and not runny. If it seems thin, add up to another ¼ cup flour to thicken it, then stir in the palm oil. (I balk at using the full cup of palm oil, instead using part of it to grease the pan well on the bottom and sides using a pastry brush.)
6. Let the batter rest in the bowl for 15 minutes, then scrape it into a pan (in Ghana we made our *ofam* in loaf pans; I use a nonstick bundt pan). Bake for 30 minutes in 350 degree F oven. Let it cool on a rack about 20 minutes before removing from the pan.

To serve: Serve warm or cool, in small slices by itself or accompanied by dry roasted peanuts. We eat ours both as a holiday dessert and a snack. Leftovers freeze nicely and are quickly defrosted and warmed in a microwave. When serving, I blot excess palm oil off with paper towels, but others might find that akin to scraping whipped cream or frosting off a cake.

Tea Bread

Makes 1 large or 2 small loaves

In 2002, Mrs. Spendlove (Barbara's cousin and owner of PamFram Bakery in Accra) agreed to teach me to make Ghana-style tea bread. She met me at Flair Catering to demonstrate quantities and techniques, but after returning to the U.S., my first attempt to re-create the tea bread failed miserably. Two years later I returned to be shown again, this time at her bakery, and realized her commercial mixers affected the texture of the breads. And also realized Ghana's flour has more gluten. Here we give you two adapted versions of Ghana's classic tea bread. They take basically a whole day or night to rise.

Ingredients

1 cup warm water

4 tablespoons (2 ounces) margarine or butter, melted

4 cups (1 pound) unsifted bread flour

4 teaspoons gluten

1 teaspoon salt

½ to ¾ teaspoon ground nutmeg (to taste)

3 tablespoons sugar

¾ teaspoon dry powdered yeast (preferably rapid rise)

To serve: This is called "tea bread" because it is a pleasant, not-too-sweet bread to enjoy with a hot beverage in the mornings, afternoons, or evenings.

Directions for bread machine

1. Put all ingredients in the bread maker container in the order listed. Set the timer on the "dough" setting, and wait for it to finish.
2. Remove the dough and put in a greased bowl, lightly covered, and let sit for about 8 hours in a warm draft-free place.
3. Punch the dough down. Shape into 1 large loaf or 2 small loaves with slightly tapered edges. Place on a lightly greased baking sheet and let the dough rest for about 30 minutes (lightly covered with a dishtowel, if desired).
4. Preheat oven to 375 degrees F. Bake the bread for about 30 to 40 minutes.
5. Remove from the pans and cool on a wire rack before slicing.

Directions for hand-kneading

1. Pour the warm water into a cup. Add 1 teaspoon sugar and stir to dissolve. Sprinkle the yeast on top of the liquid, mix gently and set aside for a few minutes to proof.
2. In a large bowl mix together the flour, gluten, salt, nutmeg, and remaining sugar. Make a hole in the center of the dry ingredients and add yeast mixture and melted margarine or butter. Mix with a sturdy spoon and then your hands until you have a smooth dough. (Add a little more flour or water if the dough is too sticky or dry.)
3. Knead the dough on a lightly floured surface until it is smooth and elastic, about 10 to 15 minutes. Form into a ball and proceed as from step 2 above.

Sugar Bread 1

Makes 12 to 15 servings

This rich sugar bread recipe is adapted from one taught to me by Barbara Baëta's cousin Mrs. Spendlove (aka Pamela Ayele Attipoe), the owner of the PamFram bakery in Accra.

Ingredients

1 egg

¾ teaspoon salt

2 tablespoons full-cream powdered milk (like Nido)

¾ cup sugar

3½ to 4 cups sifted bread flour

½ to ¾ teaspoon ground nutmeg (or to taste)

1 (¼-ounce) packet regular or rapid rise dry yeast (2¼ teaspoons)

6 tablespoons margarine or butter

Troubleshooting: If the bread fails to rise, activate an additional teaspoon of dry yeast in 2 tablespoons of very warm water with a pinch of sugar. When it bubbles, work into the dough, using a little more flour, if necessary. Repeat from step 6.

Directions

1. Set all ingredients out to come to room temperature.
2. Break the egg into a large mixing bowl. Add the salt, powdered milk, and ½ cup water, stirring with a fork until the powder is dissolved. Add sugar and mix again vigorously until slightly foamy.
3. In a second bowl, measure out 3 cups of the sifted flour. Add nutmeg and stir together.
4. Make a hole in the center of the flour and add the sugar mixture all at once, followed by the yeast. Mix together first with a spoon, then mixing and kneading by hand, pushing against the sides of the bowl to mix. Work the softened margarine or butter into the dough, pushing in the middle and turning repeatedly.
5. Sprinkle ½ cup of the remaining flour onto a clean work surface and knead the dough, gradually working in the remaining flour if needed, to achieve a smooth and elastic dough, about 10 to 15 minutes.
6. Leave the dough to rest, covered with a damp cloth, for 30 minutes in a warm, humid place away from drafts. It might need to be put in a slightly warm oven along with a bowl of water.
7. After 30 minutes, punch the dough down and knead lightly. Form into desired shape—this makes 1 medium loaf (9 x 5 x 2¾ inch pan), 1 braided loaf, 2 smaller loaves, or 12 to 15 rolls.
8. After shaping the dough, place in a greased/oiled baking pan or on a baking sheet, cover loosely, and leave to rise in a warm place until doubled in size—this will likely take several hours.

9. Preheat an oven to 350 degrees F. Bake a loaf until nicely browned, about 30 to 45 minutes. Check the loaf after 20 or 25 minutes and if it is browning too quickly, cover it with foil (for rolls, check after 15 or 20 minutes). When the bread is ready, remove it from oven and turn out to cool on a wire rack.

Variations:

Substitute mace for the nutmeg

Replace the powdered milk and water with whole milk at room temperature.

Sugar Bread 2 (Bread Machine Version)

Mr. Willis Taylor, whose father is an honorary chief in the Brong Ahafo region, generously shared this (slightly adapted) easy bread machine version of sugar bread.

Ingredients

2¼ teaspoons regular or rapid-rise yeast or 1 (¼-ounce) packet

1 cup water

1 teaspoon lemon or lime juice

2 tablespoons vegetable oil (such as canola)

¾ cup sugar

1 teaspoon salt

1½ tablespoons full-cream powdered milk (e.g., Nido)

¾ teaspoon ground nutmeg

3 cups all-purpose or bread flour

Directions

1. Put the yeast in a cup with 2 tablespoons of warm water and ½ teaspoon of the sugar. Set aside to activate.
2. Put all the other ingredients in the bread machine in the order listed.
3. When the yeast has begun frothing pour it on top of the other ingredients, using a spatula to scrape it out if necessary.
4. Set the bread machine time for 1 medium loaf, medium crust.
5. Remove loaf when baked and cool on a wire rack before slicing. (

Variation: To make rolls or braided bread, set the bread machine for dough only and remove to shape the bread into other desired shapes. Bake in a 350 degree F oven until baked.

GLOSSARY

This glossary provides an introduction to some classic Ghanaian dishes, cooking equipment, techniques, and ingredients. More information is frequently included with individual recipes and can be found by referring to the index.

Abɛ: *see* palm nuts, palm fruit

Ablemamu: toasted corn flour(page 29; also the porridge made from the flour (recipe, page 197)

Abodoo (Abolo): baked corn dough loaf wrapped in plantain leaves and baked; eaten with stew, fried fish, or roasted meat

Aboboe: stewed bambara groundnuts, commonly eaten hot or cold with *tatale*, *kakro*, or *kenkey*; one of the few snack dishes in Ghana to which sugar may be added (Recipe, page 142)

Adinkra: Ghanaian *adinkra* symbols are icons that represent visually traditional wisdom and themes, concepts, proverbs, nature, or behavior. They are frequently stamped/carved on cloth, pottery, jewelry, and walls or incorporated into furniture, signs, and used as logos. Originating among the Asante people, they are now widely embraced throughout the country. The two symbols used in this book are:

 Gye nyame ("except God"), referring to the omnipotence of God

 Asase ye duru ("the earth has weight"), referring to the importance of mother earth in sustaining life.

(Source: www.adinkra.org/htmls/graphics.htm)

Aflata: partly cooked corn dough, used in making *kenkey* (page 187)

Agidi: fermented corn-based gel-like starchy food eaten in Northern Ghana, boiled in plantain leaves (*agidi* is the Ibo word, *komu* in Hausa, *eko* in Yoruba, *akasan* in Benin)

Agushi (Yoruba: *egusi*; Hausa: *agusi*; *citrullus colocynthis*): type of melon seed native to Africa; dried and ground and used as a thickener in soups and stews, or roasted and eaten as a snack (hulled pumpkin seeds can be used as a substitute)

Ahaban: plantain leaves (often used to wrap and steam dishes, such as *kenkey* or *tubaani*); the word means "leaf" and may also refer to greens used in cooking

Akara: Yoruba name for West African cowpea/black-eyed pea fritters; known as *akara, akla, accra, koose* or *kose* in Ghana (Recipe, page 78)

Akasua: tiny green and bitter eggplant; Ashanti people use it to thicken soups

Akoko besa: African basil (*ocimum canum*) used to flavor soups and stews (aka *akokoo mesa*); "*akoko*" means chicken and *besa* means "to end" (the chicken will be consumed/finished when this herb is added to the soup. Thyme is sometimes substituted.

Akple: cooked corn and cassava dough, popular among Ewes (Recipe, page 189)

Akpeteshie: locally made gin from distilled palm wine

Ampesi: boiled starchy vegetables cooked together and eaten with stew; commonly includes green and ripe plantains, yams, sweet potatoes, cocoyams, and/or cassavas (see sidebar, page 185)

Apɔtoyewa/apotoriwa: the wooden mashing tool used to grind vegetables in an *asanka*

Aprapransa: type of one-pot dish made with palmnut soup and beans and cooked with *ablemamu* (toasted corn meal), and/or smoked herrings and crab (Recipe, page 162)

Asanka: clay grinding bowl with ridges on it used with an *apoteyewa* for grinding herbs and vegetables, commonly black or terracotta in color; also used as a serving bowl; some are now made of metal

Ashanti pepper (*Piper guineense*): spice also known as "false cubeb pepper" in English, *masoro* in Hausa, or *soro wisa* in Twi

Attiéke: fermented cassava granule that is steamed (a "*gari*" couscous); popular in Cote D'Ivoire, Benin, and parts of Ghana (Recipe, page 178)

Atwemo (atsomo): type of deep-fried cookie popular for parties and holidays; a less-sweet version is sold as a snack (Recipe, page 222)

Awiewa: traditional clay pot for making soup

Ayoyo: name for the leaves of *tossa jute* (*Corchorus olitorius*), a popular green cooked in soups

Bambara beans (*Vigna* or *Voandzeia subterranea*0 [aka bambara groundnuts, Congo groundnut, Congo goober, Madagascar groundnut, earth pea, baffin pea, njugo bean (S. Africa), *voandzou, nzama* (Malawi), *indhlubu*]: a legume similar to peanuts (groundnuts) thought to have originated in Mali, West Africa

Banku (baŋku): stirred porridge made from fermented corn dough often served with okra stew and grilled tilapia (Recipe, page 186)

Baobab: ancient tree found growing throughout the savannas of sub-Saharan Africa with massive trunk and distinctive branches, and serving multiple culinary, social, and environmental purposes

Bissap: beverage made from dried red hibiscus flowers (sorrel or roselle), steeped in water and sweetened and flavored (Recipe, page 205)

Calabashes: hollowed out and dried bottle gourds used as cups and bowls

Cassava [aka manioc, mandioca, or yucca]: a tropical root crop originating in the new world and now a staple food in sub-Saharan Africa where both its leaves and tubers are eaten; cassava is said to be the third most important carbohydrate crop after rice and maize (corn) in tropical countries of Africa, the Americas, and Asia; in North America this root crop is most commonly eaten in tapioca pudding, or as a thickener for sauces

Chichinga: grilled meat kebabs commonly dipped in a spicy rub called *tankora* powder; traditionally made from beef or liver, but now chicken and shrimp also (Recipe, page 74)

Chili peppers (*mako, shito*): common chili peppers used in Ghana include habanero peppers, Scotch bonnet peppers, *kpakpo shito*, and cayenne (see Cooking with Peppers, page 35)

Chop bars: informal, semi-enclosed restaurants in western Africa; "*chop*" is the pidgin English word for "to eat"

Cocoyam [aka taro, taro root, dasheen, edda]: root plant introduced into Africa from the Americas whose roots and leaves are eaten; there are four different roots called taro, the one commonly found in Africa is *Xanthosoma taro*

Corn (Maize): corn commonly consumed in Ghana is mostly white dent or flint corn, not sweet or yellow corn

***Dawadawa*:** in Ghana the locust bean, also known as carob, is processed into a fermented seasoning made from locust beans and soybeans that is often added to soups and stews and has numerous health benefits and serves as a nutritious alternative to seasoning cubes

Dried shrimp/crayfish/herrings (includes smoked and dried, ground and whole): important traditional seasonings in Ghana that provide umami flavor

***Fonio*:** hardy, tasty, nutritious West African cereal grain grown in northern Ghana that is difficult and time-consuming to dehull

***Fufu*:** in Ghana, refers to a stiff dumpling eaten with soup and made by cooking and pounding a variety of starches from root crops (Sidebar, page 190; Recipe, page 191)

***Gari (garri, gali)*:** a type of coarse cassava meal similar to Brazil's *farofa*, but fermented; *gari* can be bought online; there is no substitute for it (see sidebar, page 174)

Gari foto [aka *gari jollof*]: popular one-pot meal in which a tomato gravy is mixed with *gari* (Recipe, page 152)

Garden eggs: small, egg-shaped eggplants, usually creamy white to yellow in color

Grasscutter: type of cane rat (*Thryonomys swinderianus*), a wild game rodent long considered a delicacy in Ghana, but due to fear that bush meat may promote the spread of ebola, is beginning to be domesticated and use of wild grasscutter has decreased

Greens: Ghanaians eat forty-seven different kinds of leafy green vegetables, among them young tender leaves of cassava, cocoyam, okra, cowpeas, garden eggs, sweet potatoes, pumpkin, as well as *efan*, *akatewa* (a kind of spinach), and *bowene* (bitterleaf)

Groundnuts: peanuts often roasted and ground into a paste to thicken soups and stews

Guinea fowl: an indigenous West African bird, related to pheasants, common in northern Ghana

***Homowo*:** a Ga thanksgiving festival that literally means to "hoot at hunger"

***Hwentia*:** the Twi name for the seeds and aromatic seedpod of an African tree/shrub *Xylopia aethiopica*, also known as Grains of Selim, kimba pepper, African pepper, Moor pepper, Negro pepper, Kani pepper, Kili pepper, Sénégal pepper, or Ethiopian pepper; can be purchased online

***Jollof* rice:** one-pot rice dish whose name is derived from the Wolof ethnic group, but that is eaten throughout West Africa where rice is available; often made with chicken and/or shrimp in Ghana (Recipe, page 156)

Kaklo / Kakro: a savory fritter or beignet made from over-ripe plantains or yams (Recipe, pages 54)

Kelewele: seasoned ripe plantain cubes deep-fried and often eaten as a snack accompanied by dry roasted unsalted peanuts (Recipe, page 52)

Kenam / Kyenam: fried fish served with gravy, and often stuffed with ground pepper, onions and salt (Recipe, pages 138 and 139)

Kenkey (dokono / dɔkono): steamed fermented corn dough commonly wrapped in corn husks (Ga-style) or banana leaves (Fante-style); often eaten with fresh pepper sauces or *shito* and fried fish (Recipe, page 187)

Kobi: salted tilapia, a common ingredient in soups and stews (a substitute is salted cod or other salted fish)

Koko: a thin porridge commonly made from fermented corn, millet, or sorghum dough, also used as a weaning food for babies (Recipe, pages 195 and 196)

Kola (cola): West African seed kernels from a tree in the cocoa family containing stimulants like caffeine; they are chewed and are important in social and ceremonial life in much of West Africa, especially in Muslim areas

Kokonte: dried cassava flour

Kontomire: cocoyam leaves, also a component of stews by the same name

Kpakpo shito: a type of chili pepper from Ghana

Kpokpoi: traditional ceremonial Ga corn dish eaten with palmnut soup, associated with the Homowo festival

Margarine: cattle are not widely raised in Ghana thus imported butter is very expensive and rarely used, so Ghanaians make liberal use of margarine, especially when using wheat products; for making these recipes outside of Ghana, butter may be substituted

Melegueta pepper [aka Grains of Paradise, Guinea pepper]: small African seed related to cardamom, and also a member of the ginger family, once used as a substitute for black peppercorns; used for seasoning food and as a medicine in Africa, in Europe during the 1400s, and to treat and prevent slave illnesses during the Middle Passage; still grown and used in Ghana

Momoni: known in Ghana as "stinking fish," *momoni* is a fish that is left fermenting in the sun for a day, salted for a day or two, and then dried in the sun; has a pungent smell and adds a unique flavor (a dash of Thai fish sauce and/or a bit of salted cod may substitute)

Mpotompoto (nyoma): one-pot dish in which cocoyam or African yam are cooked in a soup (Recipe, page 155)

Nkwan: Twi and Fante word for "soup" (in Ga: *wonu*; in Ewe: *detsi*)

Nutmeg: an "African" nutmeg, called "*wediaba*" in Twi [aka "calabash nutmeg," "Jamaican nutmeg," or "*ehuru*" in Nigeria; scientific name is *monodora myristica*] has a sweet smell but is spicier and more pungent than regular nutmeg

Ofam: a ripe plantain loaf (Recipe, page 226)

Omo tuo: rice balls (Recipe, page 179)

Ɔtɔ: ceremonial dish commonly made from hard-boiled eggs, mashed African yam, and palm oil; may also be made from plantains (Sidebar, page 164; Recipe, page 165)

Palaver sauce: a type of stew often mixing greens, *agushi*, meat, and fish together (Recipe, page 128)

PREPARING FRESH PALM NUTS

For anyone fortunate to live in a part of Africa where fresh red palm nuts are available, the process for preparing them to use in soup or stew is as follows:
1. Wash them, then boil in water to loosen the skins and until they are softened and their color changes.
2. Put the palm nuts into a specially shaped tall wooden mortar and pound them with a wooden pestle.
3. Pour the pounded nuts into a large bowl and add a little warm water. Squeeze the fibers by hand to remove as much liquid as possible, then remove the fibers and discard. (Some people would then repeat the process with the fibers to extract a bit more juice.)
4. Strain the liquid in the bowl once to remove any remaining nuts and discard them. Strain the mixture again to make sure no fiber remains.

Palm fruit, palm nut, palm oil (abɛ): from the red palm tree, *Elaeis guineensis*; when the fruit/nuts are cooked and strained, the liquid is called "palm fruit juice" or "palm fruit butter." The palm oil rises to the top and may be skimmed off and used separately or stirred back into the juice. Fresh palm fruit is not available in the U.S. so we must content ourselves with imported canned cream of palm fruit concentrate. It is sold in African or many international markets, or can be ordered from online suppliers. Palm oil is recently becoming available at U.S. grocery stores in health food sections. A special Ewe-variety spice-infused palm oil is known as *dzomi* or *zomi*. (See recipe for Palm Nut Soup / Twi: *Abɛ Nkwan*, page 107)

Palmwine: beverage made from the sap of the oil palm tree in western and central Africa; ranges from unfermented to fermented

Peanut flour: new product on the market in U.S. health food stores that takes the place of the laborious task of grinding your own peanut powder (eg., Protein Plus); this is a fabulous innovation but make sure that you find one that does not include sugar or chocolate

Peanut paste: one can prepare peanut paste "from scratch" but I prefer the ease of using commercially prepared "natural-style" organic unsalted unsweetened creamy peanut butter

Pestle (*warma*): used with a mortar to pound vegetables, starches, dried fish, etc.

Prɛkɛse: seed of a West African flowering plant in the pea family *Tertrapleura tetraptera*, frequently used as a spice, added to soups in powdered form; has been shown to have multiple health benefits

Seasoning cubes: popular for seasoning soups and stews, found in many flavors, including traditional *shito*, *dawadawa*, and shrimp as well as beef and chicken; also called bouillon cubes; two popular brands are Maggi and Royco

Shea butter: a whitish or yellowish fat from the seeds of the shea tree, often used for cooking in West Africa, but used in the West primarily for cosmetics

Saltpeter (aka *kanwa*): from the Latin for "stone salt," potassium nitrate mineral used in Ghana to thicken soups and stews and to soften food such as beans and tough meat to speed cooking time; recently, there have been health concerns expressed

Shito (*shitɔ*): Ga word for "pepper," this commonly refers to a dark-colored hot pepper sauce also popularly called "black pepper," "student's pepper sauce," or "engine oil"; very popular with boarding school students and often found on tables in restaurants as a condiment (Recipe, page 170)

Sorghum: ancient African cereal grain that is now the fourth most valuable cereal crop globally; in Ghana, it is also used to make a kind of beer known as *pito*

Stirring stick: wooden stick much sturdier than standard wooden spoons, used to make *banku*, *akple*, and other thick starches

Tankora (*yaji* / *chichinga*) powder: a spicy rub used on kebabs in Ghana, as well as a dipping seasoning, made of dried powdered spices (Recipe, page 24)

Tatale (*Tetare*): ripe plantain pancakes often served with boiled bambara beans (Recipe, page 50)

Tiger nuts (*chufa, Cyperus esculentus*): eaten as a snack, and made into tiger nut pudding (*atadwe milkye*; recipe, page 218)

Togbei (aka **bofrot**): a spongy type of round Ghanaian doughnut ball; "*togbei*" is said to mean "goat ball" and "*bofrot*" to mean "ball float" (Recipes, pages 84 and 86)

Tubaani: steamed cowpea (black-eyed pea) balls; popular in Northern Ghana (Recipe, page 76)

Tuo zaafi (aka **TZ**): a preferred carbohydrate-based accompaniment for soups and sauces in Northern Ghana, commonly prepared as a thick porridge from millet or corn and cassava flours; less elastic than *fufu*, it ranges from soft like *banku* to a loaf that can be cut with a knife; also made from *fonio*, one of the so-called "lost crops of Africa" (Recipe, page 182)

Twi: Akan language widely spoken in Southern Ghana (and also in parts of Côte d'Ivoire); its dialects include Asante (Ashanti) Twi, Akuapem Twi, and Fante.

Waakye (*watche*): a popular rice and bean dish originally from Northern Ghana, traditionally made with millet leaves and commonly garnished with pasta called *talia* (presumably derived from the word "Italia,") and accompanied with a tomato sauce or gravy (Recipes, pages 160 and 161)

Wasawasa: steamed yam flour, eaten in Northern Ghana, served with a sauce

Wele: smoked cow hide that many Ghanaians love to chew; often included in soups as a delicacy; some health concerns about *wele* are arising however

Yams (African): The major yams grown in Ghana are *Dioscorea alata, Dioscorea rotundata, Dioscorea esculenta,* and *Dioscorea dumetorum,* all of which are quite distinct from the *Ipomoea batatas* or sweet potatoes often called yams and eaten in the United States; local names in Ghana include water yam, *afaso*, and *puna*; also sometimes called "*name*"; can be found in the U.S in some African, Latin, and Asian markets.

Weights and Measures Conversions

Standard U.S. Unit	Metric Equivalent
$1/8$ teaspoon	.5 milliliter (ml)
$1/4$ teaspoon	1 ml
$1/2$ teaspoon	2 ml
1 teaspoon	5 ml
1 tablespoon (3 teaspoons)	15 ml
$1/8$ cup (2 tablespoons)	30 ml
$1/4$ cup (4 tablespoons)	50 ml
$1/3$ cup (5 tablespoons)	75 ml
$1/2$ cup (8 tablespoons)	125 ml
1 cup (16 tablespoons)	250 ml
4 cups (1 quart)	1 liter (actually .95 liter)
1 ounce (oz)	30 grams (g)
1 pound (lb)	500 grams
2 pounds	1 kilogram (kg)
1 inch	2.5 cm

U.S. and British Measuring Systems

1 U.S. cup (8 ounces) = $5/6$ English cup

10 ounces = 1 English cup

$1\frac{1}{4}$ U.S. teaspoons = 1 English teaspoon

$1\frac{1}{4}$ U.S. tablespoons = 1 English tablespoon

1 U.S. pint = 16 fluid ounces = $4/5$ English pint

20 fluid ounces = 1 English pint

Resources

West African grocery stores are located in most large U.S. metropolitan areas or near universities, especially in areas with large West African immigrant or student populations.

Some international stores also cater to West Africans. Explore local Latin, Caribbean, and Asian stores as they often carry some ingredients used in Ghanaian cooking.

West African ingredients are increasingly available in the U.S. at large grocery chains such as Trader Joe's or Whole Foods.

Health food stores and/or gluten-free aisles now stock numerous items used in Ghanaian cooking (corn, millet, rice, cassava flours, peanut powder, palm oil, coconut oil, tiger nuts, etc.

Nina International, headquartered in Silver Springs, Maryland, has become one of the largest U.S. suppliers of African foods, many directly from Ghana: http://www.ninainternational.com.

Search for specific items online, such as at Amazon.com.

If all else fails, try posting at BETUMIblog (http://www.betumiblog.blogspot.com) and activate a worldwide community of folks interested in promoting and preserving African cuisines. Maybe someone there can help. Good luck!

GHANAIAN RECIPE NAME INDEX

RECIPE INDEX

var. = variation

*The recipes listed here under chili peppers are the ones in which they are a primary ingredient; but if you are want to use up some chili peppers you have on hand, most of the savory dishes in this book and even one of the desserts incorpoate them in some way.

*The recipes listed here under tomatoes are the ones in which they are a primary ingredient; but if you are looking to use up some tomatoes from your garden most of the soups, stews, and one-pots in this book use them as their base in some way.